The SAGE Dictionary of
Cultural Studies

The SAGE Dictionary of
Cultural Studies

Chris Barker

SAGE Publications
London ● Thousand Oaks ● New Delhi

SAGE Publications Ltd
1 Oliver's Yard
55 City Road
London EC1Y 1SP

SAGE Publications Inc.
2455 Teller Road
Thousand Oaks, California 91320

SAGE Publications India Pvt Ltd
B-42, Panchsheel Enclave
Post Box 4109
New Delhi 110 017

British Library Cataloguing in Publication data

A catalogue record for this book is available from the
British Library

ISBN 0 7619 7340 0
ISBN 0 7619 7341 9 (pbk)

Library of Congress Control Number: 2003115420

Typeset by M Rules
Printed and bound in Great Britain by
TJ International Ltd, Padstow, Cornwall

CONTENTS

CONTENTS

N

O

P

Q

R

S

xii

Y

INTRODUCTION

SPEAKING OF CULTURAL STUDIES

When I am introduced to someone I have not met before and give my name, I find I am then commonly asked what I do for a living. As a consequence, I am inevitably next asked, 'so, what is **cultural studies**?'[1] Not wanting to bore the pants off my new-found friend, I usually mumble something about it being a bit like anthropology but in industrialized cultures or liken it to the more familiar sociology, 'but with a stress on **culture**'. It never feels very satisfactory but it is enough for the **social** talk of the occasion. However, it would not be an adequate answer in the context of a more professional intellectual inquiry. Thus, from its inception writers involved with cultural studies have been interrogated as to its character and have obligingly asked themselves the same question as my acquaintance, 'what is cultural studies anyway'?

Though the asking of the question is understandable, it is to some extent misguided. I would suggest that when we ask about what cultural studies 'is' we are being tricked by the grammar of everyday English language into taking a mistaken pathway. Rather, the topic is more auspiciously pursued with the query 'how do we talk about cultural studies and for what purposes?' than by asking the question 'what is cultural studies?'. This is so because the word 'is' comes loaded with the assumptions of representationalism. When we ask the question 'what is cultural studies?' the use of 'is' implies that such a thing as cultural studies exists in an independent object world and that we can know and name it. That is, the sign 'cultural studies' actually pictures a substantive thing.

However, we cannot know what something 'is' when 'is' suggests either a metaphysical universal **truth** or an accurate **representation** of an independent object world. **Language** does not accurately represent the world but is a tool for achieving our purposes. Knowledge is not a matter of getting an accurate picture of reality, but of learning how best to contend with the world. Since we have a variety of purposes, we develop a variety of languages. Thus, in re-describing the question 'what is cultural studies?' as 'how do we talk about cultural studies and for what purposes?' we are making the switch from a question about representation to one concerning language use.

The idea that we cannot definitively say what an event 'is', and that we have different languages for different purposes, is not simply the preserve of the philosophy of language but is one shared by the 'hard' sciences. For example, at the core of quantum physics is a wave–particle duality by which all quantum entities can be treated as both waves and particles; as being in a particular place (particle) and in no certain place (wave). Under some circumstances it is useful to regard photons (quantities of light) as a stream of particles, while at other times they are best thought of in terms of wavelengths. Equally,

---

1 Throughout this Introduction, terms that appear in the body of the dictionary are highlighted in **bold** text type, and cross-references to biographical entries are set in **sans serif** type.

in classical Newtonian physics an electron is envisaged as a particle that orbits the nuclei of an atom (protons and neutrons) while in quantum mechanics it is held to be a wave surrounding the atom's nuclei. Both descriptions 'work' according to the purposes one has in mind; physical phenomena are put 'under the description' (Davidson, 1984) of different models to achieve divergent ends.

Thus, I am recommending an approach that recasts problems away from an emphasis on representation, that is, the question 'what is . . .', to the more mundane and pragmatic issues of language use, that is, 'how do we talk about X and for what purposes?'. As Wittgenstein puts it, 'Grammar tells what kind of object anything is. (Theology as grammar)' (Wittgenstein, 1957: 373). What something 'is' becomes constituted by the use of language within specific **language-games**. This therapeutic re-casting of the question 'what is cultural studies' into an inquiry about how we talk about cultural studies and its purposes enables us to see that cultural studies is not an object. That is, cultural studies is not one thing that can be accurately represented, but rather is constituted by a number of ways of looking at the world which are motivated by different purposes and values.

Historically speaking, cultural studies has been constituted by multiple voices or languages that nevertheless have sufficient 'family resemblances' to form a recognizable 'clan' connected by 'kinship' ties to other families. Thus, cultural studies can be understood as a language-game that revolves around the theoretical terms developed and deployed by persons calling their work cultural studies. In a similar argument, Stuart Hall has described cultural studies as a discursive formation, that is, 'a cluster (or formation) of ideas, images and practices, which provide ways of talking about – forms of knowledge and conduct associated with – a particular topic, social activity or institutional site in society (Hall, 1997: 6). That is, cultural studies is constituted by *a regulated* way of speaking about 'objects' that cultural studies brings into view and that cohere around key concepts, ideas and concerns.

Indeed, cultural studies has now developed to a stage where there is at least some agreement about the problems, issues and vocabulary that constitute the field. As Grossberg et al. have argued, there are a series of concepts that have been developed under the banner of cultural studies that have been deployed in various geographical sites. These form 'a history of real achievements that is now part of the cultural studies tradition. To do without them would be to willingly accept real incapacitation' (Grossberg et al., 1992: 8).

If, as many cultural studies writers argue, words give meaning to material objects and social **practices** that are brought into view by language and made intelligible to us in terms that language delimits, then the vocabulary of cultural studies performs cultural studies. Cultural studies is constituted by the language that we use when we say that we are doing cultural studies and can thus be understood in terms of **performativity**. That is, as we use a particular language so we name cultural studies and perform it. Consequently, this dictionary is in part an answer to the question 'what is cultural studies' while simultaneously performing it, manifesting it and bringing it into being in a particular way. This dictionary is a manifestation of the language-game of cultural studies that contributes to bringing its very object of inquiry into being.

A CULTURAL STUDIES CREATION STORY

In describing cultural studies as a language-game I have tried to stress two things; first that the field is defined by its ways of speaking rather than by a fixed object of study and second that cultural studies is not one thing, but rather is constituted by a plurality of lineages – though they are connected by kinship ties. Indeed, I have tried within the dictionary to be inclusive of the many traditions of cultural studies.However, it is also the case that I acquired my understanding of cultural studies in a particular way and that this history has shaped the dictionary. That is, this story of cultural studies, multi-stranded though it is, has been shaped by the who, where, when and why of its **'author'**. Thus, this dictionary is 'positioned' where the concept of **positionality** indicates that the production of knowledge is always located within the vectors of time, space and social power.

Consequently, I shall say a little about my own cultural studies creation story even while I acknowledge there are others that could be drawn on. I was an undergraduate in the sociology department of the University of Birmingham (UK) from 1975 to 1978 during which time the Centre for Contemporary Cultural Studies (CCCS) was at its high point under the directorship of Stuart Hall. I was never a member of the CCCS, but I was aware of its work; I read their papers, I attended some lectures given by Stuart Hall, I mixed in the campus political milieu in which some Centre members were active. I even secretly snuck into the occasional CCCS seminar undetected. I was somewhat in awe of Stuart Hall as he walked around the campus and thought that cultural studies was the most exciting intellectual project I had ever encountered. Later my doctoral supervisor at the University of Leeds (UK) was Janet Wolff, herself a graduate of CCCS. I have been good friends with Chris Pawling, a former Centre member and a colleague of Paul Willis at the University of Wolverhampton (UK). Thus, the so-called Birmingham School was and is *my* starting point for an exploration of cultural studies.

For me there is a line to be drawn between the study of culture and institutionally located cultural studies. The study of culture takes place in a variety of academic disciplines – sociology, anthropology, English Literature etc. – and in a range of geographical and institutional spaces, but this is not necessarily cultural studies. While the study of culture has no origins this does not mean that cultural studies cannot be named, and the formation of the **Centre for Contemporary Cultural Studies** at Birmingham University (UK) in the 1960s was a decisive organizational instance. Since that time cultural studies has extended its intellectual base and geographic scope and there are self-defined cultural studies practitioners in the United States, Australia, Africa, Asia, Latin America and Europe with each 'formation' of cultural studies working in different ways. Thus, while I do not want to privilege British cultural studies *per se,* I am pointing to the formation of cultural studies at Birmingham as an institutionally significant moment. Contemporary sociology is not the work of Marx, Durkheim and Weber any more than science is the domain of Newton and Einstein alone, but it is hard to study these subjects without discussing these figures. Likewise, contemporary cultural studies is not the Birmingham School, but any exploration of the field does need to engage with its legacy.

My version of cultural studies begins then with neo-**Marxism** and its engagement with both **structuralism** and the work of **Gramsci**. Here the key concepts for cultural studies are those of **text**, **ideology** and **hegemony**. At the same time, cultural studies developed a stream of empirical and ethnographic work which has often been less high profile than textual analysis but with which I have sympathy. Indeed, I do not see **ethnography** and textual analysis as mutually exclusive. Later, somewhat in the wake of Stuart Hall, I embraced aspects of **poststructuralism**, and the work of **Foucault** in particular, where the concepts of **discourse** and **subjectivity** are central along with issues of truth and **representation**. In this context cultural studies and I became absorbed by questions of **identity.**

The engagement with poststructuralism has led to a re-thinking of the notions of ideology and hegemony. For example Hall, **Laclau** and Mouffe have pioneered a poststructuralist-inspired **post-Marxism** with which I have sympathy, though I now have even less use for the notion of ideology or orthodox Marxism than they do. This is a relatively straightforward Birmingham-inspired inter-subjective trajectory and one that is reflected in the construction of this dictionary. However, I shall claim with **irony** a small blow for my individuality by pointing to a departure from the main trajectory of cultural studies, that is, the influence of Richard **Rorty** and neo-**pragmatism** on my thinking and through him to the work of **Wittgenstein** (who also appears in the work of Mouffe for example).

Pragmatism shares its anti-foundationalism and anti-representationalism with the poststructuralist thinking that is currently ascendant within cultural studies. However, in contrast to poststructuralism, pragmatism combines these arguments with a commitment to social reform. Pragmatism suggests that the struggle for social change is a question of language/text *and* of material practice/policy action. Like cultural studies, pragmatism attempts to render contingent that which appears 'natural' in pursuit of a 'better' world. However, unlike the revolutionary rhetoric of many followers of poststructuralism, pragmatism weds itself to the need for piecemeal practical political change. In this sense, pragmatism has a 'tragic' view of life for it does not share the utopian push of, say, Marxism. In contrast, it favours a trial and error experimentalism that seeks after new ways of doing things that we can describe as 'better' when measured against 'our' **values**. I would argue that for cultural studies those values are, or should be, a modern–postmodern mix constituted by equality, liberty, solidarity, tolerance, difference, diversity and justice.

Overall then, my own thinking hovers between post-Marxism and neo-pragmatism, and an anonymous reviewer's description of me as a 'neo-Marxist turned postmodernist' was not without foundation. For those who are interested, this mixture forms the core of my book *Making Sense of Cultural Studies: Central Problems and Critical Debates* (Barker, 2002). This is not to say that other streams of cultural studies inspired, for example, by **hermeneutics**, **feminism** and/or **postcolonial theory** are not important, they most certainly are. I am merely trying to assist the reader in the **deconstruction** of any apparent solidity in this dictionary by pointing to some of the influences that bore on its formation.

THE DICTIONARY AS TOOLBOX

This book is centred on a series of concepts that I take to be important to cultural studies. Other cultural studies writers will differ about how to deploy these concepts and about which are the most significant. I also recognize that members of the cultural studies community may well disagree with my inclusion/exclusion of certain ideas. At the same time, I would be very surprised if we could not agree that a good deal of the concepts are a necessary part of cultural studies as it is currently constituted. I doubt that we would recognize a domain of study that did not include certain words – articulation, culture, discourse, hegemony, identity, ideology, popular culture, power, representation, sign, subjectivity, texts, to name but a few – as cultural studies.

These are amongst the theoretical concepts that constitute the framework within which cultural studies writers understand the world and might carry out empirical research and interpret their evidence. Thus it is this theoretical language of cultural studies that gives it its distinctive cast. This is a toolbox that is drawn from a number of different theoretical streams and methodological approaches that constitute the field. Broadly speaking, the tributaries of cultural studies are:

Ethnography	Feminism	Marxism
Philosophy of language	Political economy	Postcolonial theory
Post-Marxism	Poststructuralism	Pragmatism
Psychoanalysis	Structuralism	Textual analysis

Consequently, it has always been difficult to pin down the boundaries of cultural studies as a coherent, unified, academic discipline with clear-cut substantive topics, concepts and methods. However, the problems of definition and disciplinary boundaries are not uniquely problematic for cultural studies nor do they pose problems of unique complexity. It is just as difficult to achieve this task for sociology, women's studies, physics, linguistics and Buddhism. Thus, in trying to establish sociology as a coherent discipline Durkheim instituted a stream of thought that has been influential across time and space. Nevertheless, he did not define sociology for all time since this particular language-game has mutated and splintered.

Cultural studies has always been a multi- or post-disciplinary field of inquiry that blurs the boundaries between itself and other 'subjects'. Further, cultural studies has been something of a magpie; it has its own distinctive cast, yet it likes to borrow glittering concepts from other nests. However, the current vocabulary or toolbox of the field suggests that cultural studies is centrally concerned with culture as constituted by the **signs**, **meanings** and representations that are generated by signifying mechanisms in the context of human practices. Further, cultural studies is concerned with the construction and consequences of those representations and thus with matters of **power** since patterns of signifying practices constitute, and are constituted by, institutions and virtual structures. Here cultural studies is very much concerned with **cultural politics**.

Knowledge is not simply a matter of collecting facts from which **theory** can be deduced or against which it can be tested. That is, 'facts' are not neutral and no amount of stacking up of `facts' produces a story about our lives without theory. Indeed, theory is precisely a story about humanity with implications for action and judgements about consequences. Yet, theory does not picture the world more or less accurately; rather, it is a tool, instrument or logic for intervening in the world (Foucault, 1980). Theory construction is a self-reflexive discursive endeavour that seeks to interpret and intercede in the world: its construction involves the thinking through of concepts and arguments with the objective of offering new ways by which to think about ourselves. Theoretical work can be thought of as a crafting of the cultural signposts and maps by which we are guided and theoretical concepts are tools for thinking and acting in the world. As such, this dictionary can be thought of as a toolbox to help with the job of thinking.

And yet words are very slippery instruments indeed, as **Derrida** (1976) reminds us with his concept of **différance** – `difference and deferral'. For Derrida there is no original meaning outside of signs, and signs do not possess clear and fixed meanings. Here the production of meaning in the process of signification is continually deferred and supplemented so that meaning slides down a chain of signifiers abolishing a stable signified. Words carry multiple meanings, including the echoes or traces of other meanings from other related words in other contexts. Indeed, using a dictionary is a useful way of exploring the concept of différance. If we look up the meaning of a word in a dictionary we are referred to other words in an infinite process of **intertextual** deferral. There is no one fixed meaning to any of the concepts in this dictionary. This is not a dictionary that claims to give definitive meanings to words. At best, given that meaning lies in use, I offer some signposts to the common uses of the concepts in the context of cultural studies.

THE PURPOSES OF CULTURAL STUDIES

If the concepts that form the field of cultural studies are tools, then we might ask about the purposes for which they are wielded. That is, what is the nature of cultural studies as practice? Most writers in the field would probably agree that the purposes of cultural studies are analytic, pedagogic and political. In particular, cultural studies has sought to develop ways of thinking about culture and power that can be utilized by forms of social **agency** in the pursuit of change. This engagement with **politics** is, for Hall (1992), what differentiates cultural studies from other subject areas. Hence, cultural studies can be thought of as a body of theory generated by thinkers who regard the production of theoretical knowledge as a political practice.

The main direction taken by cultural studies, as enacted through teaching and writing, is intellectual clarification and legitimization. Cultural studies writers offer a variety of storytelling that can act as a **symbolic** guide or map of meaning and significance in the cosmos. As such, cultural studies has the potential to assist in comprehending and changing the world; it can act as a tool for activists and policy makers through problem solving, that is, re-definition and re-description of the world. Nevertheless, we should be careful not to confuse **writing** as a politically inspired endeavour with other kinds of civic and governmental political practices.

The prime locations of cultural studies as a set of practices are academic institutions, for example, universities and publishing houses. Consequently, as it has become something to be taught, so cultural studies has acquired a multitude of institutional bases, courses, textbooks and students. In due course, this process leads to a certain 'disciplining' of cultural studies. The courses now offered by universities for undergraduate students constitute a broad 'definition' of the parameters of cultural studies. The textbooks that follow, including my own (Barker, 2000), reinforce this process. Many cultural studies practitioners have felt ill at ease with the forging of institutional disciplinary boundaries for the field. Professionalized and institutionalized cultural studies might, feared Hall, 'formalize out of existence the critical questions of power, history and politics, (Hall, 1992: 286).

However, although higher education is a branch of government and thus teachers are an arm of the state, higher education remains, at least within **liberal** democracies, a privileged site of critical inquiry. Writers, researchers and teachers in higher education may not be the 'organic' **intellectuals** that the 'pioneers' of cultural studies hoped for. However, they are in a position to speak with, and provide intellectual resources for, **New Social Movements**, workers in cultural industries and those involved with the forging of **cultural policy**. To some extent, cultural studies is constrained by its institutionalization, yet, it retains a critical edge. Likewise, while cultural studies is to a degree an academic discipline of the university system, it nevertheless continues to slip away from its moorings and slide across the surface of culture, its infinite object of inquiry and desire.

In sum, cultural studies can be understood as an intellectual enterprise that is constituted by a set of overlapping language-games. Nevertheless, for those readers frustrated by my evasion in refusing to define cultural studies, I shall now make the claim that an exploration of the contemporary vocabulary of cultural studies suggests that we might understand it thus:

> Cultural studies is concerned with an exploration of culture, as constituted by the meanings and representations generated by human signifying practices, and the context in which they occur. Cultural studies has a particular interest in the relations of power and the political consequences that are inherent in such cultural practices. The prime purposes of cultural studies, which is located in the institutions of universities, publishing houses and bookshops, are the processes of intellectual clarification that could provide useful tools for cultural/political activists and policy makers.

Of course, the tools of cultural studies are words and concepts – hence, in my view, the significance of a dictionary.

FEATURES OF THE DICTIONARY

This dictionary follows the format of most others, in that there is an alphabetical list of concepts that can be consulted whereupon one will find a discussion of the meanings and uses associated with that concept in the context of cultural studies. However, I have already argued that the meanings and uses of such terms are relational and located within a network of other concepts. Consequently, at the end of the entry I provide a list of ideas that are connected to the one that has been consulted. I have called these 'links' in the manner of a hypertext to suggest that these concepts are multi-dimensional and that one can go on pursuing their meanings in the manner implied by the notion of différance (above). Although here, of course, there is an arbitrary limit to the internal referentiality of a dictionary and thus to the trail of meaning.

In addition to the key concepts involved, I have also provided some short descriptions of key writers who have in one way or another been associated with the development of cultural studies. This list is in no way exhaustive and I am not wishing to provide an 'A-list' of the good and the great in cultural studies. It is more of a taster than a hearty meal. Further, some of the people involved are clearly connected with the development of cultural studies (for example, **Fiske**, **Gilroy**, Hall, Willis etc.) while others have provided important philosophical ideas to cultural studies though they have never identified their work with cultural studies *per se* (for example, Derrida, Foucault, **Giddens**, Rorty etc.).

In deciding whom to include and whom to omit I have tried to present a cross-section of writers from different times, places and philosophical stances that have influenced cultural studies, rather than a comprehensive list. I have also inevitably indulged some of my own preferences and been restricted by the limitations of my knowledge. My apologies to those who merit inclusion but were omitted. Still, I want to maintain that the core of the work is to do with thinking about concepts rather than people. I also want to suggest that the concepts in cultural studies do not belong to anyone. Rather, they circulate amongst a community of thinkers who forge and amend their meanings in the course of their work. Consequently, I have chosen not to reference ideas in the normal academic fashion but to claim them all as collective property not in need of attribution.[2]

As such, this dictionary is a mélange or **bricolage** of ideas, examples, themes etc. raided from the collective library of cultural studies – or rather, that which I have chosen to designate as cultural studies. Thus, on the one hand a dictionary such as this manifests a certain arbitrary character and yet on the other it is dependent on an interpretive community. Similarly it seeks to pin down the meaning of words while all along claiming that meaning is intertextual and resists closure. But then oscillating between individuality and community and between fixity and fluidity are key themes of cultural studies.

REFERENCES

Barker, C. (2000) *Cultural Studies: Theory and Practice*. London and Thousand Oaks, CA: Sage.
Barker, C. (2002) *Making Sense of Cultural Studies: Central Problems and Critical Debates*. London: Sage.

---

2 Nevertheless, where a line of thought has been pursued by a writer who is included in the dictionary I have maintained the practice of internal reference by highlighting their name by way of suggesting that readers might like to explore their work further.

Davidson, D. (1984) *Inquiries into Truth and Interpretation*. Oxford: Clarendon Press.

Derrida, J. (1976) *Of Grammatology* (trans. G. Spivak). Baltimore, MD: Johns Hopkins University Press.

Foucault, M. (1980) *Power/Knowledge*. New York: Pantheon.

Grossberg, L., Nelson, C. and Treichler, P. (1992) 'Cultural Studies: An Introduction', in L. Grossberg, C. Nelson, and P. Treichler (eds), *Cultural Studies*. London and New York: Routledge. pp. 1–22.

Hall, S (1992) 'Cultural Studies and its Theoretical Legacies', in L. Grossberg, C. Nelson, and P. Treichler (eds), *Cultural Studies*. London and New York: Routledge. pp. 277–94.

Hall, S. (1997) 'The Work of Representation', in S. Hall (ed.) *Representations*. London and Thousand Oaks, CA: Sage. pp. 13–74.

Wittgenstein, L. (1957) *Philosophical Investigations*. Oxford: Basil Blackwell.

RECOMMENDED READING: AN INTRODUCTION TO CULTURAL STUDIES

For those who are relatively unfamiliar with the field of cultural studies and who want an introduction to it, the following ten books may be useful.

Barker, C. (2000) *Cultural Studies: Theory and Practice*. London and Thousand Oaks, CA: Sage.

Du Gay, P., Hall S., Janes, L., Mackay, H. and Negus, K. (1997) *Doing Cultural Studies*. London and Thousand Oaks, CA: Sage.

Gray, A. (2003) *Research Practice for Cultural Studies*. London and Thousand Oaks, CA: Sage.

Hall, S. (ed.) (1997) *Representations*. London and Thousand Oaks, CA: Sage.

Hartley, J. (2003) *A Short History of Cultural Studies*. London and Thousand Oaks, CA: Sage.

Jordan, G. and Weedon, C. (1995) *Cultural Politics: Class, Gender, Race and the Postmodern World*. Oxford: Blackwell.

Lewis, J. (2002) *Cultural Studies: The Basics*. London and Thousand Oaks, CA: Sage.

McGuigan, J. and Gray, A. (eds) (1990) *Studying Culture: An Introductory Reader*. London: Edward Arnold.

Storey, J. (ed.) (1997) *What is Cultural Studies?* London: Routledge.

Woodward, K. (ed.) (1997) *Identity and Difference*. London and Thousand Oaks, CA: Sage.

I have also provided a reference in relation to each of the named authors in the dictionary, so that constitutes another fifty texts to be going on with . . .

A

Active audience The concept of the active audience indicates the capability of 'readers' to be dynamic creators of significance rather than being understood as simple receptors of textual meaning. This paradigm emerged in reaction to communications research that studied audiences as if they simply absorbed the meanings and messages of popular media (as identified by critics) in a passive way. This was colloquially known as the 'hypodermic model' of audiences because the meanings of texts appear to be injected directly into the minds of readers without modification. Overall, the active audience paradigm represented a shift of interest from numbers to meanings and from the general audience to particular audiences.

The active audience paradigm was theoretically informed by the encoding–decoding model of communications and by hermeneutic theory. Subsequent empirical studies by David **Morley** and Ien **Ang** in the 1980s argued that the cultural context in which reading took place provided the framework and cultural resources for differential understandings of texts. Consequently, meaning was not to be located in the text *per se,* but in the interplay of the text and the audience. Thus Ang's study of women viewers of *Dallas* found that they held a range of understandings and attitudes. Her central argument is that *Dallas* viewers are actively involved in the production of a range of meanings and pleasures that are not reducible to the structure of the text, an 'ideological effect' or a political project.

Various studies of national/ethnic cultural identity and television viewing provide evidence of divergent readings of narratives founded in different cultural backgrounds. That is, audiences use their own sense of national and ethnic identity as a position from which to decode programmes so that US television is not necessarily uncritically consumed by audiences with the destruction of 'indigenous' cultural identities as the inevitable outcome. There is now a good deal of mutually supporting work on audiences within the cultural studies tradition from which one can draw the following conclusions.

- The audience is conceived of as active and knowledgeable producers of meaning not as products of a structured text.
- Meanings are bounded by the way the text is structured and by the domestic and cultural context of the viewing.
- Audiences need to be understood in the contexts in which they read texts, both in terms of meaning construction and the routines of daily life.
- Audiences are easily able to distinguish between fiction and reality, indeed they actively play with the boundaries.
- The processes of meaning construction and the place of texts in the routines of

daily life alter from culture to culture, and in terms of gender and class within the same cultural community.

Links **Consumption, encoding-decoding, hermeneutics, reading, resistance, text**

Acculturation The ability to 'go on' in a culture requires the learning and acquisition of language, values and norms through imitation, practice and experimentation. The concept of acculturation refers to the social processes by which we learn the knowledge and skills that enable us to be members of a culture. Key sites and agents of acculturation would include the family, peer groups, schools, work organizations and the media. The processes of acculturation represent the nurture side of the so-called 'Nature *vs* Nurture' debate, and are looked to by cultural theorists as providing the basis on which actors acquire a way of life and a way of seeing.

The central argument of cultural studies is that being a person requires the processes of acculturation. Here personhood is understood to be a contingent and culturally specific production whereby what it means to be a person is social and cultural 'all the way down'. While there is no known culture that does not use the pronoun 'I', and which does not therefore have a conception of self and personhood, the manner in which 'I' is used, what it means, does vary from culture to culture. Thus, the individualistic sense of uniqueness and self-consciousness that is widespread in Western societies is not shared to the same extent by people in cultures where personhood is inseparable from a network of kinship relations and social obligations. Subjectivity can thus be seen to be an outcome of acculturation.

Links **Constructionism, culture, identity, language, subjectivity**

Adorno, Theodor (1903–1969) As co-director (with Max Horkheimer) of the Institute for Social Research at the University of Frankfurt, the German-born Theodor Adorno was a key figure in the so-called 'Frankfurt School' that later relocated to the United States under threat from the Nazis. Adorno explores culture through a combination of Marxist and psychoanalytic theory to argue that commodity culture is a form of mass deception that generates standardized reactions that affirm the status quo. This involves not just the overt meanings of ideology but the structuring of the human psyche into conformist ways. By contrast, critical art for Adorno is that which is not oriented to the market but challenges the standards of intelligibility of a reified society. Specifically, Adorno praises the 'alien' nature of avant-garde modernist art such as the atonal music of Schoenberg.

- **Associated concept** Avant-garde, capitalism, commodification, culture industry.
- **Tradition(s)** Critical theory, Marxism, psychoanalysis.
- **Reading** Adorno, T.W. and Horkheimer, M. (1979; orig. 1946) *The Dialectic of Enlightenment*. London: Verso.

Advertising Advertising is at the core of contemporary culture and at the heart of debates about postmodernism, globalization and consumer culture. Thus, amongst the markers of postmodern culture are the increased emphasis given to the visual over the verbal and the general aestheticization of cultural life in which advertising plays a key role. Further, the globalization of communications technologies and of television in particular has placed visual-based advertising at the centre of an increasingly world-wide consumer culture. This, it has been argued, is a 'promotional culture' focused on the use of visual imagery to create value-added **3** brands or commodity-signs.

The term 'Coca Cola culture' encapsulates the global reach of this promotional culture and highlights the alleged link between global capitalism, advertising and cultural homogenization. However, the global circulation of consumer goods should not lead us to assume that their impact is the same the world over since consumer goods are subject to the processes of 'localization'. That is, globalized meanings are amended at local levels in ways that generate a variety of meanings. Similarly, within the West, the creative consumption of symbolic culture makes the outcome of advertising less certain than it may at first appear. The majority of commodities launched and advertised fail, yet it is also the case that without advertising they are unlikely to succeed in the contemporary market place.

The textual and ideological analysis of advertising within cultural studies has stressed the selling not just of commodities but of ways of looking at the world. Thus the job of advertising is to create an 'identity' for a product amid the bombardment of competing images by associating the brand with desirable human values. Acquiring a brand is not simply about purchasing a product, rather, it is also concerned with buying into lifestyles and values. Thus, objects in advertisements are signifiers of meaning that we decode in the context of known cultural systems associating products in adverts with other cultural 'goods'. While an image of a particular product may denote only beans or a car, it is made to connote 'nature' or 'family'. In buying commodities we emotionally invest in the associated image and so contribute to the construction of our identities through consumption.

However, **Baudrillard** suggests that sign-value has replaced the use-value or exchange-value of commodities that is central to this analysis. In his view, consumerism is at the heart of a postmodern culture that is constituted through a continual flow of images that establishes no connotational hierarchy and thus no sense of value. This is said to be a culture in which no objects have an 'essential' or 'deep' value, rather, value is determined through the exchange of symbolic meanings. That is, commodities have sign-value established through advertising that confers prestige and signifies social value, status and power. A commodity is not an object with use-value but a commodity-sign so that postmodern culture is literally and metaphorically 'superficial'.

Links **Commodification, consumption, globalization, ideology, postmodernism**

Aesthetics Aesthetics is a domain of philosophy concerned with questions of Art and beauty. Traditionally, aesthetic philosophy has sought to provide universal criteria for the definition of Art, as in the work of Kant, and as such tends towards essentialism. An aesthetic judgement seeks to distinguish between what is Art and what is not Art as well as between good Art and bad Art. It is thus that aesthetic judgement underpins the drawing up of the artistic or literary canon. Aesthetic philosophy also provides an account of the relationship of Art to other domains of human activity, such as morality, politics and commerce.

Cultural studies developed in part through criticism of the notion of universal aesthetic criteria and the class-based cultural elitism that it contains. The anthropologically oriented understanding of culture as 'ordinary' that forms a bedrock assumption of cultural studies was developed in opposition to the elite notion of culture as being concerned only with high culture, that is, cultural forms that elite critics defined as the aesthetically good. The policing of the boundaries of a canon of 'good works' by aesthetic theory had historically led to the exclusion of popular culture. However, writers interested in popular culture have argued that there are no universal grounds for drawing lines between the worthy and the unworthy so that evaluation is not a sustainable task for the critic. The obligation of the critic is not to make aesthetic judgements but to describe and analyse the cultural production of meaning. This stance had the great merit of opening up a whole new array of popular cultural texts for legitimate discussion.

The problem for aesthetic theory from a cultural studies perspective is that the concepts of beauty, harmony, form and quality can be applied as much to a steam train as to a novel or a painting and are thus culturally relative. As such, high culture is another subculture. Further, Art can be understood as a socially created category that has been attached to certain external and internal signals by which art is recognized. Hence the 'art gallery' and the theatre. Art is not the outcome of the mystical practices of geniuses or of a different order of work from the creation of popular culture but is an industry with its owners, managers and workers.

Cultural studies does, of course, make value judgements about culture. However, these are characteristically ideological and political judgements rather than ones based on aesthetic criteria. Thus cultural studies has developed arguments that revolve around the social and political consequences of constructing and disseminating specific discursive constructions of the world with a view to understanding the way cultural and symbolic processes are connected to power.

Links **Author, canon, cultural studies, culture, essentialism, ideology, symbolic**

Agency The concept of agency can be understood to mark the socially determined capability to act and to make a difference. Agency has commonly been associated with notions of freedom, free will, action, creativity, originality and the possibility of change brought about through the actions of sovereign individuals. However, there is an important conceptual difference between agents who are held to be free in the sense of 'not determined' and agency understood as the socially constituted capacity to act. While the former concept makes no sense, for there can be no uncaused human acts, the latter asks us to consider agency as consisting of acts that make a pragmatic difference. Here, agency means the enactment of X rather than Y course of action. Of course, precisely because socially constructed agency involves differentially distributed social resources that give rise to various degrees of the ability to act in specific spaces, so some actors have more scope for action than do others.

To enact X rather than Y course of action does not mean that we have made an undetermined selection of activity. Rather, the basis for our choice has been determined or caused by the very way we are constituted as subjects. That is, by the where, when and how of our coming to be who we are. In that sense agency is determined by the social structures of language, the routine character of modern life and by psychic and emotional narratives that we cannot bring wholly to consciousness. Nevertheless, agency is a culturally intelligible way of understanding ourselves and we clearly have the existential experience of facing and making choices.

Neither human freedom nor human action can consist of an escape from social determinants and as such it is a rather pointless metaphysical question to ask whether people are 'really' free or 'really' determined in any absolute sense. Consequently, it is useful to consider freedom and determination as different modes of discourse or different languages for different purposes. Thus, our everyday practice and existential experience of decision making are not changed by the notion that we are the products of biochemical and cultural determination. Indeed, since the language of freedom and the language of determination are culturally produced for different purposes in different realms, it make sense to talk about freedom from political persecution or economic scarcity without the need to say that agents are free in some undetermined way. Rather, such discourses are comparing different social formations and determinations and judging one to be better than another on the basis of our culturally determined values.

Investigating the problem of agency involves entering a realm of metaphors that have different applications. Thus the language of agency celebrates the cultural power and capacities of persons, encourages us to act and to seek improvement of the human condition as well as persuading us to take responsibility for our actions. It also enables institutions, for example, the courts, to hold persons accountable for specific acts. By contrast, the language of determination helps to trace causality home and points to the contours of cultural life that enable some courses of action while dis-empowering others. This is the language of the dance in which we actively and creatively perform ourselves through a cosmic choreography that has no author. Here the purposes are solidarity, the alleviation of individual responsibility and acceptance that there are limits to the plasticity of the human condition.

Links **Acculturation, determinism, identity, structuration, structure, subjectivity**

Alienation The foremost theoretical source for the concept of alienation within cultural studies is Marxism and the understanding of capitalism and the labour process that is found within it. For **Marx** the first priority of human beings is the production of their means of subsistence (and consequently themselves) through labour. The centrepiece of Marx's work was an analysis of the dynamics of capitalism wherein a propertyless proletariat must sell their labour to survive. As a consequence, they are then faced with the products of their own labour in the form of commodities that now wield power and influence over them. Here the workers are doubly alienated; first by the transformation of the core of human activity,

6

namely the labour process, into meaningless actions, and second, through separation from the products of their own labour. According to Marx, capitalism also alienated workers from each other through competition, division and individualism as well as from their 'species being,' by which he means the human potential for self-determination.

A less theoretically specific use of the concept of alienation comes with the sense that the cultural circumstances of modernity are inherently those of inauthenticity and dislocation. In particular, the cultural experience of modern urban life is understood to be one of anonymity, isolation and anxiety as expressed through the themes and aesthetic style of modernism. Here alienation connotes a psychological condition of estrangement, disaffection and emotional distance that is a consequence of the impersonality and speed of living generated by modern technology, commodification and city life.

Links **Capitalism, commodification, Marxism, modernism, modernity, urbanization**

Althusser, Louis (1918–1990) Althusser was a Marxist philosopher and theorist of the French Communist Party who is associated with the attempt to produce a structuralist Marxism. In particular he rejected what he saw as the humanism inherent in the early work of **Marx** in favour of what he understood to be the scientific structuralism of the later *Das Kapital*. His central influence within cultural studies was the argument that a social formation was constituted by a complex overdetermined relationship between different autonomous levels of practice. In particular, he was a significant figure in cultural studies' break with economic determinism and the granting of autonomy within theory to the levels of culture and ideology. Once a thinker of considerable influence, especially during the late 1960s and 1970s, his star has now waned because of the complexity of his writing and the dogmatism, scientism and reductionism of his thinking.

- **Associated concepts** Ideological state apparatus, ideology, post-humanism, social formation.
- **Tradition(s)** Marxism, structuralism.
- **Reading** Althusser, L. (1969) *For Marx*. London: Allen Lane Press.

Ang, Ien (1954–) Ang's pioneering study of the way an audience reads television, *Watching Dallas*, became one of the cornerstones of the 'active audience' stream within cultural studies. Her central argument is that *Dallas* viewers are actively involved in the production of a range of responses that are not reducible to the structure of the text. Subsequent to this study, Ang has continued to write widely on the themes of media, culture, migration and globalization. She has continued to maintain a substantial empirical emphasis in her work that includes an interest in ethnicity and migrant cultures in Australia. She is Professor of Cultural Studies and Director of the Centre for Cultural Research at the University of Western Sydney.

- **Associated concepts** Active audience, consumption, ethnicity, gender, globalization, reading.
- **Tradition(s)** Cultural studies, feminism, hermeneutics, postmodernism.

● **Reading** Ang, I. (1985) *Watching Dallas: Soap Opera and the Melodramatic Imagination*. London: Metheun.

Anti-essentialism This concept alludes to the idea that words do not have referents in an independent object world that possesses essential or universal qualities. Rather, all categories of knowledge are discursive constructions that change their meanings according to time, place and usage. In particular, there can be no truths, subjects or identities outside of language, which does not itself have stable referents, and thus there are no stable truths or identities. The 'objects' of language are not fixed or universal things but meaningful descriptions that through social convention come to be 'what counts as truth' (that is, the temporary stabilization of meaning).

7

Anti-essentialism offers an awareness of the contingent, constructed character of our beliefs and understandings that lack firm universal foundations. However, this does not mean that we cannot speak of truth or identity *per se*. Rather, the anti-essentialist argument points to both as being cultural productions that are located in specific times and places rather than being universals of nature. Thus, the speaking subject is dependent on the prior existence of discursive positions and truth is made rather than found. For example, since words do not refer to essences, identity is not a fixed universal 'thing' but a description in language that is malleable so that what it means to be a 'woman' or an 'American' is not stable but subject to constant modification.

The argument that social categories do not have universal, essential characteristics or qualities but are constituted by the way we speak about them is derived from an anti-representationalist understanding of language. That is, language does not reflect a pre-existent and external reality of independent objects but rather constructs meaning from within itself through a series of conceptual and phonic differences. Thus, the signifier 'good' has meaning not because it refers to a universal quality but by virtue of its relations with other related signifiers, notably bad, but also righteous, worthy, virtuous etc.

The philosopher **Derrida** argues that since meaning is generated through the play of signifiers and not by reference to an independent object world it can never be fixed. Words carry multiple meanings, including the echoes or traces of other meanings from other related words in other contexts, so that language is inherently unstable and meaning constantly slides away. Thus, by différance, the key Derridian concept, is meant 'difference and deferral'. In a similar vein, **Wittgenstein** argued that the meaning of words is derived not from reference to objects but through use in specific language-games and social contexts.

Links **Différance, essentialism, identity, language-game, poststructuralism, semiotics**

Archaeology In the context of cultural studies the idea of archaeology is associated with the methodology involved in the early works of **Foucault**. By archaeology he means the exploration of the specific and determinate historical conditions that form the grounds on which discourses are created and regulated to define a distinct field of knowledge/objects. A domain of knowledge requires a particular set of concepts that delimits a specific 'regime of truth '(that is, what counts as truth) and Foucault attempts to identify the historical conditions and determining rules of their formation.

8   Archaeology suggests excavation of the past in one specific site and entails 'digging up' the local sites of discursive practice. Foucault argues that archaeology is the appropriate method for the analysis of local discursivities; it is not transcendental and does not seek to identify the universal structures of all knowledge or all possible moral action, but treats the instances of discourse as historical events.

Foucault argues that his archaeological methods demonstrate that discourse is discontinuous in the transition from one historical era to another. That is, the social world is marked by different epistemes, or configurations of knowledge, so that it is no longer perceived, described, classified and known in the same way but rather is marked by historical breaks in understanding. Foucault's stress on discontinuity constitutes a questioning of the modern themes of genesis, teleology, continuity, totality and unified subjects. The tracing of the discontinuities of history is the domain of his other favoured methodology–genealogy.

Links **Discourse, episteme, genealogy, power/knowledge, poststructuralism, truth**

Articulation The concept of articulation has been used to theorize the relationships between discursive elements and/or components of a social formation. The notion of articulation is premised on the argument put by **Laclau** that there are no *necessary* links between discursive concepts or between the 'levels' of a social formation and that those which are forged are of a temporary nature, being articulated and bound together by custom and convention. Here, according to **Hall**, the concept of articulation suggests a temporary unity of discursive elements that do not have to 'go together' so that an articulation is the form of connection that *can* make a unity of two different elements under certain conditions. Articulation suggests expressing/representing as well as a joining together.

For example, the apparent 'unity' of identity can be understood as the articulation of different and distinct elements that, under other historical and cultural circumstances, could be re-articulated in different ways. Here individuals are understood to be the unique historically specific articulation of discursive components that are contingent but also socially determined or regulated. Since there is no *automatic* connection between the various discourses of identity, class, gender, race, age etc. they can be articulated together in different ways. Thus, all middle class white men do not necessarily share the same identity and identifications any more than all working class black women do. Further, ideas about ethnic purity may be articulated with nationality within nationalist discourse and gendered metaphors play a significant part in the construction of the nation, for example, the fatherland, mother of the nation etc.

The concept of articulation enables apparently unifying concepts such as 'society' or 'nation' to be considered as the unique historically specific temporary stabilization of relations and meanings. For example, national identity can be grasped as a way of unifying cultural diversity. That is, national culture is a discursive device that represents difference as unity or identity.

The notion of articulation is also deployed to discuss the relationship between culture and political economy so that culture is said to be 'articulated' with moments of production but not determined in any 'necessary' way by those moments and vice versa. In this model, cultural meaning is produced and embedded at each level of a 'circuit of culture' whose meaningful work is necessary, but not sufficient for, or determining of, the next moment in the circuit. Each moment–production, representation, identity, consumption and regulation–involves the production of meaning which is articulated, linked to, the next moment without determining what meanings will be taken up or produced at that level.

Links **Circuit of culture, identity, national identity, post-Marxism, social formation**

Authenticity To claim that a category is authentic is to argue that it is genuine, natural, true and pure. For example, it might be claimed that the culture of a particular place is authentic because uncontaminated by tourism, or that a youth culture is pure and uncorrupted by consumer capitalism. In this sense, the concept of authenticity is closely related to the notion of essentialism in that authenticity implies immaculate origins. It follows then that the anti-essentialism of poststructuralism and postmodernism rejects the idea of the authentic as such, replacing it with the notion of 'authenticity claims'. That is, nothing is authentic in a metaphysical sense; rather, cultures construct certain places, activities, artefacts etc. as being authentic.

The question of authenticity can be grasped through consideration of the study of youth within the field. Here cultural studies has tended to explore the more spectacular youth cultures; the visible, loud, different, avant-garde youth styles which have stood out and demanded attention. These activities have commonly been understood as an authentic expression of the resistance of young people to the hegemony of consumer capitalism and arbitrary adult authority. Subcultures have been seen as spaces for deviant cultures to re-negotiate their position or to 'win space' for themselves. In particular, youth subcultures are marked, it is argued, by the development of particular styles which, as the active enactment of resistance, relied on a moment of originality, purity and authenticity.

However, the distinction between the media, the culture industries and an oppositional and authentic youth subculture is problematic when the latter is heavily influenced and shaped by the global leisure industry. If youth cultures are thoroughly embroiled in surveillance, the mass media and the cultural industries, then claims to authenticity by members and subculture theorists look dubious. Style, it is now argued, involves bricolage without reference to the meanings of originals and has no underlying message or ironic transformation. It is the look and only the look, merely another mode of fashion, pastiche rather than parody.

The birth of youth fashion and style in the media does not necessarily reduce style to meaninglessness. Thus the end of authenticity is not the death of significance, for bricolage can involve the creative recombination of existing items to forge new meanings. This creativity takes place 'inside the whale' of postmodern consumer capitalism where the binary divisions of inside–outside and authentic–manufactured collapse. Style is on the surface, culture is industry, subcultures are mainstream, high culture is a subculture, the avant-garde is commercial pop art, fashion is retro. However, the deconstruction of authenticity at the level of theory does not prevent participants in youth subcultures from laying claim to it. Indeed, empirical research suggests that claims to authenticity remain at the heart of contemporary youth subcultures and club cultures.

Links **Anti-essentialism, author, essentialism, postmodernism, style, subculture**

Author Both the high cultural tradition and common sense understand an author to be an individual who is the creative originator of a text and whose intentions constitute a work's authentic meanings and significance. This account of an author is solidly located within the humanist tradition wherein meaning is understood to be the product of unique and unified persons who possess an inner core that is the source of significance and creativity.

However, this view has been challenged, from a number of theoretical directions, by questioning the proposition that individuals are the most appropriate level at which to explore the generation of meaning. Thus the tradition of hermeneutics disputes the idea that an 'author' has any special insight into the meanings of a text since meaning is required to be actualized by readers who may do so in ways that deviate from authorial intention. For hermeneutic theory, understanding and meaning are realized in the 'hermeneutic circle' that is constituted by the interplay between texts and readers.

Barthes, **Derrida** and **Foucault**, writers associated with poststructuralism, have also challenged the centrality of authorship. Indeed, Barthes famously announced the 'death of the author' arguing that a text does not consist of a single meaning (the 'message' of the Author–God), rather, it is better grasped as a multi-dimensional space in which a variety of writings blend and clash. In other words, textual meaning is unstable and cannot be confined to single words, sentences or particular texts. Meaning has no single originatory source but rather is the outcome of relationships between texts, that is, intertextuality. This is an idea that finds further elaboration in the work of Derrida and in particular through his notion of 'différance'. In a parallel argument, Foucault suggests that the proper name 'author' is not to be identified with a 'real and external individual' but rather is a sign that marks an 'author–function' in the context of discourses of individualism and artistic creativity. Thus the 'author' is understood to be a sign of a particular 'regime of the self' and its processes of subject formation.

To hold subjects and texts to be the products of social and cultural processes that lie outside of the individual does not mean that either persons or works of art are not original. Originality does not have to mean that subjects or texts are their own spontaneous source but rather that they demonstrate specific and unique arrangements of the cultural resources from which they are formed. Subjects all have unique patterns of family relations, of friends, of work and of access to discursive resources just as the order of words and narrative structure of one novel is not exactly the same as another. Both the self and texts are original, like a snowflake that is constructed from the common ingredients that make up snow.

Links **Différance, hermeneutics, humanism, meaning, poststructuralism, subjectivity, text**

Avant-garde The French term avant-garde is equivalent to the English word 'vanguard' and refers to the foremost part of an army that is often sent ahead of the main body to perform some special task. The idea of the avant-garde was adopted as a metaphor within aesthetic theory to refer to experimental Art movements, most notably those of the modernist movement of the early twentieth century. These would include the self-proclaimed new movements of cubism, dada and surrealism. The idea of the avant-garde carries with it the connotation of cultural leadership and progress. In particular, avant-garde movements have often sought to destroy, or at least deconstruct, the very idea of Art even while they appear to many as the height of aesthetic elitism.

Some writers associated with or drawn upon by cultural studies have embraced avant-garde Art. Thus **Adorno** praises the non-realism and the 'alien' nature of avant-garde work which, he argues, inspires us through its 'utopian negativity'. Art of this type is said to force us to consider new ways of looking at the world through its unconventional use of form. In a similar vein, **Kristeva** argues that 'transgression' is marked in certain kinds of avant-garde modernist literary and artistic practice through the rhythms, breaks and absences in texts that re-order signs in time and space and so develop a new language. Indeed 'femininity' is understood by Kristeva to be a condition or subject position of marginality that some men, for example avant-garde artists, can also occupy.

On the other hand, given its cultural populism, that is, the sense that popular culture is as valuable as high culture, cultural studies also contains a strand of thinking that is less sympathetic to avant-garde work, seeing it as obscure and condescending. Thus it is sometimes argued that the task of breaking down the barriers between Art and popular culture has been achieved rather more successfully by postmodernism with its blurring of the boundaries of Art, commerce and popular culture than by the modernist avant-garde. Postmodernism often shares with avant-garde work the use of non-linear narrative forms, montage, juxtaposition, de-contextualization of images and aesthetic self-consciousness. However, postmodernism plays with popular culture and its forms more obviously than does modernist avant-garde art and with a stronger sense of irony. Nevertheless, postmodernism in Art has remained avant-garde in its relative isolation from mainstream popular culture.

Links **Aesthetics, critical theory, modernism, popular culture, postmodernism**

B

Bakhtin, Mikhail (1895–1975) Bakhtin was born in Russia, studied at St Petersburg University and worked as a professor in the small town of Saransk after spending a significant period of his life in exile in Kazakhstan. Much of his work emanated from a group of thinkers known as 'the Bakhtin circle' and indeed some of his work is thought to have been published under other names, most notably that of Volosinov. Bakhtin was critical of formalism and instead conceives of language as a diverse, living, action-oriented phenomenon where meaning arises out of a dialogic relation between speakers and interlocutors. Heteroglossia is Bakhtin's term for the multi-voiced workings of language and culture that constitute the field of signs in which there is a struggle over meaning. For Bakhtin the renaissance 'carnivalesque', as documented by Rabelais, is a manifestation of the heterogeneity of culture and the impulse to resist the official languages of the powerful.

- **Associated concepts** Anti-essentialism, carnivalesque, dialogic, intertextuality, language, meaning, polysemy.
- **Tradition(s)** Hermeneutics, Marxism.
- **Reading** Bakhtin, M. (1965) *Rabelais and his World*. Bloomington, IN: Indiana University Press

Barthes, Roland (1915–1980) The French writer, critic, teacher and theorist Roland Barthes exerted a very significant influence on the development of cultural studies, particularly in its movement from culturalism to structuralism during the 1970s. His work was instrumental in assisting cultural thinkers to break with the notion of the text as a carrier of transparent meaning. In particular, he brought the methods of semiotics to bear on a wide range of cultural phenomena to illuminate the argument that all texts are constructed with signs in social contexts. Central to Barthes's work is the role of signs in generating meaning and framing the way texts are read. Thus he explored the way that the naturalization of connotative meanings enables that which is cultural to appear as pre-given universal truths, which he called myths. He famously declared the 'death of the author' as a way of illustrating the argument that meaning does not reside with individual writers but rather with the interplay between the wider structures of cultural meaning and the interpretive acts of readers.

- **Associated concepts** Author, meaning, myth, reading, signs, text.
- **Tradition(s)** Cultural studies, poststructuralism, semiotics, structuralism.
- **Reading** Barthes, R. (1972) *Mythologies*. London: Cape.

Base and superstructure The metaphor of the base and superstructure derives from Marxism and is a way of explaining the relationship between the economy and culture. As such it forms the basis of a perspective known as cultural materialism. Broadly speaking, it is argued that the cultural superstructure is shaped and determined by the economic base or mode of production. According to **Marx**, as people produce the means of their material subsistence, so they enter into definite forms of social relationship. Subsequently these relations of production constitute the economic structure of society which itself constitutes the base on which cultural and political superstructures arise. Thus, the mode of production of material life determines the general character of the social, political and cultural processes of living.

It is noteworthy that for Marx a mode of production is held to be 'the real foundation' of legal and political superstructures and that it determines the social, political and cultural. Thus, the economic mode of production or 'base' shapes the cultural 'superstructure' so that, for Marxism, culture is the consequence of a historically specific mode of production. As such it is not a neutral terrain because the class-based relations of production express themselves as political and legal relations. Here culture naturalizes the social order as an inevitable 'fact' so obscuring the underlying relations of exploitation. Consequently, culture is understood to be inherently the domain of ideology, a conceptualization that forms the basis of cultural studies' fascination with issues of ideology and hegemony as read through **Althusser**, **Gramsci** and **Hall**.

Most thinkers in cultural studies have rejected the economic reductionism implicit to the base and superstructure model. While the analysis of economic determinants may be necessary to any understanding of culture it is not, and cannot be, self-sufficient. Many thinkers from within cultural studies have argued that we need to examine cultural phenomena in terms of their own rules, logics, development and effectivity. This argument points to the desirability of a multi-dimensional and multi-perspectival approach to the understanding of culture. This methodology would seek to grasp the connections between economic, political, social and cultural dimensions without reducing social phenomena to any one level.

Links **Circuit of culture, cultural materialism, culture, hegemony, ideology, Marxism, reductionism**

Baudrillard, Jean (1929–) The early influences upon French theorist Jean Baudrillard, namely structuralism and Marxism, are also the prime targets of his core works where he critiques their assumptions and develops his own theories of postmodernism. Amongst Baudrillard's key themes is the idea that the Marxist distinction between use-value and exchange-value has collapsed in favour of the exchange of signs. Thus, a commodity is not simply an object with use-value for exchange but a commodity-sign. For Baudrillard, postmodern culture is constituted through a continual flow of images that establishes no connotational hierarchy but is one-dimensional and 'superficial'. Baudrillard argues that a series of modern distinctions, including the real and the unreal, the public and the private, Art and reality, have broken down (or been sucked into a 'black hole' as he calls it) leading to a culture of simulacrum and hyperreality.

- **Associated concepts** Commodification, hyperreality, irony, signs, simulacrum, symbolic.
- **Tradition(s)** Marxism, postmodernism, semiotics, structuralism.

- **Reading** Baudrillard, J. (1983) *Simulacra and Simulations*. New York: Semiotext(e).

Bennett, Tony (1947–) Bennett was a member of the Birmingham Centre for Contemporary Cultural Studies (CCCS) where he helped to develop and promote the influence of Gramsci within the field, particularly in relation to television and popular culture. Subsequently, Bennett has been critical of the Gramscian stream of cultural studies as over-emphasizing signification and consciousness at the expense of the pragmatic considerations of cultural policy. Here he draws upon the work of **Foucault** and his concept of governmentality. As Director of the 'Australian Key Centre for Cultural and Media Policy' at Griffith University, Bennett played a significant part in promoting cultural policy as a goal for cultural studies. He is currently a Professor of the Open University (UK).

- **Associated concepts** Cultural policy, culture, governmentality, hegemony, ideology, practice.
- **Tradition(s)** Cultural studies, Marxism, poststructuralism.
- **Reading** Bennett, T. (1998) *Culture: A Reformer's Science*. St Leonards: Allen & Unwin.

Bhabha, Homi K. (1949–) Homi Bhabha was born in India and educated at Bombay University and Christchurch College, Oxford (UK). He is currently Professor in the Humanities at the University of Chicago, where he teaches in the Departments of English and Art. Strongly influenced by the poststructuralism of **Derrida**, **Lacan** and **Foucault**, Bhabha argues against the tendency to essentialize 'Third World' countries into a homogeneous identity claiming instead that all sense of nationhood is narrativized. He also suggests that there is always ambivalence at the site of colonial dominance so that the colonizer and the colonized help to constitute each other. For Bhabha, the instability of meaning in language leads us to think of culture, identities and identifications as always a place of borders and hybridity rather than of fixed stable entities, a view encapsulated in his use of concepts such as mimicry, interstice, hybridity and liminality.

- **Associated concepts** Anti-essentialism, différance, ethnicity, hybridity, national identity.
- **Tradition(s)** Cultural studies, postcolonial theory, poststructuralism.
- **Reading** Bhabha, H. (1994) *The Location of Culture*. London and New York: Routledge.

Black Atlantic Paul **Gilroy** introduced the concept of the Black Atlantic into cultural studies in the early 1990s as a concrete example of the 'changing same' of a diaspora. It is also an illustration of 'identities in motion' as opposed to conceiving of them as absolutes of nature or culture. Thus a diaspora such as the Black Atlantic involves creolized and hybridized cultural forms. For Gilroy, black identities cannot be understood in terms of being American or British or West Indian. Nor can they be grasped in terms of ethnic absolutism (that there is a global essential black identity), rather, they should be understood in terms of the black diaspora of the Atlantic.

Cultural exchange within the black diaspora produces hybrid identities and cultural forms of similarity and difference within and between its various locales so that black self-definitions and cultural expressions draw on a plurality of black histories and politics. Blackness is not a pan-global absolute identity since the cultural identities of black Britons, black Americans and black Africans are different. Nevertheless, Gilroy points to cultural forms that have been historically shared within the Black Atlantic despite the different meanings and history of 'race' which have operated in Britain, America, Africa and the Caribbean. He speculates that a common experience of powerlessness experienced through *racial* categories may be enough to secure an affinity across the Black Atlantic.

Music plays a prominent part in Gilroy's exposition of the Black Atlantic. For example, rap music cannot be said to have any single point of origin or authenticity for it has developed in America, Jamaica, West Africa, South Africa, and Britain (amongst others). As such, rap is always already a cultural hybridization. For example, South African rappers take an apparently 'American' form and give it an African twist to create hybridized music that is now being exported back to the USA. Further, rap can trace its roots/routes back to the influence of West African music and the impact of slavery. Thus, any idea of clear-cut lines of demarcation between the 'internal' and 'external' is swept away since rap has no obvious point of 'origin' and its popular American form is indebted to Africa.

Links **Anti-essentialism, authenticity, diaspora, ethnicity, hybridity, identity, race**

Body The body is commonly understood to be the physical flesh and bones of an organism. However, within cultural studies it is commonly argued that the body has been stylized and performed by the workings of culture making the idea of the body as a pre-social, pre-cultural object impossible to sustain. A concern for the body within contemporary culture is manifested by organ transplants, regimes of diet, exercise, cosmetic surgery and health promotion strategies that represent narratives of self-transformation achieved through self-regulation. Thus we are constantly called upon to perform 'body work', for example involving the transformation of the body through fashion and self-decoration, as a significant aspect of contemporary identity projects.

One could understand the performance of 'body work' that is dedicated to maintaining a particular and desirable state of embodiment as being the passive consequence of disciplinary power. However, it may also be grasped as an active process of the project of identity construction. The work of **Foucault** encapsulates both these theoretical directions. Thus a good deal of Foucault's writing has been concerned with the 'disciplinary' character of modern institutions, practices and discourses that have produced what he called 'docile bodies' that could be subjected, used and transformed. In this context, a criticism of Foucault is that he turns men and women into acquiescent creatures that have no agency. However, in his later work Foucault concentrates on 'techniques of the self' that re-introduce agency and 'self-fashioning'. In particular, in his studies of ancient Greek and Roman practices he points to an ethics of 'self-stylization' centred on the body that forms a process of 'self-mastery'.

The manner in which the body has been understood by medical science illustrates our changing cultural understanding of the body as well as highlighting the issues of agency and determination. For biologically based medicine (biomedicine) the body is constituted by unchanging necessities that exist prior to culture. Here the causes of disease are internal to the body so that illness is an outcome of the objective facts of biology. It follows from this that doctors know best how to treat illness since they have has gained the appropriate scientific knowledge. Thus did medicine describe and compare bodies in ways that produced normality, pathology and disciplinary practices. Patients became cases rather than unique persons.

However it has become apparent that ill health is not simply a consequence of the hermetically sealed workings of individual bodies. It is a product of what we eat, where we work (for example, stress or chemical poisoning), levels and types of exercise, the patterns of our thinking (generated in our childhood experiences) and so forth. Thus a more holistic understanding of health practice has begun to emerge called the biopsychosocial model of medicine. The shift from biomedicine to biopsychosocial is marked by *relative* shifts from a focus on the isolated body to bodies in environmental contexts and from the curative to the preventative.

The new holistic model of medicine would appear to weaken the dominance of medical authority in favour of the active participation of lay persons. Nevertheless, health promotion can itself be grasped as a new disciplinary process involving the medicalization of lifestyles and identity management. Thus, we are exhorted, urged and disciplined into adopting the 'right' healthy attitude towards our bodies. Having the right kind of body is now not only a matter of tasteful and pleasing appearance, or even of longevity, but of moral virtue. Nevertheless, the management of health as an aspect of lifestyle can also be understood as a manifestation of reflexivity and agency as we make self-fashioning choices.

Links **Agency, consumption, culture, emotion, identity, reflexivity, self-identity**

Bourdieu, Pierre (1930–2002) Bourdieu was the leading French sociologist of culture and Professor of Sociology at the Collège de France and Director of the Centre for European Sociology. His work was unusual in its combination of empirical methods, including statistics, with more philosophical theory. Bourdieu attempted to resolve the puzzle of structure and agency in terms of what he called a generic structuralism. He argued that practice carries the mark of agency but needs to be grasped in the context of the 'objective' structures of culture and society. In particular, Bourdieu was concerned with the determining power of class as a structural constraint so that some critics regard his work as reductionist. He is perhaps best known for his argument that cultural tastes are social constructs located in the context of a class-oriented habitus.

- **Associated concepts** Agency, consumption, cultural capital, culture, habitus, structure.
- **Tradition(s)** Hermeneutics, Marxism, structuralism.
- **Reading** Bourdieu, P. (1984) *Distinction: A Social Critique of the Judgement of Taste.* Cambridge, MA: Harvard University Press.

17

Bricolage The concept of bricolage refers to the rearrangement and juxtaposition of previously unconnected signifying objects to produce new meanings in fresh contexts. Bricolage involves a process of re-signification by which cultural signs with established meanings are re-organized into new codes of meaning. That is, objects that already carried sedimented symbolic meanings are re-signified in relation to other artefacts under new circumstances. For example, cultural studies writers have pointed to the construction of the Teddy Boy appearance (that emerged during the 1950s and was re-worked in the 1960s) through a combination of the otherwise unrelated Edwardian upper class look, the bootlace tie and brothel-creepers as a form of bricolage in the context of youth cultural style. Likewise, the boots, braces, cropped hair, Stayprest shirts and Ska music of Skinheads during the 1970s was read as a stylistic symbolic bricolage which communicated the hardness of working class masculinity.

The other main usage of the term bricolage comes with the juxtaposition of signs in the visual media to form a collage of images from different times and places. Thus, the global multiplication of communications technologies has created an increasingly complex semiotic environment of competing signs and meanings. This creates a flow of images and juxtapositions that fuses news, drama, reportage and advertising etc. into an electronic bricolage. This kind of bricolage as a cultural style is a core element of postmodern culture and is observable in architecture, film and popular music video. Shopping centres have made the mixing of styles from different times and places a particular 'trade mark' while MTV is noted for the blending of pop music from a variety of periods and locations.

The term bricoleur has been used to suggest someone who constructs a bricolage and has most commonly been applied to those who stylize themselves using the clothing and artifacts of popular culture. Here the idea of the bricoleur has been deployed to discuss the ways in which commodities – notably those of the fashion world – form the basis of multiple identity construction. In doing so, attention is drawn to the meaning-oriented activity of consumers in selecting and arranging elements of material commodities and meaningful signs into a bricolage that forms part of identity construction.

Links **Articulation, identity, multiple identities, postmodernism, style, youth culture**

Butler, Judith (1960–) A US-born philosopher and feminist thinker, Butler has established herself as one of the foremost writers about sex/gender, subjectivity and identity. Her originality lies in the way that the poststructuralism of Michel **Foucault** and Jacques **Derrida** is combined with psychoanalysis (courtesy of **Lacan**) and speech act theory to generate a theory of sex as performative. Butler argues that 'sex' is a normative 'regulatory ideal' that produces the bodies it governs through citation and reiteration of hegemonic discourses (the heterosexual imperative) to generate a performativity that is always derivative. Butler's project involves the deconstruction of the compulsory gender matrix and she has cited drag as a parodic form that can destabilize gender norms. Nevertheless, for Butler, *all* identity categories are necessary fictions that must be interrogated.

- **Associated concepts** Discourse, gender, identity, performativity, power, sex, subject position, subjectivity.
- **Tradition(s)** Feminism, poststructuralism, psychoanalysis, queer theory.
- **Reading** Butler, J. (1993) *Bodies That Matter*. London and New York: Routledge.

C

Canon The idea of a canon refers to a body of work held to be the most important within a particular tradition, or sometimes to the parameters that surround the work associated with a given author. The concept derives from the Greek word *kanon* that means measure or rule and was further developed in the context of fourth-century Christian scholars concerned with the orthodox and the heretical. Thus, a canon is centrally involved with questions of inclusion and exclusion and in the context of contemporary culture that process of selection centres on questions of aesthetic value. That is, an item is selected for inclusion in the canon of, say, literature on the basis of the quality of its expression of 'universal' aesthetic values. Such a list of 'great books' would include the work of Chaucer, Homer, Shakespeare and T.S. Eliot amongst others while Bach, Beethoven and Mozart form the core of the European classical music canon.

The formation of a canon involves a process of judgement and discrimination the authority and grounds for which have been challenged not least from within the domain of cultural studies. The whole idea of a canon as 'the good and the great' has been questioned on the grounds that there are no universal grounds for aesthetic judgements so that those which are employed can be understood as distinctions of taste and power associated with class-based groups. In particular, the policing of the boundaries of a canon of 'good works' had led to the exclusion of popular culture. Ironically, while challenging the very idea of a canon, there has also been an attempt to widen the boundaries of the traditional canon to include the works of, for example, postcolonial and feminist works in the canon of literature or to include film under the rubric of Art. From a cultural studies perspective perhaps the more pertinent issue is the exploration of the conditions and processes that underpin the formation of a canon at a particular time and place.

Links **Aesthetics, cultural capital, cultural studies, popular culture, values**

Capitalism The most influential understanding of capitalism within cultural studies has come from the nineteenth-century writings of Karl **Marx**. Here capitalism is grasped as a mode of production premised on the private ownership of the means of production. In the past this would have included factories, mills and workshops while today it signals multinational corporations. Class conflict is a marker of capitalism whose fundamental division is between those who own the means of production, the bourgeoisie, and a working class or proletariat who must sell their labour to survive. Today the class structures of Western societies are considerably more complex and internally stratified than Marx described them. Class is now

20

identifiable not simply through direct ownership of the means of production but through share distribution, managerial control, income, education and lifestyles.

According to Marx, while the legal framework and common sense thinking of capitalist societies may declare that workers are free agents and the sale of labour a free and fair contract, this obscures the fundamental process of exploitation at work. This is so because capitalism aims to make a profit and does so by extracting surplus value from workers. That is, the value of the labour taken to produce goods, which become the property of the bourgeoisie, is more than the worker receives for it. The realization of surplus value in monetary form is achieved by the selling of goods (which have both 'use-value' and 'exchange-value') as commodities. A commodity is something available to be sold in the market place and commodification the process associated with capitalism by which all spheres of a culture are increasingly put under the sway of the market. Commodity fetishism is the name Marx gives to the process through which the surface appearance of goods sold in the market place obscures the origins of commodities in an exploitative relationship.

Capitalism is a dynamic system whose profit-driven mechanisms lead to the continual revolutionizing of the means of production and the forging of new markets. For Marx, this was its great merit in relation to feudalism, for it heralded a massive expansion in the productive capacities of nineteenth-century European societies and dragged them into the modern world of railways, mass production, cities and a formally equitable and free set of human relations. However, according to Marx, the mechanisms of capitalism lead to perennial crises and ultimately, or so Marx argued, to its being superseded by socialism. Problems for capitalism include a falling rate of profit, cycles of boom and bust, increasing monopoly, and most decisively, the creation of a proletariat that is set to become the system's grave-diggers.

Marx hoped that capitalism would be rift asunder by class conflict, with the proletariat's organizations of defence, trade unions and political parties overthrowing and replacing it with a mode of production based on communal ownership, equitable distribution and ultimately the end of class division. Today, Marx's dream of the demise of capitalism seems farther away than ever as rather than generating its own demise, capitalism keeps on transforming itself. This process has been explored by the theorists of 'disorganized capitalism' and post-Fordism amongst others. Indeed, capitalism is the driving force of a renewed globalization where one-half of the world's largest economic units are constituted by 200 transnational corporations who produce between one-third and one-half of world output. Thus globalization is, in part, constituted by planetary-scale economic activity which is creating an interconnected if uneven capitalist world economy.

Links **Alienation, commodification, disorganized capitalism, globalization, Marxism, post-Fordism**

Carnivalesque The carnivalesque is a concept appropriated into cultural studies from the work of Mikhail **Bakhtin** and his study of Rabelais. The idea derives from the medieval carnival when a degree of otherwise unpermitted freedom was granted to ordinary people to lampoon the figures of authority associated with the church and state. Thus, the carnivalesque involves a temporary reversal of the order of power enacted through the rituals, games, mockeries and profanities in which the polite is overthrown by the vulgar and the king up-ended by the fool. The carnival introduces a topsy-turvy world of reversals of power and authority in tandem with the pleasures of excessive eating, drinking and sexual activity that offend the borders of polite decorum.

The contemporary use of the term carnivalesque is a metaphorical one that connotes a form of resistance to power and authority from within popular culture. The power of the carnivalesque does not lie in a simple reversal of social and cultural distinctions but rather resides in the invasion of the high by the low that is marked by the creation of 'grotesque' hybrid forms. Here the challenge is not simply to the high by the low but to the arbitrary character of the very act of cultural classification by power. This is a challenge attributed by **Hall** to the very concept of the 'popular' that transgresses the boundaries of cultural power (for it is of value though 'officially' classified as low). Thus, aspects of spectacular youth cultures such as Punk could be seen as carnivalesque subversions of the order of power.

Links **Dialogic, popular culture, power, resistance, youth culture**

Centre for Contemporary Cultural Studies (1964–1988) There is a difference between the study of culture and an institutionally located 'cultural studies' that named itself as such. Though that naming marks only a cut or snapshot of an ever-evolving intellectual project, this moment was the work undertaken at the Centre for Contemporary Cultural Studies (CCCS) at the University of Birmingham (UK). CCCS was founded in 1964 as a postgraduate centre initially under the directorship of Richard **Hoggart** (1964–1968) and later Stuart **Hall** (1968–1979). It is during the period of Hall's Directorship that one can first speak of the formation of an identifiable and distinct domain called cultural studies.

The initial focus of CCCS was on 'lived' culture, with an emphasis on class cultures that chimed with the work of Hoggart and Raymond **Williams**. However, this moment of 'culturalism' – formed from an amalgam of sociology and literary criticism – was surpassed by the influence of structuralism, particularly as articulated with Marxism. Here the decisive intellectual resources were drawn from **Barthes**, **Althusser** and, most crucially, **Gramsci**. The key conceptual tools were those of text, ideology and hegemony as explored through the notion of popular culture as a site of both social control and resistance. The substantive topics of research included the mass media, youth subcultures, education, gender, race and the authoritarian state.

Since the moment of CCCS cultural studies has acquired a multitude of institutional bases on a global scale. Further, the influence of poststructuralism has eclipsed structuralist Marxism as the decisive theoretical paradigm. In 1988, CCCS ceased being a postgraduate research centre and became a university department that included undergraduate teaching before it too was closed in the 1990s.

- **Associated concepts** Cultural politics, culture, encoding–decoding, hegemony, ideology, popular culture, resistance, text.
- **Tradition(s)** Cultural studies, culturalism, Marxism, poststructuralism, psychoanalysis, structuralism.
- **Reading** Hall, S. (1992) 'Cultural Studies and its Theoretical Legacies', in L. Grossberg, C. Nelson and P. Treichler (eds), *Cultural Studies*. London and New York: Routledge.

Circuit of culture The idea of a 'circuit of culture' has developed from the debates about cultural materialism and specifically the relationship between the economy and culture. The metaphor of the circuit of culture is an attempt to move away from the determinism and reductionism implicit in the Marxist 'base and superstructure' model while retaining an explanatory link between material and cultural production and consumption. The model grew out of the description of a social formation (put forward by structuralist Marxism in the 1970s) as constituted by complex structures or regularities that are articulated or linked together. The emphasis is on the irreducible character of cultural practices which are at the same time in a relationship of mutual determination with other practices.

The metaphor of the 'circuit of culture', which emerged in embryonic form in the early 1980s and was developed to greater maturity in the 1990s, adapts this basic idea of the articulation of levels of practice to the question of economy and culture. Here, cultural meaning is produced and embedded at each level of the circuit that is, production–representation–identity–consumption–regulation, so that the production of significance at each moment of the circuit is articulated to the next moment without determining what meanings will be taken up or produced at that level. Thus, culture is autonomous but articulated to other practices to form a whole. The challenge is to grasp just how the moment of production inscribes itself in representation in each case without assuming that it can be 'read off' from economic relations. The model is also concerned with how culture as representation is implicated in the forms and modes of organization that production takes. That is, we need to grasp the ways in which 'the economic' is formed culturally.

Thus commodities may be analysed in terms of the meanings embedded at the level of design and production which are subsequently modified by the creation of new meanings as the commodity is represented in advertising. In turn, the meanings produced through representation connect with, and help constitute, the identities of its users. Meanings embedded at the moments of production and representation may or may not be taken up at the level of consumption, where new meanings are again produced. Thus, meanings produced at the level of production are available to be worked on at the level of consumption. However they do not determine them. Further, representation and consumption shape the level of production through, for example, design and marketing.

The advantage of the circuit of culture metaphor is that it allows for analysis of the specificities of each moment of the circuit while at the same time considering the relations between them. This model is more flexible, more useful and more sophisticated than a crude base–superstructure model. However, it does carry with it the danger of losing sight of the fact that 'levels' or 'moments' are only a heuristic device and not organizational aspects of an otherwise non-separable 'whole way of life'

Links **Base and superstructure, cultural materialism, reductionism, structuralism**

Citizenship A form of political identity by which individuals are endowed with social rights and obligations within political communities. Needless to say, the meaning of citizenship changes according to the language-game and cultural contexts in which it is deployed. For example, the classical Liberal conception of citizenship focuses on the rights and duties of individuals and includes such issues as residency, freedom of movement, freedom of speech and voting rights. The social democratic usage of the term adds to this list those collective rights associated with the welfare state, including the rights to education, relief from poverty, medical services and so forth. Today one also hears of the cultural rights of identity groups that are said to flow from the claims of citizenship. Thus it is important to recognize that the scope of citizenship rights and the habits and routines that are attendant on it are progressively formed over time and are not universal givens. Indeed, the extension of the scope of citizenship to cover increasing numbers of persons and the enlargement of the rights with which it is concerned have commonly been the focus of social and political struggles.

The concept of citizenship has been etymologically linked with notions of civility, as the proper way to live with others, and civilization, as the habits and routines of cooperative life. As such, citizenship has been historically restricted to those considered to be civilized and denied to others, for example slaves. Though the concept of citizenship was initially connected to the emergence of the city, the modern usage derives from the workings of the nation-state, within which the aforementioned rights and obligations obtain. In particular, the modern discourse of citizenship stresses that with citizenship comes equality. That is, one cannot legitimately divide citizenship into first and second class varieties, for it is said to be universal and indivisible. Consequently, the language of citizenship is useful to the cultural politics of subordinated groups who are seeking greater freedom and recognition within the bounds of the nation-state.

In the context of the modern democratic tradition, citizenship can be understood as one aspect of our multiple selves whereby a civic 'identity of citizenship' seeks to hold together a diversity of values and life-worlds within a democratic framework. The commitment by diverse groups to the procedures of democracy and to inter-subjectively recognized rights and duties of citizenship in the social, civil and political domains advances democracy and provides the conditions for particularistic identity projects. As such, the concept of citizenship is a mechanism for linking the micro-politics of representation and identity with the official macro-politics of institutional and cultural rights.

Links **Cultural politics, identity politics, Liberalism, nation-state, public sphere**

City The growth of the contemporary city is an aspect of the urbanization processes inherent within modernity and with the associated culture of modernism. Of particular interest for cultural studies has been (a) the inner city, (b) the postmodern city and (c) the global city.

24   *Inner city*   The 'modern' Anglo-American city has commonly been understood in terms of zones that expand radially from the centre and which are inhabited by particular types or classes of people. In effect, various social class groups are allocated specific residential zones by income selection. In recent years it has become commonplace to discuss the 'inner city' as being a poor, non-white zone of decay paralleled by the growth of suburbs populated predominantly by the middle class.

Typically, the formation of the inner city has involved a degree of 'white flight' from the city to the suburbs. At its most extreme, a city like Detroit (USA) has a poor black inner zone with whole sections not supplied with basic services like electricity and water. In the popular imagination these are dangerous places of gang wars, drug abuse and crime that have emerged as a sign of intensified social polarization, including the abandonment of an 'underclass' to mass unemployment, drug trafficking, poverty and homelessness. Here are the conditions for the urban rioting witnessed during the 1980s and 1990s in British and American cities.

However, some parts of the inner city, especially those areas that have been most effected by de-industrialization, have been taken over by middle class groups who have benefited from the regeneration of former industrial or dockland areas in a process of gentrification. This has involved an increase in house prices and the generation of cultural activities based on the lifestyles of a college-educated group. At the same time so-called 'inner city' poverty is increasingly located across the urban landscape.

Postmodern city   According to some writers, most notably Soja, major changes took place in cities during the last quarter of the twentieth century that can be described as postmodern. Los Angeles is commonly understood to be the archetypical case. Thus de-industrialization and re-industrialization in the context of a global economy have shifted the economic base of the city towards a combination of high-technology industries and low-skill, labour-intensive, design-sensitive industries. The postmodern city is also marked by the restructuring and redistribution of jobs, affordable housing, transport systems and lines of racial/ethnic divide. This has spread the attributes of formally distinct urban zones across the city so that, for example, the 'inner city' poor zone is not necessarily located within the physical inner city and residential suburbs are increasingly the site of new forms of industrial development.

The restructuring of the urban economy is implicated in new patterns of social fragmentation, segregation and polarization marked by an enlarging managerial technocracy, a shrinking middle class and a growing base of the homeless, welfare dependants and cheap labour. The backbone of a cheap and weakly organized labour force is the growing proportion of migrants. In this context the perception of rising crime, violence and ethnic difference has led to an increasingly security conscious city marked by walled-in estates, armed guards, patrolled shopping centres, surveillance cameras and wire fences. Finally, on the level of cultural representation, LA is marked by the rise of hyperreality and simulacra courtesy not only of Hollywood or Disneyland but also of spin doctors, virtual reality, cyberspace, sound bites and pop culture.

Global city Underpinning the concept of the global city is the sense that the urban world economy is dominated by a small number of centres which act as command and control points for an increasingly dispersed set of economic activities. Thus, the idea of the global city is illustrative of the structuring and re-structuring of space as a created environment through the spread of industrial capitalism. In particular, capitalist corporations are sensitive to questions of location and their relative advantages. Thus, lower labour costs, weaker unionization and tax concessions will lead firms to favour some places over others as locations for plants, markets and development. Similarly, the need to find alternative forms of investment, and the particular conditions of markets and state intervention, assists some sectors of the economy (and thus some places) in gaining preference over others.

The key contemporary global cities – London, New York, Tokyo, Seoul, Los Angeles, Frankfurt, Paris, Singapore – have significance not because of population size or volume of business but because key personnel and activities are located within them. That is, they are sites for the accumulation, distribution and circulation of capital where information and decision making functions are more telling than size. Ten cities host the headquarters of nearly half of the world's largest 500 transnational manufacturing corporations and the top four cities, London, New York, Tokyo and Seoul, account for 156 of these. This is a consequence of a growth in the number and range of the institutions of global capital, the geographical concentration of capital and an extension of global reach via telecommunications and transport. In particular, finance and banking have become the crucial facets of a city's claim to global significance.

Links **Capitalism, globalization, post-industrial society, postmodernism, urbanization**

Civil society After Hegel, the idea of civil society gains its currency from a contrast with the realm of the state as the domain of social relations and public participation. Civil society is understood to be an arena of engagement in which individuals pursue their private interests and form relationships in pursuit of their subjective needs. However, this brings with it a sense of shared interests as individuals recognize their duties to others as a condition of their own freedoms. Broadly speaking, **Marx** took over this understanding of civil society from Hegel but gave more emphasis to its penetration by market relations and commodification. Thus, civil society is understood to be the province of ideological conflict which is both implicated in the workings of capitalism and the state whilst simultaneously offering itself as a possible site of resistance.

In work that was significant and influential within cultural studies, Gramsci understood civil society to be constituted by affiliations outside of formal state boundaries including the family, social clubs, the press, leisure activities, etc. Here civil society is the realm of ideology as lived experience rooted in day-to-day common sense, cultural conditions and practical activities. As a consequence, Gramsci makes the distinction between a *war of position* that involves the winning of hegemony within the sphere of civil society and a *war of manoeuvre* constituted by an assault on state power. The latter is dependent on the former so that civil society is the critical domain of ideological struggle.

Following Gramsci, key cultural studies theorists conceived of popular culture as a substantive element of civil society and the site on which hegemony was won and lost. By now the concept of civil society has been transformed from its Hegelian use, where it indicated a domain between the state and the family, and comes instead to connote the heterogeneous arena of personal life that encompasses the family, sexual relationships, leisure pursuits, the mass media, youth culture and so forth.

Links **Common culture, hegemony, ideology, nation-state, public sphere**

Class In general terms class can be understood as a classification of persons into groups based on shared socio-economic conditions. However, classes do not exist as stand alone groups but are to be understood in relation to other classes in the context of an overall stratification system. As such, class can be grasped as a relational set of inequalities with economic, social, political and ideological dimensions. Since class is a cultural classification rather than an 'objective' fact, post-Marxist writers such as **Laclau** and Mouffe approach it as a discursive construct.

Within cultural studies, the most influential understanding of class has been that associated with Marxism where class is broadly defined as a relationship to the means of production. Here the organization of a mode of production is not simply a matter of coordinating objects but also of the relations between people. These relations, while social, that is, cooperative and coordinated, are also matters of power and conflict. Indeed, Marxists regard class antagonisms, which are an intrinsic part of a mode of production, as the motor of historical change. For **Marx**, class is constituted by an objective relation to property ownership and the mode of production. Nevertheless, he also recognizes that consciousness of those circumstances is significant. Thus he makes a distinction between class-in-itself and class-for-itself where the latter includes a self-consciousness that is absent from the former.

The core of Marx's work was his analysis of the dynamics of capitalism wherein the fundamental class division is between those who own the means of production, the bourgeoisie, and those who, being a propertyless proletariat, must sell their labour. Although, for Marxists, capitalists and workers form the core of the contemporary class system, it is acknowledged that other class divisions are also in evidence. For example, small shopkeepers, clerks and students form part of what Marx called the 'petite bourgeoisie' while the unemployed and the criminal fraternity are at the heart of the so-called 'lumpen-proletariat'.

It is now widely felt that the class system of contemporary capitalism is much more complex than that envisioned by Marx during the mid-nineteenth century and involves a more graduated set of unequal relations. That class is constituted by more than one's relationship to the means of production has long been the argument of Weber and his subsequent followers. Here, though class is considered to be founded on divisions associated with ownership of the means of production, it also includes lifestyle differences based on income, occupation, status, education, qualifications and so forth that cluster together to form class.

In particular, class relations today include the much-expanded middle classes who, while they are not owners of the means of production, are nevertheless distanced from the manual working class by income and lifestyle. This has been the consequence of both a sectoral redistribution of labour from the primary and secondary sectors to the service sector and a shift in the make-up of labour towards white-collar work. Indeed, the working class has itself become highly stratified by transformations in the occupational structures of industrial capitalism and the increased though differential consumption that an ever-expanding capitalism has enabled. To a considerable extent these transformations are implicated in the displacement of industrial manufacturing by service industries centred on information technology and by a more general alteration of emphasis from production to consumption.

The increased productivity of capitalism has meant that the majority of the populations of Western societies have sufficient housing, transportation and income to be in a post-scarcity situation. This has contributed to an increased consumption-centredness amongst the working class that has led to its fragmentation as their differential incomes and consumption capabilities are expressed in the market. Further, as its relative prosperity has risen so the employed working class has become dislocated from the unemployed urban underclass. In this context, it has been argued by the theorists of 'New Times' that (at least in the heartlands of Western capitalism) we are witnessing the emergence of a two-thirds: one-third society. That is, two-thirds of the population are relatively well off while one-third are either engaged in de-skilled part-time work or form a new underclass of the unemployed and unemployable.

With this re-construction of class relations has come a new uncertainty regarding the relationship between class position and political behaviour. Thus there has been a steady decline in allegiance between occupational class categories and the major political parties. More generally, we have witnessed the demise of a revolutionary working class politics that could realize an alternative social order. Nevertheless, class does retain a powerful and important place in social life that cannot be ignored. There are still inequalities in educational access and outcome that are underpinned by social class and there are still differences in cultural tastes and practices that mark out class boundaries.

Links **Capitalism, Marxism, New Times, political economy, post-industrial society, post-Marxism**

Code The customary usage of the term code refers to a set of signs that stand in for another set of signs and their meanings. Thus a code involves translation and concealment. Within cultural studies a code is understood to be a system of representation by which signs and their meanings are arranged by cultural

28

convention and habituated to the extent that meaning is stabilized and naturalized. Here the concept of code draws from the semiotic argument that the relations between signifiers and the signified, or signs and their meanings, are arbitrary but temporarily 'fixed' by convention.

A commonly cited illustration of this thesis concerns the organization and regulation of colours into the cultural code of traffic lights. Colours are classifications of gradations in the light spectrum that we name with signs such as red, green, amber and so forth. However, there is no universal reason why the sign 'red' should refer to a specific colour, for the sign 'rojo' can designate the 'same' colour. Hence the relationship between sign and colour is arbitrary. Subsequently the signs red, green and amber are organized into a sequence that generates meaning through the cultural conventions of their usage within a particular context. Thus, traffic lights deploy 'red' to signify 'stop' and 'green' to signify 'go'. This is the cultural code of traffic systems that temporally fixes the relationship between colours and meanings so that signs become naturalized codes. The apparent transparency of meaning (we 'know' when to stop or go) is an outcome of cultural habituation, the effect of which is to conceal the practices of cultural coding.

Semiotics, and subsequently cultural studies, has argued that all cultural objects convey meaning and all cultural practices depend on meanings generated by signs. Hence the concept of code is extended to cover all manner of cultural practices. For example, everyday objects are commonly gender coded: washing machine (female), drill (male), cooker (female), car (male). Here the operation of habituated cultural codes is such that not only objects but also practices (for example, household tasks as female) are associated with a particular gender. In that sense, naturalized codes seek to essentialize the meanings of male and female. Critical cultural practice seeks to undo and take apart those naturalized cultural codes to reveal the arbitrary character of their classifications, arrangements and meanings.

Links **Culture, deconstruction, meaning, myth, semiotics, signs**

Commodification The process associated with capitalism by which objects, qualities and signs are turned into commodities where a commodity is an item whose prime purpose is sale in the market place. The study of culture has long involved a strand of thinking critical of the commodification of culture by which the culture industry turns people and meanings into commodities that serve its interests. Thus, in a process that **Marx** called commodity fetishism, the surface appearance of goods sold in the market place is said to obscure the origins of those commodities in an exploitative relationship at the level of production.

The critique of commodification is often pursued by contrasting the shallowness and manipulation of commodity culture to an authentic 'people's culture' or to the 'civilizing' qualities of high culture. For example, Richard **Hoggart** offers a sympathetic, humanist and detailed chronicle of the lived culture of the British working class of the1950s that contrasts starkly with his acid account of the development of 'commercial culture' figured by the 'juke box boy', the 'American slouch' and loud music. Likewise, **Adorno**'s concept of the 'culture industry' is deployed to argue that highly standardized commodities that encourage authoritarianism and conformism dominate Western capitalist culture.

In a more contemporary vein, **Habermas** argues that the increased commodification of life by giant corporations transforms people from rational citizens to 'non-rational' consumers in a way that subordinates social-existential questions to money. Thus, one of the central criticisms of the commodification of culture is that it not only shapes and disciplines cultural meanings but also turns people into commodities. For example, the promotion of the 'slender body' as a disciplinary cultural norm for women centres on diet as a commodity as well as self-monitoring. Paradoxically, commodity culture offers us images of desirable foods while proposing that we eat low calorie items and buy exercise equipment. In the face of this contradiction the capacity for self-control and the containment of fat is posed in moral as well as physical terms.

Traditionally, within Marxist theory commodities are said to have both 'use-value' and 'exchange-value'. Thus, while a spade may be sold, that is, exchanged for money, it also has uses, such as digging a hole. However, the postmodern theorist **Baudrillard** argues that sign-value has replaced both the use-value and exchange-value of commodities in contemporary culture. Here, it is argued, is a culture in which value is determined through the exchange of symbolic meanings rather than through usefulness. Thus a commodity is not an object with use-value but a commodity-sign. In this view, all spheres of life are penetrated by commodification so that external validation 'authenticated' by formal canons or socially formed cultural authority collapses and choice between values and lifestyles becomes a matter of taste and style operating within a self-referential world of commodities.

For much of its life then cultural studies and its forebears have been critical of the commodification of culture. However, with the growing interest in active audiences and the processes of consumption it has been argued by some writers that the meanings generated by consumers are not necessarily those that critics identify as being embedded in commodities. Further, with the wholesale commodification of Western culture there is no longer a very strong case for looking to an authentic non-commodified culture of the people. Rather, the crucial questions surround what consumers do with commodities and what meanings are created in the interplay of commodity and customer. Hence an increasing interest in the processes of creative consumption.

Links **Authenticity, capitalism, common culture, consumption, culture industry, Marxism**

Common culture There is an ambiguity about the notion of a 'common culture'. On the one hand a common culture constitutes the collective or community (for example, nation, youth group, class etc.). On the other hand a shared democratic and participative common culture is that which is yet to be built since numerous lines of difference also mark out culture.

In the first sense the idea of common culture is connected to notions of community and the idea that 'culture is ordinary', as described by Raymond **Williams**. Indeed, the whole notion of common culture within cultural studies is associated with 'culturalism' and the stress on a common community element to culture in the face of the selective tradition of elite class culture. In so far as culture is a common whole way of life, its boundaries are largely locked, at least in the work of Williams, into those of nationality and ethnicity.

The work of Paul **Willis** has maintained the idea of 'common culture' in the tradition of Williams. However, whereas the initial stress in the notion of a common culture for Williams was on the generation of meaning at the moment of production, for Willis a common culture is forged through the practice of creative consumption. For example, Willis argues that young people have an active, creative and symbolically productive relation to the commodities that are constitutive of youth culture. Meaning, he suggests, is not inherent in the commodity but is produced through actual usage in a process called 'grounded aesthetics'. For Willis, contemporary culture involves the active creation of meaning by all people as cultural producers through acts of symbolic creativity.

Under the influence of poststructuralism cultural studies has begun to emphasize not so much commonality as difference. As cultural studies has engaged with structuralism and poststructuralism so it has been widely accepted that meaning is generated through the play of difference down a chain of signifiers. Further, subjects are formed through difference so that we are constituted in part by what we are not. In this context, there has been a growing emphasis on difference rather than commonality in cultural life. This is a culture that is not 'One' but rather is divided by class, gender, race, age and other forms of 'difference'. Indeed, though once grasped as a 'whole way of life', culture is now understood to be fractured into a kaleidoscope of distinctions.

Links **Consumption, cultural studies, culturalism, culture, difference, poststructuralism**

Common sense The category of 'common sense' has been a significant one in the context of Gramscian-influenced cultural studies and its concern with questions of ideology and hegemony. Here the notion of common sense refers to the embedded, incoherent beliefs and assumptions that characterize a given social order. That is, common sense involves the deeply held terrain of the 'taken-for-granted' aspects of cultural life.

For **Gramsci**, all people reflect upon the world and it is through the 'common sense' of popular culture that they organize their lives and experience. Thus, common sense becomes a crucial site of ideological conflict. In particular, common sense is the site of struggle on which Gramsci hoped to see the forging of a 'good sense' that would involve the recognition of the class character of capitalism. Common sense is the most significant site of ideological struggle because it is the domain of that practical consciousness which guides the actions of the everyday world. More coherent sets of philosophical ideas are contested and transformed in the domain of common sense so that every philosophical current leaves behind it a sediment of common sense. Of course, common sense is not rigid and immobile but is continually transformed and enriched with scientific ideas and philosophical opinions that have entered ordinary life.

The deployment of Gramscian concepts proved to be of long-lasting significance to cultural studies in part because of the central importance given to popular culture as a site of common sense and thus of ideological struggle. Here common sense is the place where hegemony needs to be constantly re-won and renegotiated in an ongoing process making popular culture a terrain of a continuous struggle over meanings.

Links **Capitalism, hegemony, ideology, popular culture**

Communication From a cultural studies perspective communication is concerned with the production, consumption and exchange of meaning. The idea of 'meaning' is an important one to cultural studies in so far as the concept of culture is based on the notions of 'maps of meaning' and 'shared meanings'. Communication takes place in a socially and culturally formed world that in turn makes it possible, so that communication and culture constitute each other. That is, every time we communicate we do so using cultural assumptions and tools just as that very culture is enabled by communication.

Of course, meanings are not simply 'out there' waiting to be found and exchanged, rather, they are generated through the organization of signs, most notably those of language. Hence the strong interest that cultural studies has had in semiotics (the study of signs), discourse (regulated ways of speaking) and the philosophy of language. However, signs do not have transparent and authoritative meaning but are polysemic, that is, signs are able to generate more than one set of meanings. Indeed, the meanings of signs are always unstable and continuously slip away. Further, the texts that are constituted by signs have to be read by people to activate any meanings and it is now an axiom of cultural studies that audiences are active and knowledgeable producers of meaning not products of a structured text. How an audience reads signs will depend on the cultural competencies they bring to the text and the context of communication.

From a cultural studies perspective then, ambiguity is built into communication processes. This stress on ambiguity, circularity and meaning in the cultural studies approach to communication is in stark contrast to the early 'classical' models of communication that centred on the passage of information and/or the sending and receiving of messages.

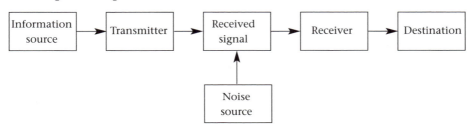

Figure 1 *Shannon and Weaver's model of communication*

Thus the model of communication proposed by Shannon and Weaver in the 1940s (Figure 1) presents the process as a linear one in which the informational message itself is clear and can be understood unambiguously by its receiver provided it is not subject to interference (noise).

The study of communication within cultural studies has taken place at the levels of production (political economy), text (semiotics, discourse analysis) and reception (or consumption). Although debate has raged about the relative significance of each level, it is clear that the processes of communication and culture need to be explored at all these levels in a multi-perspectival examination of the circuit of culture.

Links **Circuit of culture, culture, encoding–decoding, meaning, polysemy, signs**

Constructionism A generic name given to anti-essentialist theories that stress the culturally and historically specific creation of meaningful categories and phenomena. This is in contrast to theories that appeal to universal and biological explanations for objects and events. For example, the body, which is commonly held to be a simple biological given of nature, is understood by constructionism to be also an outcome of the forces of culture. The functioning of 'emotions' for example is said to show evidence for differential responses within divergent cultures or social situations.

Similarly, identities are held to be discursive constructions that do not refer to an already existent 'thing'. That is, identity is not a universal entity but a culturally specific discursive construction. Indeed, even sexual identity is not thought to be a reflection of a natural state of being but rather is a matter of representation. Thus, there can be no biological 'sex' that is not also cultural since there is in principle no access to biological 'truths' that lie outside of cultural discourses. Sexed bodies are always already represented as the product of regulatory discourses of sexuality.

Constructionism is grounded in the anti-representationalist account of language. That is, language does not act as a mirror able to reflect an independent object world but is better understood as a tool that we use to achieve our purposes. Language 'makes' rather than 'finds' and representation does not 'picture' the world but constitutes it. Here, the limits of language are said to mark the edge of our cognitive understanding of the world, for our acculturation in and through language is constitutive of our values, meanings and knowledge. As such, for constructionism there are no culturally transcendental or ahistorical elements to what it is to be a human being.

For constructionism the very notion of what it is to be a person is a cultural variable since the resources that form the materials of personhood are the languages and cultural practices of specific times and places. Indeed, the very concept of 'I' as a self-aware object is held to be a modern Western conception that emerged out of science and the 'Age of Reason'. In short, we are constituted as individuals in a social process using culturally shared materials, and meaning is formed in the joint action of social relationships, accounting practices and conversations. Consequently, our maps and constructs of the world are never simply matters of individual interpretation but are inevitably a part of the wider cultural repertoire of discursive explanations, resources and maps of meaning available to members of cultures. Even fundamental psychological notions such as attitudes, emotions and the inner mind can be approached through the examination of shared language.

Links **Anti-essentialism, body, discourse, emotion, identity, language, representation, sex**

Consumption To consume suggests to use or to ingest. Thus the process of cultural consumption in capitalist societies concerns the use to which the commodities that circulate in the market place are put. In particular, consumption in the context of cultural studies is centred on the generation of meanings in the process of consumption.

The critique of the consuming practices of contemporary Western cultures is tightly linked to the analysis of both capitalism and commodification. That is, it has commonly been argued (for example by **Marx** in the 1850s, **Adorno** in the 1940s and **Althusser** in the 1970s), that commodities carry embedded ideological meanings that serve the interests of capitalism and which are taken on board by consumers through the very act of consumption. However, during the 1980s and 1990s this view of consumption within capitalist social formations has been the subject of criticism on two fronts. First, it has been argued that commodities do not of necessity carry ideological meanings supportive of the social order but may themselves be the basis for transgression and resistance. Second, it has been suggested on the basis of empirical research that consumers are active creators of meaning. That is, consumers do not simply take on those meanings that critics have identified as being 'within' commodities but are capable of generating their own meanings through the interplay of commodities and consumers' cultural competencies.

Consumption-oriented cultural studies argues that while the production of popular music, film, television and fashion is in the hands of transnational capitalist corporations, meanings are produced, altered and managed at the level of consumption. For example, **Fiske** argues that popular culture is constituted by the meanings that people construct rather than those identifiable within texts. While he is clear that capitalist corporations very largely produce popular culture, he is more concerned with the tactics by which these forces are evaded or are resisted. Fiske argues that the culture industries have to work hard to get us to consume mass culture and that consumers are not passive dopes but discriminating active producers of meaning.

The work of **McRobbie** illustrates the transformation in thinking that has taken place within cultural studies. In her early work, she is suspicious of the consumer culture from which 'girl-culture' stems. For example, the teen-oriented magazine *Jackie* is held to operate through the codes of romance, domesticity, beauty and fashion, thereby defining the world of the personal sphere as the prime domain of girls. In her account of working class girls, McRobbie explores the way in which this culture of femininity is used by them to create their own cultural space while at the same time securing them for boyfriends, marriage, the family and children. Later, she critiques her own reliance on the analysis of documents and suggests that girls

34

are more active and creative in relation to magazines and other forms of consumer culture than she had given them credit for. She points to the productive, validating and inventive bricolage of fashion style that women originate and to the dynamic character of shopping as an enabling activity.

Ironically, as **Willis** has argued, it is capitalism and the expansion of consumerism that have provided the increased supply of symbolic resources for young people's creative work. Capitalism (in the world of work) may be that from which escape is sought but it also provides the means and medium (in the domain of consumption) by which to do so. Thus, it is argued that the consumption practices of youth cultures are able to offer resistance to the apparent passivity and conformity of consumer culture.

Links **Active audience, commodification, common culture, ideology, popular culture, resistance**

Convergence The concept of convergence, that is the coming together or joining of previously discrete items, has taken on a particular set of meanings during the 1990s in the context of changes within the communications industries and their related technologies. One use of the concept of convergence refers to the breaking down of barriers between technologies that had once been separate. For example, this can be seen in the merging of television sets and computers to produce PC-TV and the super-information highway. That is, television with built-in computers linked to cable which will allow us to order and pay for shopping, transfer e-money, keep an eye on our bank accounts, call up a selection of films and search the Internet for information.

To a considerable extent this kind of convergence has been enabled by digital technology that organizes information electronically into bytes or discrete bundles of information that can be compressed during transmission and decompressed on arrival. This enables more information to travel down any given conduit (be that cable, satellite or terrestrial signals) at greater speed over larger distances. The impact of new technologies in general, and digital processes in particular, can be summed up in terms of speed, volume and distance. That is, more information at greater speed over larger distances.

The concept of convergence also refers to the consequences of the re-structuring of the communications industries so that corporate activities, and corporations, that had been distinct have come together in order to accrue for themselves the benefits that flow from synergy. This involves bringing together the various elements of the communications industries at the levels of production and distribution so that they complement each other to produce lower costs and higher profits. Indeed, it is becoming apparent that the technologies having the most impact are those concerned with distribution. Organizations that control the distribution mechanisms are eclipsing the power of producers because no one is willing to commit expensive resources to a project that has not secured a distribution agreement. For this reason, traditional producers are becoming distributors and vice versa.

In recent years the processes of convergence, which include diversification by financial, computer and data processing companies into telecommunications, have created multi-media giants that dominate sectors of the market. For example, the 1989 merger of Time and Warner created the largest media group in the world. **35** This was followed in 1995 by Time-Warner's acquisition of Turner Broadcasting (CNN) and in 2000 by its merger with the major Internet company America On-Line (AOL). Similarly, the acquisition by News Corporation during the 1990s of the Hong Kong based Star TV for $525 million has allied Rupert Murdoch's European and American television interests, primarily BskyB (UK) and Fox TV (USA), with a satellite footprint over Asia and the Middle East. Thus News Corporation's global television interests have a reach of some two-thirds of the planet.

Links **Mass media, multimedia corporation, synergy, television**

Conversation The notion of conversation has two dimensions that are of significance to cultural studies; namely, 'conversation analysis' as a methodology for exploring cultural categories and the 'conversation' as a metaphor for understanding culture. Conversation analysis emerged from a domain called ethnomethodology that has been concerned with the 'ethnomethods' or local 'folk' understandings that people deploy to construct and maintain social and cultural life. One of the core arguments of ethnomethodology is that the social order is constructed in and through the everyday activities and accounts (in language) of skilful and knowledgeable actors (or members). The ethnomethods or resources that members draw on are also those that constituted them and the wider social and cultural patterns.

Needless to say the primary focus of conversation analysis is on the organization and structuring of conversations and the way that these form the very fabric of cultural activity. In order to do this practitioners have developed a particular mode of conversational transcription, notation and analysis. Although conversation analysis has not played a significant part in the development of cultural studies as a 'discipline', it does throw useful light on the workings of culture and has been deployed to explore some of the crucial categories used by cultural studies. For example, conversation analysis has been used to demonstrate the way in which identity (a key concern of cultural studies during the 1990s) involves the ascription, avowal and display of identity categories in the structures of conversations. Thus conversation analysis explores how identity is achieved in the everyday flow of ordinary talk.

The metaphor of 'culture as a conversation' grasps the dynamic and language-oriented character of culture and allows us to consider the formation of meaning and culture as formed in the joint action of social relationships. It directs us to the constitutive and action orientation of language in the context of social dialogue and underscores the importance of the social practice of reason-giving in the justification of action. As such, culture is understood to involve agreement, contestation and conflict over meanings and actions and highlights the variability of accounts to which any state of affairs can be put. In particular, it assists us to

36

think through cross-cultural communication in terms of the learning of language skills and the development of what **Rorty** calls 'the cosmopolitan conversation of human kind'.

Like all metaphors, that of the conversation is better suited to some kinds of purpose or object than others so that there are limitations to the analogy between culture and conversations. The commonly understood connotations of 'conversation' may lead us to prioritize declarative voice over conduct, the verbal above the visual and the utterance before the body. Indeed, what we say is only occasionally the product of intentionality and self-conscious reflection for it is more often than not the outcome of pragmatic routines, habits and ritualized or unconscious processes. Further, objects and spaces, which are very much part of cultural analysis, are in danger of disappearing from view in this metaphor.

Links **Communication, dialogic, discourse analysis, language, meaning, performativity**

Counterculture The idea of a counterculture refers to the values, beliefs and attitudes, that is, the culture, of a minority group that is in opposition to the mainstream or ascendant culture. Further, a counterculture is articulate and self-conscious in its opposition to the values of the governing culture in a way that distinguishes it from a subculture. The term is particularly associated with the cultural and political movements and formations of the 1960s and early 1970s in the United States and Britain, from whence the concept emerged.

The counterculture of the 1960s was primarily constituted by the anti-materialistic Hippie movement with its themes of dropping-out, sexual liberation, drug use and the display of hairstyle and clothing as self-conscious cultural and political statements. The city of San Francisco (most notably the district of Haight-Ashbury), the music of the Grateful Dead, Jefferson Airplane, Bob Dylan and Janis Joplin, along with the writings of Allen Ginsberg, Timothy Leary and Herbert Marcuse, were component parts of a cultural movement whose symbolic high point was the Woodstock festival.

The counterculture of the time also included the political activists of the anti-Vietnam war movement, the 'Students for a Democratic Society' and a nascent Women's Liberation Movement. As such the counterculture of the 1960s is the forerunner of contemporary New Social Movements and the onset of the self-conscious cultural politics that marks cultural studies. Indeed, cultural studies emerged in Britain during much the same time period, so that a number of significant figures in its history were influenced by the 1960s counterculture.

Links **Cultural politics, life-politics, New Social Movements, postmaterialism, subculture, women's movement**

Critical theory The term 'critical theory' has been associated with the work of the 'Frankfurt School', a research institute that began its work in Germany in 1923 but later transferred to the United States under the threat of Nazism. The leading figures of the Frankfurt School, **Adorno**, Horkheimer and Marcuse, were indebted to Marxism but also critical of it. A mixture of Marxism, critical philosophy and psychoanalysis was drawn upon to present a critique of the capitalist social order and of the 'culture industry' in particular.

The notion of a 'critique' was familiar to the Frankfurt School through the German philosophical tradition and especially Marxism, wherein it involves seeking to find the contradictory tendencies of a theory. Here one seeks both to criticize but also to retain that which remains valuable in a given tradition. Given that the Frankfurt School was also highly critical of capitalism and the social order, it is a short step from the notion of a critique to the idea of 'critical' theory.

Today the idea of critical theory is less obviously connected to the work of the Frankfurt School, though its contemporary heir **Habermas** would still attract the term, but it has also become associated more widely with contemporary cultural and textual analysis that carries a critical edge. This would include structuralism, poststructuralism and postmodernism. Used in this way, the idea of critical theory has taken on a sense of being critical of the symbolic order and of the traditions of Western philosophy rather more than of the capitalist order.

Links **Culture industry, Marxism, postmodernism, poststructuralism, structuralism**

Cultural capital A concept associated with **Bourdieu**, for whom cultural capital acts as a social relation within a system of exchange that includes the accumulated cultural knowledge that confers power and status. For example, education and/or the ability to talk knowledgeably about high culture has traditionally been a form of cultural capital associated with the middle classes. Cultural capital is distinguished from economic capital (wealth) and social capital (whom you know). Here distinctions of cultural taste are understood to be classifications based on lines of power rather than being founded on either universal aesthetic criteria or individual choice. Thus taste differentiation is never simply about differences that are of equal standing but rather entails claims to authority and authenticity.

Thornton has applied the concepts of cultural capital and distinction to an analysis of youth subcultures and to the dance cultures of the late 1980s and early 1990s in particular. She argues that club cultures are taste cultures marked by a whole series of internal authenticity claims and distinctions. These include claims regarding the authentic versus the phoney, the 'hip' versus the 'mainstream', and the 'underground' versus 'the media'. Here dance culture distinctions invoke forms of 'subcultural capital' such as clothes, records, haircuts, dance styles and knowledges to confer status and power on young people. Subcultural capital involves distinctions between 'us' (alternative, cool, independent, authentic, minority) and 'them' (mainstream, straight, commercial, false, majority). It also involves distinctions *within* club culture: knowing the latest releases and dances, wearing the most fashionable clothes, seeing the coolest DJs, and attending the right clubs. So fast moving is contemporary club culture as it undergoes metamorphosis after metamorphosis that maintaining subcultural capital is a highly skilled task.

Links **Authenticity, consumption, habitus, postmodernism, power, youth culture**

Cultural imperialism Cultural imperialism is said to involve the domination of one culture by another and is usually thought of as a set of processes involving the ascendancy of one nation and/or the global domination of consumer capitalism. This argument stresses a loss of cultural autonomy for the 'dominated' nation and the worldwide growth of cultural homogeneity or 'sameness'. The principal agents of cultural synchronization are commonly said to be transnational corporations and particularly those of US origin. Consequently, cultural imperialism as domination is regarded as the outcome of a set of economic and cultural processes implicated in the reproduction of global capitalism.

Herbert Schiller, one of the leading proponents of the cultural imperialism thesis since the late 1960s, has argued that US-controlled corporations dominate the global communications industries. He points to the interlocking network that connects US television, defence subcontractors and the Federal government. Schiller's case is that the mass media fit into the world capitalist system by providing ideological support for capitalism in general and transnational corporations in particular. That is, they are said to act as vehicles for corporate marketing along with a general 'ideological effect' that purportedly produces and reinforces local attachment to US capitalism.

There are three central difficulties with the cultural imperialism thesis under contemporary conditions. First, it is no longer the case, if it ever was, that the global flows of cultural discourses are constituted as one-way traffic. Second, in so far as the predominant flow of cultural discourse remains from West to East and North to South, this is not *necessarily* a form of domination. Third, it is unclear that the current period of globalization represents a simple process of homogenization since the forces of fragmentation and hybridity are equally as strong.

There can be little doubt that the first waves of economic, military and cultural globalization were part of the dynamic spread of Western-originated capitalist modernity. The early phases of globalization certainly involved Western interrogation of the non-Western 'Other', while colonial control manifested itself as military dominance, cultural ascendancy and the origins of economic dependency. However, though the economies of the world are integrated into a world economic order in which developing nations occupy a subordinate position, it is not clear that cultural homogenization is the inevitable consequence.

While the values and meanings attached to place remain significant, we are increasingly involved in networks that extend far beyond our immediate physical locations. Though we are not yet part of a world-state or unitary world culture, we can identify global cultural processes, of cultural integration and disintegration, which are independent of inter-state relations. Here metaphors of uncertainty, contingency and chaos are replacing those of order, stability and systemacity so that global cultural flows cannot be understood through neat sets of linear determinations but are better comprehended as a series of overlapping, over-determined, complex and chaotic conditions. Indeed, for a number of cultural studies writers the disjunctive cultural flows that mark globalization are best characterized in terms of the emergence of cultural hybridity rather than of homogenization and cultural imperialism.

Links **Capitalism, globalization, hybridity, ideology, modernity, postcolonial theory**

Cultural materialism The concept of cultural materialism draws our attention to the idea that the meanings and representations that we designate as 'culture' are generated through material processes under particular physical and social circumstances. Thus cultural materialism is concerned to explore the questions of how and why meanings are inscribed at the moment of production. That is, cultural materialism explores signifying practices in the context of the means and conditions of their construction. Traditionally, this has focused on the connections between cultural practices and political economy, though strictly speaking this is a rather narrow definition of cultural materialism. Thus **Williams** understands cultural materialism to involve the analysis of all forms of signification within the actual means and conditions of their production.

The debates about the place of culture in social formations and its relationship to other practices, notably economics and politics, has its roots in cultural studies' Marxist legacy. Marxism, or historical materialism, is a philosophy that attempts to relate the production and re-production of culture to the organization of the material conditions of life. Here culture is a corporeal force tied into the socially organized production of the material conditions of existence and refers to the forms assumed by social existence under determinate historical conditions. In particular, the material 'base' is said to shape the parameters of the cultural 'superstructure' of ideas, politics, arts and so forth. Expressed in this way, the relationship between the economic base and the cultural superstructure is a rather mechanical and economically deterministic one.

The influence of such a mechanistic and reductionist model has waned in cultural studies. Indeed, the narrative of cultural studies from the 1960s onwards involves a moving away from economic reductionism towards an analysis of the autonomous logic of language, culture, representation and consumption. This in part reflects the influence of structuralism within cultural studies during the 1970s wherein the emphasis is on the irreducible character of the cultural as a set of distinct practices with their own internal organization or structuration.

The analysis of economic determinants may be necessary to any understanding of culture but it is not, and cannot be, self-sufficient. Nevertheless, culture remains the consequence of a range of material activities embedded within material circumstances. Thus, what we require is a multi-dimensional and multi-perspectival approach to the understanding of culture that would grasp the connections between economic, political, social and cultural dimensions without reducing social phenomena to any one level. Hence the metaphor of 'circuit of culture' involves the articulation of moments of production and consumption. In this model, cultural meaning is produced and embedded at each level of the circuit – production, representation, identity, consumption and regulation – and articulated, linked to, the next moment without determining what meanings will be taken up or produced at that level.

Links **Articulation, base and superstructure, circuit of culture, Marxism, reductionism, structuralism**

Cultural policy Cultural policy is concerned with the regulation and management of culture and in particular with the administration of those institutions that produce and govern the form and content of cultural products. This would include organizations like the Arts Council in the UK, the Federal Communications Commission in the United States, museums, government departments of education/arts/culture/media/sport etc., schools, institutions of higher education, theatre administration, television organizations, record companies and advertising agencies. However, within the context of cultural studies, questions of policy formation and enactment are connected to wider issues of cultural politics. That is, cultural policy is not only a technical problem of administration, but also one of cultural values and social power set in the overall context of the production and circulation of symbolic meanings.

Although cultural studies has been much concerned with critical thinking and cultural politics, not many of its practitioners have, at least until recently, taken cultural policy or the possibility of working with state or commercial organizations particularly seriously. Indeed, many cultural studies writers have often appeared contemptuous of such an idea, holding an engagement with policy to be somehow impure or corrupting. However, during the 1990s a significant discussion about cultural policy was prompted by the work of Tony **Bennett**, amongst others.

Bennett argued that the textual politics with which cultural studies has traditionally been engaged ignores the institutional dimensions of cultural power. He was particularly critical of cultural studies for displacing its politics onto the level of signification and text which, he suggested, has been at the expense of a material politics in relation to the institutions and organizations that produce and distribute cultural texts. For Bennett, cultural studies has been too concerned with consciousness and the ideological struggle and has not paid enough attention to the material technologies of power and of cultural policy.

In this view, culture is caught up in, and functions as a part of, cultural technologies that organize and shape social life and human conduct; a cultural technology being part of the 'machinery' of institutional and organizational structures that produces particular configurations of power/knowledge. Here, culture is not just a matter of representations and consciousness but of institutional practices, administrative routines and spatial arrangements. Thus, the processes of social regulation are themselves constitutive of self-reflective modes of conduct, ethical competencies and social movements. Culture in this reading is best understood in terms of a 'governmentality' that, for Bennett, is the relation of culture and power that most typically characterizes modern societies.

The debate about cultural policy that Bennett and others initiated often appeared to counterpoise the development of cultural policy to the more long-standing generation and elaboration of cultural criticism within cultural studies. However, there is no necessary reason why cultural studies cannot attend to the important pragmatic calls of policy without relinquishing the role that 'critical cultural theory' has to play. Indeed, it remains important to consider and debate the values that are to guide policy formation and enactment as an integral part of the policy process itself.

Cultural politics Cultural politics is about the power to name, and thus legitimate, objects and events, including both common sense and 'official' versions of the social and cultural world. One of the central arguments of cultural studies is that culture is a domain in which competing meanings and versions of the world have fought for ascendancy. In particular, meaning and truth are constituted within patterns of power and subject to processes of contestation. Thus, cultural politics can be understood in terms of the ability to represent the world and to make particular descriptions 'stick'. Here social change becomes possible through rethinking and re-describing the social order and the possibilities for the future. *41*

All forms of cultural representation are intrinsically 'political' because they are bound up with the power that enables some kinds of knowledge and identities to exist while denying it to others. For example, to describe women as full human beings and citizens with equal social rights and obligations is quite a different matter from regarding them as sub-human domestic workers with bodies designed to please men. To use the language of citizenship to describe women is a different representation of common sense and official ideology from one in which they are described as whores, tarts and servants. The language of citizenship legitimates the place of women in business and politics while the language of sexual and domestic servitude denies this place, seeking to confine women to the traditional spheres of domesticity and as objects of the male gaze.

As a form of cultural politics, cultural studies has sought to play a deconstructive and de-mystifying role by pointing to the fabricated character of cultural texts. It has aimed to highlight the myths and ideologies embedded in texts in the hope of producing subject positions, and real subjects, who are enabled to oppose subordination. Deconstructing texts helps us to understand how they work and in particular to be aware of their political implications. Thus we are enabled to grasp the culturally constructed nature of the descriptions that regulate our understanding of the world and their possible consequences in terms of politics, values and purposes.

At its best, the development of critical positions and new theory aims to be linked to communities, groups, organizations and networks of people who are actively involved in social and cultural change. Indeed, as a political theory cultural studies has hoped to organize disparate oppositional groups into an alliance of cultural politics. Given that the emergence of cultural studies as an institutionally located enterprise did not coincide with an upsurge of class struggle, it has been the 'new' social and political movements of identity politics which have more often than not attracted the attention of cultural studies writers. Here cultural politics has been conceived of as a series of collective social struggles organized around gender, race, sexuality, age etc. which seek to re-describe the social in terms of specific values and hoped for consequences.

Links **Cultural policy, deconstruction, dialogic, hegemony, identity politics, ideology, politics, polysemy**

Cultural populism At one level the idea of cultural populism is simply that assumption central to cultural studies that popular culture is valuable and worthy of serious study. However, the concept was given a twist by McGuigan in the early 1990s and made into the centrepiece of a critique of the direction being taken by cultural studies at that time. In particular, the respect accorded to popular culture by cultural studies was said to have turned into uncritical valorization of the consumption of commodity culture. Further, cultural studies was said to lack an adequately materialist understanding of culture and was thus unable to grasp the material circumstances and power relations of the contemporary world.

The argument was that cultural studies rightly took issue with ideas of 'mass culture' that denigrated popular culture as unworthy of either participation or study. However, the increased 'postmodernization' of culture was said to have itself collapsed the high–low division. Further, the celebration of the productive and resistive capacities of audiences by cultural studies writers was argued to have gone too far so that it had become complicit with the ideology of consumer sovereignty. For McGuigan, cultural studies was unable to critique the products of consumer culture because it had lost sight of any profound conception of cultural value from which to critique texts. Further, it over-endowed audiences with the cultural competencies to deconstruct ideology.

Links **Common culture, consumption, cultural materialism**

Cultural studies The domain of cultural studies can be understood as an interdisciplinary or post-disciplinary field of inquiry that explores the production and inculcation of culture or maps of meaning. However, 'cultural studies' has no referent to which we can point; rather, it is constituted by the language-game of cultural studies. That is, the theoretical terms developed and deployed by persons calling their work cultural studies constitutes that which is 'cultural studies'. These are concepts which have been deployed in the various geographical sites of cultural studies and which form the history of the cultural studies tradition as it emerged from the **Centre for Contemporary Cultural Studies** and proliferated across the globe from the 1960s onwards.

Cultural studies can be also be grasped as a discursive formation; that is, a group of ideas, images and practices, that provide ways of talking about, and conduct associated with, a particular topic, social activity or institutional site. That is, cultural studies is constituted by a regulated way of speaking about objects (which cultural studies brings into view) and coheres around key concepts, ideas and concerns that include articulation, culture, discourse, ideology, identity, popular culture, power, representation and text. Indeed, the production of this dictionary forms a part of the process by which cultural studies constitutes itself.

Clarifying the boundaries of cultural studies as a coherent and unified discipline with clear-cut substantive topics, concepts and methods which differentiate it from other disciplines remains difficult. Cultural studies is, and always has been, a multi- or post-disciplinary field of inquiry which blurs the boundaries between itself and other 'subjects'. Indeed, cultural studies draws important concepts from other theoretical domains critical amongst which have been Marxism, structuralism, poststructuralism, and psychoanalysis.

Today, a good deal of cultural studies work is centred on the question of how the world is socially constructed and in particular with the themes of 'difference' and identity. As such, the central strand of cultural studies can be understood as an exploration of culture, as constituted by the meanings and representations generated by human signifying practices, and the context in which they occur, with a particular interest in the relations of power and the political consequences that are inherent in such cultural practices.

Even though cultural studies can be understood as a kind of intellectual magpie, it cannot be said to be anything. It is not physics, it is not sociology and it is not linguistics, despite drawing upon these subject areas. For **Hall**, that which differentiates cultural studies from other subject areas is its connections to matters of power and politics and in particular to the need for social and cultural change. In this view, cultural studies is a body of theory generated by thinkers who regard the production of theoretical knowledge as a political practice. Thus **Bennett** understands cultural studies to be an interdisciplinary field in which perspectives from different disciplines can be selectively drawn on to examine the relations of culture and power. Here cultural studies is concerned with those practices, institutions and systems of classification that enable a population to acquire particular values, beliefs, competencies and routines of life. Further, cultural studies seeks to develop ways of thinking about culture and power that can be utilized by agents in the pursuit of change

Links Cultural politics, culturalism, culture, Marxism, poststructuralism, power, structuralism

Culturalism This is a *post hoc* term that, within the development of cultural studies, owes its sense to a contrast with structuralism and has little currency outside of that debate. Thus within the mythology of cultural studies the figures of Richard **Hoggart**, Raymond **Williams** and Edward Thompson are held to represent the moment of culturalism that emerged during the 1960s and which is later contrasted with the 'structuralism' of the 1970s. Theoretically, culturalism is associated with the adoption of a broadly anthropological definition of culture that takes it to be an everyday lived process not confined to 'high art'. Thus, culturalism stresses the 'ordinariness' of culture and the active, creative, capacity of people to construct shared meaningful practices. Methodologically, culturalism has favoured concrete empirical research and ethnography in particular with a focus on lived experience in order to explore the way that active human beings create cultural meanings.

In the hands of Williams, culturalism is a form of historically oriented cultural materialism that traces the unfolding of meaning over time and investigates culture in the context of its material conditions of production and reception. Additionally, there is an explicit partisanship in exploring the class basis of culture that aims to give 'voice' to the subordinated and to examine the play of class power within culture. However, this form of 'left culturalism' was also nation-centred in its approach and there is little sense of either the globalizing character of contemporary culture or the place of race within national cultures.

Links **Cultural materialism, culture, ethnography, experience, structuralism**

Culture Culture is a complicated and contested word because the concept does not represent an entity in an independent object world. Rather it is best thought of as a mobile signifier that enables distinct and divergent ways of talking about human activity for a variety of purposes. That is, the concept of culture is a tool that is of more or less usefulness to us as a life form and its usage and meanings continue to change as thinkers have hoped to 'do' different things with it.

The multitudinous ways that culture has been talked about within cultural studies include culture as a whole way of life; as like a language; as constituted by representation; as a tool; as practices; as artefacts; as spatial arrangements; as power; as high or low; as mass and as popular. This variety of ways of comprehending culture does not represent cases of objective right versus objective wrong, for none of the definitions of culture is erroneous in the sense of mis-describing an object. However, they do achieve different purposes and may be more or less applicable in different times and places. The concept of culture is thus political and contingent and to explore its meaning(s) is to trace its uses and the consequences that follow from this. In so far as contemporary cultural studies has a distinguishing take on the concept of culture, it is one that stresses the intersection of power and meaning with a view to promoting social change and improving the human condition.

Raymond **Williams** has suggested that the word culture began as a noun of process connected to growing crops, that is, cultivation. Having germinated from the soil, the concept of culture grew to encompass human beings so that to be a cultivated person was to be a cultured person. However, during the nineteenth century it was apparent to the 'cultured' that not all persons were equally civilized. At worst the capability to be cultured was held to be a product of natural selection, at best it was a condition to be aspired to and acquired by, in practice, the educated classes. Hence Matthew Arnold's view that acquiring culture was the means toward moral perfection and social good. Here culture as human 'civilization' is counterposed to the 'anarchy' of the 'raw and uncultivated masses'. Later, the English literary critic F.R. Leavis was to hold that high or literary culture, captured in the artistic and scholarly tradition, kept alive and nurtured the ability to discriminate between the best and the worst of culture; that is, between the canon of good works and the 'addictions' and 'distractions' of mass culture.

By contrast, Raymond Williams utilized the spirit of a nineteenth-century anthropological understanding of culture associated with Malinowski and Radcliffe-Brown to designate culture as 'a whole and distinctive way of life'. For Williams, it was the meanings and practices of ordinary men and women that composed culture. In this view, culture is constituted by the tapestry of texts, practices and meanings generated by every one of us as we conduct our lives. The implication of applying an anthropological understanding of culture to modern Western industrialized cultures (rather than to the cultures of colonized peoples) is to say that we are all cultured. We all know 'how to go on' within our form of life. Further, within the context of modernity, an anthropological definition of culture offered a critical and democratic edge, since to comprehend culture as a 'whole way of life' involves splitting off the concept from the 'Arts'. This argument helps to legitimize the study of popular culture and to put questions of cultural democracy to the fore.

Culture is commonly held to concern questions of shared social meanings, that is, the various ways we make sense of the world. However, meanings are not simply floating 'out there', rather, they are generated through signs. Hence the investigation of culture has become closely entwined with the study of signification. Cultural studies has argued that language is not a neutral medium for the formation of meanings and knowledge relating to an independent object world outside of language, but rather is constitutive of those very meanings and knowledge. That is, language gives meaning to material objects and social practices that are brought into view by language and made intelligible to us in terms which language delimits. These processes of meaning production are signifying practices and to understand culture is to explore how meaning is produced symbolically as forms of representation.

Consequently, cultural studies has, for many of its proponents, become centred on questions of representation with an especial emphasis on the ways by which the world is socially constructed and represented to and by us. This requires us to explore the textual generation of meaning in tandem with its subsequent consumption in a variety of contexts. Further, cultural representations and meanings have a certain materiality; they are embedded in sounds, inscriptions, objects, images, books, magazines and television programmes. They are produced, enacted, used and understood in specific social and material contexts. Thus, the central strand of cultural studies can be understood as the study of culture where this concept is understood to mean the signifying practices of representation set within the social and material contexts of production, circulation and reception.

Significantly, the sites of contemporary cultural production and reception are no longer confined within the borders of nation-states. Rather, in the era of globalization culture is best thought of not as a bounded unit but as a set of overlapping performative language-games that flow with no clear limits or determinations within the global whole of human life. Culture is becoming less a matter of locations than of hybrid and creolized cultural meanings and practices that span global space. Cultures are syncretic and hybridized products of interactions across space and are increasingly thought of as carving routes rather than possessing roots. They are constellations of temporary coherence, or knots in the field of social space that are the product of relations and interconnections from the local to the global.

Links **Cultural studies, language, meaning, performativity, popular culture, representation, signs**

Culture industry: The notion of the 'culture industry' is associated with the work of the quasi-Marxist Frankfurt School and their version of critical theory. Indeed, **Adorno** and Horkheimer wrote a famous essay called 'The Culture Industry – Enlightenment as Mass Deception', a title that sums up their line of thinking on the matter. Published in 1946, the essay argues that culture is dominated by the commodities produced by the culture industry and that these commodities, while purporting to be democratic, individualistic and diversified, are in actuality authoritarian, conformist and highly standardized. Thus the culture industry impresses the same stamp on everything and produces an apparent diversity of products only so that 'none may escape'.

For example, Adorno regarded the popular music of the 1940s as stylized, lacking in originality and requiring little effort by its audience. For Adorno, the aim of standardized music is standardized reactions that affirm life as it is, including the structuring of the human psyche into conformist ways. He argued that the culture industry, in tandem with the family, produces 'ego weakness' and the 'authoritarian personality'. By contrast, critical art is said by Adorno to be a form of expression that is not oriented to the market but which challenges the standards of intelligibility of a reified society. Thus Adorno contrasts what he thinks of as the critical music of Schoenberg with the alleged conformism of jazz.

A more contemporary use of the term 'culture industry' may not necessarily refer to the work of the Frankfurt School but more simply to the production of popular music, film, television and fashion by transnational capitalist corporations. Here one is concerned with the political economy of culture. That is, with issues of who owns and controls the institutions of economy, society and culture and the way in which the corporate ownership and control of the culture industries moulds contemporary culture. In this sense the study of the culture industries forms a necessary part of cultural studies. Nevertheless, many cultural studies writers have wanted to argue that the meaning of culture cannot be reduced to a concern with political economy but must also focus on the domain of consumption where consumers generate their own meanings. Thus, consideration of culture as an industry raises a series of questions about cultural materialism and the commodification of culture but also about creative consumption and the dangers of reductionism.

Links **Circuit of culture, commodification, cultural materialism, political economy, reductionism**

D

De Certeau, Michel (1925–1986) French writer Michel De Certeau trained as a Jesuit priest at the University of Lyons and continued his studies at the Sorbonne before becoming a Professor at the Catholic Institute of Paris and the Universty of Paris-vii. He also worked at the University of San Diego, California. His writings about power, resistance and everyday life, which carry the mark of **Foucault**, have been influential within cultural studies. De Certeau argues that there are no 'margins' outside of power from which to lay an assault on it or from which to claim authenticity so that the poetic and resistant practices of everyday life are always already in the space of power. De Certeau makes the distinction between the *strategies* of power by which power marks out a space for itself distinct from its environs and the resistive *tactics* of the poacher operating within a terrain organized by the law of a foreign power.

- **Associated concepts** Cultural politics, cultural populism, popular culture, power, resistance.
- **Tradition(s)** Poststructuralism, psychoanalysis.
- **Reading** De Certeau, M. (1984) *The Practice of Everyday Life*. Berkeley, CA: University of California Press.

Deconstruction This concept is associated with the work of **Derrida** and his 'undoing' of the binaries of Western philosophy as well as its extension into the fields of literature (for example, De Man) and postcolonial theory (for example, **Spivak**). To deconstruct is to take apart, to undo, in order to seek out and display the assumptions of a text. In particular, deconstruction involves the dismantling of hierarchical binary conceptual oppositions such as man/woman, black/white, reality/appearance, nature/culture, reason/madness etc. that serve to guarantee the status and power of truth-claims by excluding and devaluing the 'inferior' part of the binary.

The purpose of deconstruction is not simply to reverse the order of binaries but to show how they are implicated in each other. Deconstruction seeks to expose the blind spots of texts, the unacknowledged assumptions upon which they operate. This includes the places where a text's rhetorical strategies work against the logic of a text's stated arguments. That is, deconstructionism highlights the tension between what a text means to say and what it is constrained to mean.

One of the central problems of deconstruction is that it must use the very conceptual language it seeks to undo. For example, to deconstruct Western philosophy is to use the very language of Western philosophy. To mark this tension, Derrida places his concepts 'under erasure'. The use 'under erasure' of accustomed and known concepts is intended to de-stabilize the familiar, marking it as useful, necessary, inaccurate and mistaken. Thus does Derrida seek to expose the undecidability of meaning.

Links Différance, meaning, poststructuralism, text, under erasure, writing

Deleuze, Gilles (1925–1995) and Guattari, Félix (1930–1992) The French philosopher Deleuze and the psychoanalyst/philosopher Guattari made their greatest impact on cultural theory together in their two-volume tome *Capitalism and Schizophrenia*. The strong theme of their work is multiplicity and resistance to reductionism and reification through the imposition of fixed forms, such as the triangular Oedipal model, on multi-directional desire. Through concepts such as 'schizo-analysis', 'nomadology' and the Rhizome they stress that which is moving, fleeing and becoming in the form of multiple deterritorialized flows of energy that transcend fixed relationships of identity. Deleuze worked at the Sorbonne, the University of Lyons and the University of Paris while Guattari spent most of his career working in La Borde, a psychiatric clinic. Both were politically active on the 'Left' and Guattari joined the Green Party in his later years.

- **Associated concepts** Anti-essentialism, capitalism, Oedipus complex, post-humanism, reductionism (anti-), resistance, rhizome.
- **Tradition(s)** Psychoanalysis, structuralism.
- **Reading** Deleuze, G. and Guattari, F. (1988) *A Thousand Plateaus*. Minneapolis, MN: University of Minnesota Press.

Deregulation The idea of deregulation refers, in a communications context, to the relaxation of state prescriptions governing the ownership and content of the mass media. In recent times it has involved the replacement of existing regulations by others that were less stringent in their restrictions. Thus deregulation is also re-regulation. For example, the 1980s and early 1990s were a period of deregulation of the media that saw the emergence of multimedia conglomerates in search of synergy and convergence. This process was assisted by the relaxation of state regulations restricting cross-media ownership and the entry of new players into the market.

This deregulatory process was occasioned by the growth of 'new' technologies that invalidated the argument that communications required state ownership based on a 'natural' monopoly. This was so since digital technology allows frequencies to be split and alternative delivery systems employed. Further, various court rulings upheld the legal rights to communicate and the adoption of diversity as a key public principle. Above all, there was a new governmental enthusiasm for the market which included a preference for the funding of the media by commercial means rather than through taxation.

Deregulation has been an aspect of the increased commercialization of communications that has reshaped the media landscape. For example, outside of the United States, the 'old order' was marked by the subordination of broadcasting to public service goals set in the context of a broadly political process of regulation. Thus, television was of a largely national character and was generally noncommercial in principle. In contrast, the 'new order' involves the co-existence of public and commercial broadcasting. In particular the deregulation of commercial television has fuelled the increasing power of multimedia transnational companies whose influence adds to the pressure on public service television to operate within a commercial logic. These are the world-wide trends that underpin the emergence of a global electronic culture.

Links **Convergence, globalization, multimedia corporation, public sphere, synergy**

Derrida, Jacques (1930–) Derrida is an Algerian-born French-speaking philosopher whose work has been influential within cultural studies and who is associated with the themes of deconstruction and poststructuralism. The main influence that Derrida has had on cultural studies is his anti-essentialism, by which words do not refer to objects that possess essential qualities. Derrida undoes the structuralist trope of the stable binary structures of language, arguing that meaning slides down a chain of signifiers and is thus continually deferred and supplemented. Derrida seeks to deconstruct the epistemological base of Western philosophy, including the idea that there can be any self-present transparent meaning outside of 'representation'. He also deconstructs the hierarchical conceptual oppositions of philosophy such as speech/writing, reality/appearance, and argues for the 'undecidability' of binary oppositions.

- **Associated concepts** Anti-essentialism, deconstruction, différance, logocentricism, under erasure, writing.
- **Tradition(s)** Postmodernism, poststructuralism.
- **Reading** Derrida, J. (1976) *Of Grammatology*. Baltimore, MD: Johns Hopkins University Press.

Determinism Determinism is a form of analysis that explains one kind of phenomenon in terms of another. In its weaker form, determinism simply amounts to the attribution of a chain of cause and effect to occurrences. To point to causal links between items, for example between material conditions and human actions, is not to deny the specificity of the other term. That phenomena have material causes does not reduce their significance to the causal agent nor take away their specificities. For example, each of us can trace biological, historical and cultural explanations for our own being, yet, at no time are we anything less than unique persons who are capable of action.

In its stronger formulation the designation and ascription of causes appears to deny human beings 'free will' or agency. That is, human actions are understood to be the consequence of the structures of society. This is the problem of structure and agency explored by **Giddens**'s structuration theory (amongst others). Where an account is determinist in excluding the creative power of human action it is a sibling of reductionism. Paradoxically, the strong form of determinism faces the problem of including its own production in the explanatory account of human behaviour.

Another way of considering the question of determinism revolves around the issue of predictability. That is, determinism would appear to make the objects of analysis subject to predictable outcomes and indeed some aspects of human action do seem to be relatively predictable and thus open to structural explanations. Yet an explanation that includes human motives, meanings, reasons, emotions etc. cannot assume predictability because of the instability of human intent and the unintended consequences of action. The complexity and overdetermination of human behaviour makes entirely reliable prediction impossible to achieve.

Since there is no Archimedean place outside of ourselves from which to ascertain the conditions of our own being we cannot answer the metaphysical question as to whether people are 'really' free or 'really' determined in any absolute metaphysical sense. Rather, discourses of freedom and discourses of determination are socially produced narratives that have different purposes and are applicable in different ways. The languages of freedom and determination are socially produced for different purposes in different realms. For example, the language of agency encourages us to act, to seek improvement of the human condition and to take responsibility for our actions. The language of determination might help us to understand and empathize with others or to make policy recommendations that would change social conditions outside of a given person. Paradoxically agency is itself determined yet it is also a culturally intelligible way of understanding the existential experience of facing and making choices.

A more substantive application of debates about determinism within cultural studies can be seen in relation to discussions about cultural materialism where the Marxist model of the base and superstructure has been understood as economically determinist. The general direction of cultural studies has been to move away from economic determinism by which cultural products and practices are explicable simply in terms of the production process. Cultural studies has also been opposed to biological determinism (for example, the early forms of sociobiology) by which human behaviour is said to be explicable solely by recourse to genetics.

Links **Agency, base and superstructure, cultural materialism, structuration**

Dialogic The concept of the dialogic is drawn from the work of Bakhtin and refers to the idea of the 'two-directionality' or 'multi-accentuality' of signs and meaning. Here words are directed simultaneously towards another speaking subject and towards another word. Thus the meaning of signs is an aspect of the relationship between one sign and another as well as between a speaker and the audience to whom an utterance is addressed. The concept of the dialogic draws our attention to the inherent ambiguities of language and to the means by which subjects create meaning dialogically through the socially derived and shared medium of language. Dialogism involves the continuous state of dialogue into which every word is placed.

Bakhtin argues that all meaning is essentially dialogic; it has been passed from mouth to mouth, as well as been used in different contexts and with different intentions. Here meaning is the outcome of the relations between signs and the negotiation of meaning between speaker and addressee. Language takes shape and becomes meaningful in the space between ourselves and our audience while a text is to be analysed as a dialogic relationship between subject–addressee and text–context. Thus one of Bakhtin's other key concepts, heteroglossia, refers to the diversity and stratification of languages or voices to be found within a work. As such the notion of the dialogic provided the key foundational idea for the concept of 'intertextuality' as developed by **Kristeva** and also resonates with **Derrida**'s notion of 'différance'.

Inherent in the way Bakhtin understands language is a critique of **Saussure**'s semiotics as involving a dead, neutral and static object of investigation that appears to foreshadow a number of the claims of poststructuralism. Thus 'the dialogic' emphasizes the construction of meaning as an active, dynamic process involving signs that are able to take on a range of different meanings and connotations for different social actors in different social, cultural and historical situations. Indeed, signs are the site of a continuous struggle over meaning so that powerful groups try to fix the meanings of words (monoglossa) in ideological ways that serve their interests. The influence of the notion of the struggle over the multiple meanings of words as expressed by the notion of the dialogic (that is, polyglossia or the contestation of languages) can be seen in the post-Marxist understanding of ideology and hegemony in the work of **Hall**, **Laclau** and Mouffe.

Bakhtin also argued that individual linguistic performances, both written and oral, are the outcome of an internal process whereby the various voices of our past and present are intertwined through the cultural web of language. Indeed, he argues that we acquire language by internalizing the voices of others, and then spend much of our lives re-externalizing these incorporated forms in a continuous dialogue with others. As such the subject is constituted as a dialogic self.

Links **Carnivalesque, différance, ideology, intertextuality, meaning, polysemy, post-Marxism**

Diaspora The concept of diaspora is deployed to indicate a dispersed network of ethnically and culturally related peoples. As such, this term is concerned with ideas of travel, migration, scattering, displacement, homes and borders. Diasporas are formed as networks comprised of transnational identifications that encompass 'imagined' communities and as such are often engaged in the politics and social dynamics of remembrance and commemoration. Commonly, but not always, the idea of a diaspora also connotes notions of aliens, displaced persons, wanderers and those engaged in forced and reluctant flight. Globalization provides the context for an increased interest in the study of diaspora in recent years, notably during the 1990s. In particular, patterns of population movement and settlement instituted during colonialism and its aftermath established diaspora populations at the heart of Western cultures and nation-states.

The strength of the concept of diaspora lies in its encouragement to think about identities in terms of contingency, indeterminacy and conflict, of identities in motion rather than of absolutes of nature or culture. **Gilroy** describes this process as involving routes rather than roots; a 'changing same' of the diaspora that involves hybridized cultural forms. His prime example is the concept of the Black Atlantic. Here, cultural exchange within the black diaspora produces hybrid identities and cultural forms of similarity and difference within and between its various locales.

It is a sign of our times that forms of hybrid cultural identity associated with diaspora populations are appearing all across the world; from the United States to Australia and from Europe to South Africa. The physical meeting and mixing of peoples across the globe that is exemplified by diaspora throws the whole notion of pure national or ethnic cultures into doubt. For example, in a Caribbean context the idea of the 'Creole continuum' has gained in significance. That is, a series of overlapping language uses and code switching that deploys not only the specific modes of other languages, say English and French, but invents forms peculiar to itself. Here, neither the colonial nor colonized cultures or languages are best understood as 'pure' forms separated from each other but rather as elements in the construction of new hybrid cultural forms.

Links **Black Atlantic, ethnicity, globalization, hybridity, identity, race**

Différance The concept of différance – difference and deferral – is central to the work of the philosopher **Derrida** and the influence of poststructuralism within cultural studies. Derrida's starting point is the argument derived from structuralism that language is to be understood as a system of differential signs that generate meaning through phonetic and conceptual difference rather than by correspondence with fixed transcendental meanings or by reference to an independent object world. Derrida goes on to argue that since meaning is generated through the play of signifiers and not by reference to an independent object world it can never be fixed. Words carry multiple meanings including the echoes or traces of other meanings from other related words in other contexts. Language is non-representational and meaning is inherently unstable so that it constantly slides away.

One way to understand the notion of différance is to look up the meaning of a word in a dictionary. Here we are referred to other words and then other words and then other words in an infinite process of deferral so that meaning slides down a chain of signifiers abolishing a stable signified. That is, the production of meaning in the process of signification is continually deferred and supplemented in the play of more-than-one.

Here the logic of the 'supplement' forms a challenge to the logic of identity. While the latter takes meaning to be identical with a fixed entity to which a word refers, a supplement adds to and substitutes meanings. That is, the meaning of a word is supplemented by the traces of other words. Nevertheless, even this use of 'the supplement' is problematic for it assumes that the supplement adds to an already existent self-present original meaning. Instead, the supplement is always already part of the thing supplemented. Meaning is always displaced and deferred. The continual supplementarity of meaning, that is the continual substitution and adding of meanings through the play of signifiers, challenges the identity of noises and marks with fixed meaning.

One of Derrida's purposes is to illustrate the argument that the very idea of literal meaning is based on the idea of the 'letter', that is, writing. Literal meaning is thus underpinned by metaphor – its apparent opposite. Here Derrida critiques what he calls the 'logocentrism' and 'phonocentrism' of Western philosophy. At the same time, the endless play of signification that Derrida explores is arguably regulated and partially 'fixed' as the marks and noises of language take on pragmatically stabilized meanings related to the achievement of purposes in the context of social practice.

Links **Deconstruction, logocentricism, meaning, poststructuralism, under erasure**

Difference A concern with ideas of difference gained ground during the 1990s to the point that it is the word of the hour for cultural studies in the twenty-first century. Difference is about the non-identical and dissimilar. It is about distinction, division, multiplicity and otherness. As such, difference is not an essence or attribute of an object but a relationship and position or perspective of signification. The importance of difference as a concept also lies in the way it links the themes of contemporary cultural studies. Thus, the significance of difference for cultural studies lies in two connected directions: the linguistic generation of meaning and the co-existence of variant cultural identities.

As described by structuralism and poststructuralism difference is the mechanism for the generation of meaning. That is, meaning is not generated because an object or referent has an essential and intrinsic meaning but is produced because signs are phonetically and conceptually different from one another. In language, it is said, there are only differences without positive terms, that is, signs do not have fixed meanings by dint of reference to an independent object. **Derrida** extends this idea with his concept of différance (above), whereby meaning generated through the play of signifiers can never be fixed but is continually supplemented and deferred.

It follows from these primary arguments of structuralism and poststructuralism that all the categories that had been used to describe and talk about human beings – 'culture', 'identity', 'women', 'class', 'society', 'interests', etc., can no longer be conceived of as having fixed meanings. That is, we cannot understand these categories in terms of unitary objects with single underlying structures and determinations; rather they are understood to be discursive constructs. This is the basis of the anti-essentialism that pervades contemporary cultural studies.

A central concern of cultural studies during the 1990s and into the new millennium has been identity. The word identity in common parlance connotes sameness. However, within cultural studies it has been understood much more through the notion of difference. Here, identity is not a fixed 'thing' that we possess but an emotionally charged symbolic description of ourselves. Subject to the idea of difference and deferral (différance) identity is never stable but a process of *becoming*. This signals to **Hall** the 'impossibility' of identity as well as its 'political significance'. The latter lies in the meanings attached to difference and the actions

54

that flow from them so that, he argues, the central task for contemporary cultural studies is to learn how to live with difference as manifested in various forms of cultural identity. Hence the concern with the cultural politics of race, gender, sexuality etc.

Links **Anti-essentialism, différance, identity, poststructuralism, structuralism**

Discourse The routine day-to-day usage of the term discourse simply refers to a stretch of text or spoken utterances that cohere into a meaningful exposition. However, cultural studies practitioners are, more often than not, using the concept of discourse in a more technical way that derives from the work of the historian and philosopher **Foucault**. Here, discourse is said to 'unite' language and practice and refers to regulated ways of speaking about a subject through which objects and practices acquire meaning. The production of knowledge through language that gives meaning to material objects and social practices we may call discursive practice.

Foucault is determinedly historical in his insistence that language develops and generates meaning under specific material and historical conditions. He explores the particular and determinate historical conditions under which statements are combined and regulated to form and define a distinct field of knowledge/objects requiring a particular set of concepts and delimiting a specific 'regime of truth' (that is, what counts as truth). Foucault attempts to identify the historical conditions and determining rules of formation of regulated ways of speaking about objects that he calls a discourse.

Foucault argued that discourse regulates not only what can be said under determinate social and cultural conditions but also who can speak, when and where. Here, through the operation of power in social practice, meanings are temporarily stabilized or regulated. Repeated motifs or clusters of ideas, practices and forms of knowledge across a range of sites of activity constitute a discursive formation. This is a pattern of discursive events that refer to, or bring into being, a common object across a number of sites. They are regulated maps of meaning or ways of speaking through which objects and practices acquire significance. For example, Foucault's study of discourses of madness included:

- Statements about madness which give us knowledge concerning madness.
- The rules which prescribe what is 'sayable' or 'thinkable' about madness.
- Subjects who personify the discourses of madness, that is, the 'madman'.
- The processes by which discourses of madness acquire authority and truth at a given historical moment.
- The practices within institutions which deal with madness.
- The idea that different discourses about madness will appear at later historical moments producing new knowledge and a new discursive formation.

Discourse is not a neutral medium for the formation and transfer of values, meanings and knowledge that exist beyond its boundaries, rather, it is constitutive of them. That is, discourse is not best understood as an innocent reflection of non-linguistic meaning, nor simply in terms of the intentions of language users. Rather, discourse constructs meaning. Though material objects and social practices have a material existence outside of language, they are given meaning or 'brought into view' by language and are thus discursively formed. Discourse constructs, defines and produces the objects of knowledge in an intelligible way while excluding other forms of reasoning as unintelligible. It structures which meanings can or cannot be deployed under determinate circumstances by speaking subjects.

Links **Discourse analysis, language, poststructuralism, power/knowledge**

Discourse analysis Discourse analysis is a form of linguistic investigation that inquires into the workings of stretches of text. Here the concept of discourse is not necessarily being used in the way developed by **Foucault** (above) but more often than not in the more mundane sense of an expanse of language larger than the unit of the sentence. Technically speaking, discourse in this context involves the conjoining of linguistic elements so as to constitute a structure of meaning larger than the sum of the parts.

Discourse analysis is based on a close examination of texts, whether written or spoken, so that the textual metaphor need not preclude analysis of speaking subjects. Thus discourse analysis can be brought to bear on social actions accomplished by language users who communicate within specific social and cultural situations. Discourse analysis is interested in naturally occurring text (written) and talk (verbal) that is studied within its global and local context. Naturally occurring discourse is a form of social practice the accomplishment of which is linear and sequential where the constitutive units of discourse may also be productive of larger units. Consequently, discourse analysis is interested in levels or layers of discourse and their relations. Discourse analysts are interested in the generation of meaning as the consequence of rule-governed activities the exploration of which illuminates the micro processes by which people make claims about themselves. Thus discourse analysis can demonstrate our participation in patterns of the linguistic dance of which we are not self-conscious.

Links **Conversation, discourse, language, meaning, representation, text**

Disorganized capitalism This is an idea (associated with Lash and Urry) that seeks to connect widespread contemporary economic, organizational and technological change to the restructuring and regeneration of global capitalism. Disorganized capitalism involves the reorganization of capitalism on a world-wide scale involving in particular the dispersal of capital through globalized production, financing and distribution. In the West this has been associated with de-industrialization, a sectoral shift towards the service sector and a rise in flexible forms of work organization. In this respect the concept shows a similarity to that of the 'post-industrial society'. However, it departs from it by stressing the continued significance of capitalist social relations and the processes of capital accumulation rather than the role of information or knowledge management, as is commonly found in theories of post-industrialism.

56

Disorganized capitalism involves a world-wide de-concentration of capital in the context of the fact that the growth of capitalism in the 'developing world' since the early 1970s has led to increasing competition for the West in the extractive and manufacturing industries and a consequent decline in those sectors of Western economies. Subsequent sectoral reorganization has led directly to the decrease in the absolute and relative size of the core working class, along with the emergence of a service class. It has also led to a reduction in regional and urban concentration together with a rise in flexible forms of work organization and a decline in national bargaining procedures.

These changes in economic practices and class composition are said to have an affinity with alterations in political thinking. This is manifested in the increased independence of large corporations from state regulation, the breakdown of state corporatist authority and challenges to the centralized welfare provision. The change in the role of the state is an aspect of the general decline in the salience and class character of politics and political parties. This arises from an educationally based stratification system that disorganizes the traditional links between occupation and class politics.

Links **Capitalism, globalization, post-Fordism, post-industrial society**

E

Écriture feminine The concepts of *écriture feminine* (woman's writing) and *le parler femme* (womanspeak) are associated with the feminist theorist Luce Irigaray and her attempt to inscribe the feminine, or, as she would see it, to write the unwritable. **Irigaray** theorizes a pre-symbolic 'space' or 'experience' for women constituted by a feminine *jouissance* or sexual pleasure, play and joy, which is outside of intelligibility. This is founded on the pre-Oedipal imaginary as the source of a feminine that, it is argued, cannot be symbolized because it precedes entry into the symbolic order. Since it is pre-symbolic it cannot be written, but through *écriture feminine* Irigaray must try to do so.

Irigaray speculates on what she understands to be the 'Otherness' of the feminine, and she seeks to ground this in the female body. Women are 'Other' because they are outside the specular (visual) economy of the Oedipal moment and thus outside of representation (that is, of the symbolic order). Given that the symbolic order lacks a grammar that could articulate the pre-Oedipal mother–daughter relationship, the feminine, according to Irgaray, can return only in its regulated form as man's 'Other'.

Irigaray explores the feminine as the constitutive exclusion of philosophy and seeks to deconstruct a Western philosophy that she reads as guaranteeing the masculine order and its claims to self-origination and unified agency. However, Irigaray, like **Derrida**, is faced with the problem of trying to critique philosophy for its exclusions while using the very language of that philosophy. Her strategy is to 'mime' the discourse of philosophy, that is, to cite it and talk its language but in ways that question the capacity of philosophy to ground its own claims. Thus *écriture feminine* mimes 'phallogocentrism' only to expose what is covered over.

Links Deconstruction, logocentricism, Oedipus complex, Other, phallocentric, psychoanalysis

Emotion The concept of 'emotion' is not one commonly associated with culture or cultural studies. However, it is included here as an example of how that which is commonly associated with the body can also be understood in terms of culture. Emotion has largely been thought of as a manifestation of brain biochemistry that involves and invokes a range of physiological changes. As such, an emotion has been thought to be in the domain of universal bodily responses that have been forged in the context of our evolutionary history. On this basis, many contemporary evolutionary theorists think that we have a set of 'hard-wired' basic emotions (sadness, surprise, disgust, anger, anticipation, joy, acceptance, fear), and a number of newer emotions that are a blend of the 'basic' emotional states (friendliness, alarm, guilt, sullenness, delight, anxiety etc.).

58

While emotion certainly does have a biological and evolutionary foundation, it also involves cognitive classificatory and appraisal functions that involve learned responses. Thus, though we have a number of bodily responses (for example, the heart is racing) that form the components of a variety of emotions, these are organized and named by higher cognitive functions (appraisals). Thus to a set of bodily responses we add a conscious 'feeling' from our working memory along with words that not only label context-specific responses as 'fear', 'anger', 'love' etc. but which can themselves set off further emotional responses. Indeed, discourses of emotion organize and regulate how we should understand bodily responses in given contexts. As such, emotions show evidence of cultural differences in terms of expression and display. Thus writers committed to social constructionism tend to regard emotions as culturally formed, citing as evidence the different emotional responses found within divergent cultures or social situations

Emotion works at the permeable interface between language, that is, culture, and the body, with causal flows taking place in either direction. That is, thinking generates and can change biochemical emotional responses while these chemical actions can set off a stream of thoughts. Current thinking in neuroscience suggests that all thoughts have an affective dimension so that the concept of 'emotion-thought' is a useful one. Language digs deep down into the body so that questions concerning biochemistry are pertinent to human emotions and the cultural quest for meaning.

This is relevant to cultural studies, a discipline whose central concern is Western culture, since many of the major problems faced by this culture involve psychological distress rather than material deprivation (which is not to say that the two do not often go hand in hand). These difficulties concern our relations with others (isolation, failed marriages, aggression and violence), our sense of meaninglessness, our addictions and our mental health. In other words, contemporary Western culture is plagued by emotional discontents.

Links **Body, constructionism, culture, discourse, evolutionary psychology**

Encoding–decoding It is a foundational argument of semiotics, and subsequently of cultural studies, that the relations between signifiers and the signified, or signs and their meanings, though arbitrary in principle, are in practice arranged by cultural convention so that meaning is stabilized and naturalized into codes of meaning. Thus encoding refers in general to the process by which signs are organized into codes, while decoding refers to the process of reception by which readers make sense of codes and generate meaning from them. More specifically, the encoding–decoding model of communication as developed by Stuart **Hall** in the late 1970s and early 1980s refers to the relationship between texts, their producers, and their readers or audiences. In general terms, the encoding–decoding model suggests that whatever analysis of textual meanings a critic may undertake, it is far from certain which of the identified meanings, if any, will be activated by actual readers/audiences/consumers.

Hall conceives of the process of television encoding as an articulation of the linked but distinct moments of production, circulation, distribution and reproduction each of which have their specific practices which are necessary to the circuit but which do not guarantee the next moment. In particular, the production of meaning does not ensure consumption of that meaning as the encoders might have intended because television texts are polysemic. In short, television messages carry multiple meanings and can be interpreted in different ways. That is not to say that all the meanings are equal among themselves, rather, the text will be 'structured in dominance' leading to a 'preferred meaning', that is, the one the text guides us to.

Here the audience is conceived of as socially situated individuals whose readings will be framed by shared cultural meanings and practices. To the degree that audiences partake of cultural codes in the same way as producers/encoders they will decode messages within the same framework. However, where the audience is situated in different social positions (for example, class and gender) with different cultural resources, the audience is able to decode programmes in alternative ways. Hall proposed a model of three hypothetical decoding positions:

- The dominant-hegemonic decoding, which accepts the 'preferred meanings' of the text.
- A negotiated code, which acknowledges the legitimacy of the 'preferred meanings' in the abstract but makes its own rules and adaptations under particular circumstances.
- An oppositional code, where people understand the preferred encoding but reject it and decode in contrary ways.

David **Morley**'s research into the audience for the British news 'magazine' programme *Nationwide* published in 1980 was based on Hall's encoding–decoding model and gave empirical backing to it. For example, it was argued that dominant decodings had been made by a group of conservative print managers and bank managers while negotiated readings were made by a group of trade union officials. The latter's readings remained negotiated rather than oppositional because they were specific to a particular industrial dispute while remaining within the general discourse that strikes were a 'bad thing for Britain'. According to Morley, oppositional decodings were made by a group of shop stewards whose political perspective led them to reject wholesale the discourses of *Nationwide* and by a group of black further education students who felt alienated from the programme by virtue of its perceived irrelevance to their lives.

Links **Active audience, code, consumption, hermeneutics, semiotics, television**

Enlightenment (the) A stance in European philosophy that can be explored through the writings of key seventeenth- and eighteenth-century philosophers such as Voltaire, Rousseau, Hume and Bacon. Enlightenment thinkers valued the power of reason – especially science – to demystify the world over and against superstition, myth and religion. Here, human creativity, rationality and scientific exploration are understood to be the forces that mark the break with tradition and herald the coming of modernity. The philosophers of the Enlightenment period sought after truths that could be seen as leading to progress, that is, an improvement in the human condition. As such, the French Revolutionary slogan 'Equality, Liberty, Fraternity' best encapsulates the moral-political agenda of the Enlightenment. In both its scientific project and its moral-political project, Enlightenment philosophy sought universal truths, that is, knowledge and moral principles that applied across time, space and cultural difference.

One of the legacies of the Enlightenment is what **Habermas** calls 'instrumental rationality'. This can be understood as a process by which the logic of rationality and science is put to work in the service of the regulation, control and domination of human beings. Thus **Adorno** and Horkheimer argued that the Enlightenment impulse to control nature is a manifestation of the will to control and dominate human beings. In this view the logic of Enlightenment thinking leads not only to industrialization but also to the concentration camps of Auschwitz and Belsen. However, Habermas also suggests that the Enlightenment generates a *critical* rationality capable of liberating human beings from exploitation and oppression. Thus the Enlightenment promotes the development of universal education, political freedom and social equality as well as that rationality which is capable of critiquing domination.

The main criticism of Enlightenment philosophy is that it seeks after universal truth and, in declaring that it has found it, then seeks to eradicate any alternative points of view. Consequently, post-Enlightenment philosophy – Nietzsche, **Wittgenstein, Derrida, Foucault, Rorty** – argues that knowledge is not metaphysical, transcendental or universal but specific to particular times and spaces. Thus there can be no one totalizing knowledge that is able to grasp the 'objective' character of the world. Rather, we both have and require multiple viewpoints by which to interpret a complex heterogeneous human existence.

Nevertheless, Foucault suggests that we do not have to be 'for' or 'against' the Enlightenment and challenges the idea that there is a clear, distinctive and final break between Enlightenment and post-Enlightenment thought. It is not a question of accepting or rejecting Enlightenment rationality but of asking about what reason is and how it is used along with exploration of its historical effects, limits and dangers.

Links **Modernity, postmodernism, postmodernity, poststructuralism, rationality, truth**

Episteme A term associated with the work of **Foucault** that denotes a form or order of knowledge. An episteme is constituted by the prevailing ways of knowing that give an historical epoch or intellectual era its distinctive and systematic cast where specific rules of formation shape a field of knowledge/objects. Foucault was interested in exploring the historical conditions under which statements are combined and regulated to form and define a distinct episteme as constituted by a particular set of concepts. The notion of an episteme is thus closely connected to the idea of discourse (regulated ways of speaking), 'regime of truth' (that is, what counts as truth) and discursive formation (the repeated motifs or clusters of ideas, practices and forms of knowledge across a range of sites of activity). According to Foucault, the modern episteme is most obviously marked by a humanism that underpins paradigms such as psychology and sociology as well as governing what counts as truth or knowledge in contemporary life.

Links **Discourse, epistemology, humanism, post-humanism, poststructuralism, truth**

Epistemology Epistemology is a branch of philosophy that is concerned with the source and status of knowledge. Thus, the question of what constitutes truth is an epistemological issue. The most significant debate concerning epistemology within cultural studies has been between representationalism (realism) and those opposed to it (poststructuralism, postmodernism and pragmatism). Thinkers who maintain a realist stance argue that a degree of certain knowledge about an independent object world (a real world) is possible even though methodological vigilance and reflexivity need to be maintained. In contrast, poststructuralism and postmodernism adopt Nietzsche's characterization of truth as a 'mobile army of metaphors and metonyms'. That is, sentences are the only things that can be true or false. Knowledge is not a question of true discovery but of the construction of interpretations about the world that are taken to be true. In so far as the idea of truth has an historical purchase, it is the consequence of power, that is, of whose interpretations come to count as truth.

Modern realist truth-claims exhibit contradictory tendencies. On the one hand, they are universalizing and assert their truths for all people in all places. On the other hand, they also embody the methodological principle of doubt by which knowledge is subject to chronic and continual revision. Poststructuralism and postmodernism emphasize the production of truths within the language-games in which such truths are founded and as such they accept the legitimacy of a range of truth-claims, discourses and representations of 'reality'. This postmodern understanding of knowledge is on the ascendant within cultural studies but remains disputed.

Links **Pragmatism, postmodernism, poststructuralism, representation, realism, truth**

Essentialism The concept of essentialism, along with its partner anti-essentialism, derives its meaning from an understanding of the way language functions in relation to an independent object world (reality). Thus, essentialism assumes that signs have stable meanings that derive from their equally stable referents in the real. In that way, words refer to the essence of an object or category which they are said to reflect. Or, to put it another way, words and their referents are identical. Posed in this way, it is easy to see why, in the context of cultural studies, debates about essentialism and anti-essentialism have focused on questions of cultural identity. In that context, the concept of essentialism refers to the argument that there are fixed truths to be found about identity categories so that there exists an essence of, for example, women, Australians, the working class and Asians. Here words refer to fixed essences and thus identities are regarded as being stable entities.

By contrast, poststructuralism seeks to deconstruct the very notion of the stable structures of language. Meaning, it is argued, cannot be confined to single words, sentences or particular texts but is the outcome of relationships between texts. Thus, signs do not make sense by virtue of reference to entities in an independent object world, but rather, they generate meaning by reference to each other. Meaning is understood to be a social convention organized through the relations between signs. Consequently, social categories do not have universal, essential characteristics or qualities but are constituted by the way we speak about them. It is this anti-essentialism that leads cultural studies to describe identity as a becoming, a never-to-be-fixed category that derives its meaning from a 'cut' or temporary stabilization of otherwise endlessly unfolding meanings of language. Thus, what it means to be a man or a woman, black or white, old or young is an ever-changing construction of language.

A stress on the practical value of conventionalized meaning has given rise to the notion of *strategic essentialism,* by which we act *as if* identities were stable entities for specific political and practical purposes. Thus it has been suggested that while we can deconstruct the notion of 'woman' this does not stop people from mobilizing around the idea of 'woman' for political purposes. This argument has some merit for practical purposes and may be what happens in practice. However, strategic essentialism is open to the criticism that at some point certain voices have been excluded. Thus, the strategic essentialism of feminism, that it takes women to be an essential category for tactical reasons, may lead to some women, for example black or Hispanic women, saying to white women they have not taken account of our differences as well as our similarities. As such, strategic essentialism tends towards ethnic or gender 'absolutism'.

What is required is a certain oscillation between a theoretical objectivism that tries to offer an independent description of language, and which in doing so illuminates the fact that meaning cannot be fixed in the abstract, and linguistic practices themselves in which meaning becomes temporally fixed for practical purposes. Thus, for **Wittgenstein**, while the meanings of language do derive from relations of difference (that is, there are no fixed essences), they are given a degree of regulated stability through pragmatic narratives. For example, in so far as the meaning of the word 'friend' is generated through the relationship of signifiers – colleague, companion, acquaintance, associate, confidant, etc. – it is volatile and undecidable. Nevertheless, in practice its meaning is stabilized by social knowledge of the word friend, of what it is used for, when, under what circumstances and so forth. Thus, words do not have stable meanings but rather have diverse functions.

Links **Anti-essentialism, identity, language-game, poststructuralism, pragmatism, structuralism**

Ethnicity A term that suggests cultural boundary formation between groups of people who have been discursively constructed as sharing values, norms, practices, symbols and artefacts and are seen as such by themselves and others. The concept of ethnicity is connected to the concept of race but is more cultural in its connotations. As such, ethnicity is centred on the commonality of cultural beliefs and practices. The formation of 'ethnic groups' relies on shared cultural signifiers that have developed under specific historical, social and political contexts and which encourage a sense of belonging based, at least in part, on a common mythological ancestry.

The anti-essentialist arguments of cultural studies suggest that ethnic groups are not based on primordial ties or universal cultural characteristics possessed by a specific group but are formed through discursive practices. That is, ethnicity is formed by the way we speak about group identities and identify with the signs and symbols that constitute ethnicity. Thus, ethnicity is a relational concept concerned with categories of self-identification and social ascription. Here, what we think of as our identity is dependent on what we think we are not so that, for example, Serbians are not Croatians, Bosnians or Albanians. However, to suggest that ethnicity is not about pre-given cultural difference but a process of boundary formation and maintenance does not mean that such distinctiveness cannot be socially constructed around signifiers that do connote universality, territory and purity. For example, discourses of ethnicity often invoke metaphors of blood, kinship and homeland.

The significance of the concept of ethnicity lies in its acknowledgment of the place of history, language and culture in the construction of subjectivity and identity. However, it does have some problems of usage and it remains a contested term. For instance, white Anglo-Saxons frequently use the concept of ethnicity to refer to *other* people, usually with different skin pigmentation, so that Asians, Africans, Hispanics and African Americans are ethnic groups but the English or white Anglo-Saxon Americans or Australians are not. In contrast, it is important to maintain that white English, American or Australian people *do* constitute ethnic groups. Thus the value of studying whiteness lies in making it strange rather than taking it for granted as the universal touchstone of humanity.

Critics have also argued that the notion of ethnicity sidelines questions of power and racism when it is used to suggest, as in some discussions about multiculturalism, that a social formation operates through plurality and equality rather than with hierarchical groups. Consequently, some writers prefer the concept of 'racialization', not because it corresponds to any biological or cultural absolutes, but because it connotes, and refers investigation to, issues of power.

Discourses of ethnic centrality and marginality are commonly articulated with those of nationality so that history is littered with examples of how one ethnic group has been defined as central and superior to a marginal 'other'. While Nazi Germany, apartheid South Africa and 'ethnic cleansing' in Bosnia are clear-cut examples, the use of ethnicity as a metaphor of superiority and subordination is also applicable within contemporary Britain, America and Australia.

Links **Difference, diaspora, hybridity, identity, national identity, race, representation**

Ethnocentrism The general use of the term ethnocentrism refers to the process by which values and ways of seeing the world that are founded in one culture are used to comprehend and judge another. Ethnocentrism therefore asserts the centrality and implied superiority of a particular cultural identity over others. Here the concept describes how subjects constitute the 'Other' as alien and impose a world-view upon them. The use of the term in this way can be seen in the work of Edward **Said** on Orientalism and in the critique of anthropology and other forms of intellectual inquiry that seek to place themselves outside of and apart from their culture of origin. In particular the idea of ethnocentricism has been used to critique the assumed privilege of white European ethnic groups and as such has been taken to involve a critique of racism.

However, the use of the term has become more complex with the writings of **Derrida**, **Rorty** and others, arguing that knowledge is inherently ethnocentric. For Rorty truth, knowledge and understanding are located within the particular language-games of specific cultures. He argues that no 'skyhook' provided by any contemporary or future forms of knowledge is able to free us from the contingency of having been acculturated as we are. Thus, when he argues that knowledge is ethnocentric he is saying something akin to the concept of 'positionality' in cultural studies. To say that knowledge is ethnocentric is thus to say that it is culture-bound.

The danger of course is that truth acquired through acculturation becomes a narrow loyalty to a particular culture or way of being. In order to avoid this, Rorty argues that it is desirable to open ourselves up to as many descriptions and re-descriptions of the world as possible. This enables individuals to grow through the acquisition of new vocabularies and cultures and to be increasingly able to listen to the voices of others who may be suffering. This is to strengthen 'the cosmopolitan conversation' of human kind. Likewise for Derrida, ethnocentricism, understood as a culture-centred perspective, is inevitable and inescapable. It cannot be overthrown but can be made subject to self-conscious critical rigour.

Links **Culture, ethnicity, Orientalism, Other, positionality, postcolonial theory, pragmatism**

Ethnography: Ethnography is an empirical and theoretical approach inherited from anthropology whose central purpose is to generate detailed holistic description and analysis of cultures based on intensive fieldwork. The objective of this methodology is the production of what **Geertz** calls 'thick descriptions' of the multiplicity and complexity of cultural life, including its unspoken and taken-for-granted assumptions.

Ethnographic cultural studies has been centred on the qualitative exploration of cultural values, meanings and life-worlds with the purpose of giving (mediated) 'voice' to people who are traditionally under-represented within Western academic writing. In the context of media-oriented cultural studies, ethnography has also become a code word for a range of qualitative methods, including participant observation, in-depth interviews and focus groups. Here, it is the 'spirit' of ethnography (that is, qualitative understanding of cultural activity in context) which has been invoked polemically against the tradition of quantitative communications research.

In seeking to represent the meanings, feelings and cultures of others, ethnography has tended to rely on a realist epistemology and has thus opened itself up to considerable critique. In particular, not only is ethnography inevitably 'positional' or ethnocentric knowledge but also it is a genre of writing that deploys rhetorical devices, often obscured, to maintain its realist claims. This argument has led to the examination of ethnographic texts for their rhetorical devices, along with a more reflexive and dialogical approach to ethnography which demands that writers should elaborate on their own assumptions, views and positions.

If we think that the purpose of ethnography and other forms of qualitative empirical work lies in the discovery of accurate representations of an objective reality then the critique of ethnographic realism is devastating. However, the critique of the epistemological claims of ethnography does not leave it without worth or significance for its purposes do not have to lie in the production of a 'true' picture of the world. Rather, ethnography has personal, poetic and political, rather than epistemological, justifications.

The problems of ethnography are issues of translation and justification not universal or objective truth. If we consider languages (and thus culture and knowledge) as constituted not by untranslatable and incompatible rules but as learnable skills, then ethnography can be understood as a part of the continued re-description of the world that supplies new initiatives that enrich our culture with innovative ideas.

This does not mean that ethnographic research can abandon all methodical rigour. First, evidence and poetic style are pragmatically useful warrants for truth and action epistemologically equivalent to the procedural agreements of the physical sciences. Second, the languages of observation and evidence are among the conventions that divide the genre of ethnography from the novel. Third, the rejection of a universal objective truth is based on the impossibility of word–world correspondence and therefore of accurate or adequate representation. This does not mean that we have to abandon word–word translation. That is, we can achieve 'good enough' reporting of the speech or action of others without making claims to universal truth.

Links **Ethnocentricism, methodology, positionality, representation, text, truth**

Experience The idea of experience appears somewhat paradoxically within cultural studies. On the one hand, this notion is crucial to understanding culture when grasped in terms of lived meaningful experience. On the other hand, one cannot understand experience or undergo meaningful experiences without the framing work of language. Thus experience seems to disappear as a concrete category into those of discourse and language.

For an example of the first case we may turn to Raymond **Williams**, for whom culture is best understood as 'a whole and distinctive way of life'. Here Williams stresses that culture involves 'lived experience' and he was particularly concerned with the working class and their active construction of culture. For Williams, the purpose of cultural analysis is to explore and analyse the recorded culture of a given time and place in order to reconstitute the experience and 'structure of feeling' of a culture. In more contemporary vein, feminism has often stressed that it is focused upon the distinct experience of women. Thus experience is a crucial category to feminism.

66

Yet, constructionism suggests that experience is a discursive construct so that feminism generates 'women's experience' by creating a language rather than by finding what it is to be a woman. That is, experience cannot be accessed, and thus does not exist, outside of the way we talk about it. Hence, discourse constructs our experience since it is only through discourse that we can know experience or understand it as meaningful. What we have is not so much experience but discourses of and about experience. Indeed, reflexivity can be understood as 'discourse about experience' so that to be reflexive is to engage in a range of discourses and relationships while constructing further discourses about them.

Links **Constructionism, culturalism, discourse, poststructuralism, representation, truth**

Evolutionary psychology Evolution is the processes of adaptive change made by organisms in order to survive and which structure the long-term development of species. Natural selection, the driving force of evolutionary change, is the inevitable outcome of the interaction of phenotypic variation, differential fitness and heritability. Evolutionary psychology is concerned with the evolution of the cognitive mechanisms that arose as fitness-enhancing effects in the context of our ancestral environments.

The significance of evolutionary psychology for cultural studies lies in its claim that the foundations of culture are to be found in our evolved psychological mechanisms that subsequently utilize and work over social and cultural inputs. It is the differential activation of these psychological mechanisms by divergent inputs in varied contexts that accounts for cultural diversity. For example, the class of possible human languages – so important to culture – may depend on a single 'language-acquisition device' within the brain, yet its different operations in divergent settings explain the range of human languages available to us.

The fundamental argument of evolutionary psychology is that domain-specific modules in the brain contribute to the shape of culture by providing the template for human thinking and the parameters of solutions to problems that we are likely to face. This would include the existence of specialized inference mechanisms that allow for the representations of culture to be transmitted from one mind to another through observation and/or interaction. Of course, some aspects of culture such as art, literature, film, music etc. do not seem to have much to do with survival and reproduction. Nevertheless, it can be argued that people take pleasure from shapes, colours, sounds, stories etc. whose mechanisms evolved in relation to other evolutionary tasks faced by our ancestors but which now enable us to appreciate and develop artistic endeavours.

Thus, evolutionary psychology rejects the division of labour between evolutionary and cultural theory. This is because they argue that not only is human cultural diversity less profound than it may at first appear, but also that diversity itself has evolutionary explanations. Further, the human social group constituted at least one of the crucial selection environments for our ancestors. For example, the cooperative group may well have been the primary survival strategy for humans and this would have selected for adaptations suited for cooperative living. Subsequently, because social adaptive problems were (and are) so crucial to human survival and reproduction many of the most important evolved psychological mechanisms will be social in character.

Links **Body, culture, emotion, language**

F

Femininity For cultural studies, femininity is an identity category that refers to the social and cultural characteristics associated with being female. It is a discursive-performative construction that describes and disciplines the cultural meaning of being a woman. As such, femininity is to be understood as the culturally regulated behaviour held to be socially appropriate to women. Thus, for cultural studies femininity is not an essential quality of embodied subjects but a matter of representation by which sexual identity is constituted through ways of speaking about and disciplining bodies. As such, femininity is a site of continual political struggle over meaning and there are multiple modes of femininity that are enacted not only by different women, but also by the same woman under different circumstances.

According to **Kristeva**, femininity is a condition or subject position of marginality that some men, for example avant-garde artists, can also occupy. Indeed, it is the patriarchal symbolic order that tries to fix all women as feminine and all men as masculine, rendering women as the 'second sex'. Kristeva suggests that the very dichotomy man/woman as an opposition between two rival entities may be understood as belonging to metaphysics. Sexual identity concerns the balance of masculinity and femininity within specific men and women. This struggle, she suggests, could result in the deconstruction of sexual and gendered identities understood in terms of marginality within the symbolic order.

Links Feminism, gender, identity, patriarchy, performativity, representation, sex

Feminism Feminism can be understood both as a diverse body of theoretical work and as a social and political movement. In either case, feminism has sought to examine the position of women in society and to further their interests. Feminism has become a major influence within cultural studies and indeed they share the view that knowledge production is political and positional along with the wish to engage with, or be a part of, political movements outside of the academy.

In general terms, feminism asserts that sex is a fundamental and irreducible axis of social organization that, to date, has subordinated women to men. Thus, feminism is centrally concerned with sex as an organizing principle of social life that is thoroughly saturated with power relations. Most feminists have argued that the subordination of women occurs across a whole range of social institutions and practices with a degree of regularity that makes it a structural phenomenon. This structural subordination of women has been described by feminists as patriarchy with its derivative meanings of the male-headed family, mastery and superiority.

Feminism has adopted a range of analyses and strategies of action. Thus so-called liberal feminists regard differences between men and women as social-economic and cultural constructs rather than the outcome of an eternal biology. They stress equality of opportunity for women in all spheres which, within the liberal democracies of the West, is held to be achievable within the broad structures of existing legal and economic frameworks. Socialist feminists point to the interconnections between class and gender, including the fundamental place of gender inequalities in the reproduction of capitalism. The subordination of women to men is seen as intrinsic to capitalism so that the full 'liberation' of women would require the overthrow of capitalist organization and social relations. While liberal and socialist feminists stress equality and sameness, so-called difference feminism asserts essential distinctions between men and women. These differences, regarded as fundamental and intractable, are variously interpreted as cultural, psychic and/or biological. In any case, difference is celebrated as representing the creative power of women.

One criticism of difference feminism, and indeed of the concept of patriarchy, is that the category of woman is treated in an undifferentiated way. By contrast, black feminists have pointed to the differences between black and white women's experiences, cultural representations and interests. They have argued that colonialism and racism have structured power relationships between black and white women. Thus, gender is articulated with race, ethnicity and nationality to produce different experiences of what it is to be a woman.

Feminists influenced by poststructuralism and postmodernism have argued that sex and gender are social and cultural constructions that are not to be explained in terms of biology nor to be reduced to the functions of capitalism. This anti-essentialist stance suggests that femininity and masculinity are not universal and eternal categories but discursive constructions. That is, femininity and masculinity are ways of describing and disciplining human subjects. As such, poststructuralist feminism is concerned with the cultural construction of subjectivity *per se,* including a range of possible masculinities and femininities. Femininity and masculinity, which are a matter of how men and women are represented, are held to be sites of continual political struggle over meaning.

Links **Cultural politics, gender, identity, patriarchy, post-feminism, representation, sex, women's movement**

Fiske, John (1939–) Fiske, who has worked in Britain, Australia and the United States, has been a significant voice in the dissemination of cultural studies throughout the Academy, most especially during the 1980s and 1990s. His work has been concerned with the character of popular culture, and television in particular, laying stress on the uses that people make of texts as active readers or producers of meaning. While he is clear that popular cultural texts are very largely produced by capitalist corporations he has been more concerned with the popular tactics by which these forces are coped with, evaded or are resisted so that popular culture is understood to be a site of 'semiotic warfare'. In this he was influenced by the work of **De Certeau**. According to Fiske, while the financial economy needs to be taken into account in any investigation of the cultural, it does not determine it nor invalidate the power audiences have as producers of meaning at the level of consumption.

- **Associated concepts** Active audience, consumption, popular culture, reading, resistance, television.
- **Tradition(s)** Cultural studies, hermeneutics, Marxism, poststructuralism.
- **Reading** Fiske, J. (1989) *Understanding Popular Culture*. London: Unwin Hyman.

Flâneur The name given to a crucial figure of modernism as it emerged in the late nineteenth century and early twentieth century. As understood by Baudelaire, the flâneur or stroller was one of the heroes of modern life. A flâneur was held to be an urban, contemporary and stylish person who walked the anonymous spaces of the modern city. Here he experienced the complexity, disturbances and confusions of the streets with their shops, displays, images and variety of people. This perspective emphasizes the urban character of modernism. The flâneur took in the fleeting beauty and vivid, if transitory, impressions of the crowds, seeing everything anew in its immediacy yet achieving a certain detachment from it. The idea of the flâneur directs our attention towards the way in which the urban landscape has become aestheticized through architecture, billboards, shop displays, street signs etc., and through the fashionable clothing, hairstyles, make-up etc. of the people who inhabit this world.

It has been argued by some feminist writers that the flâneur was a male figure who walked spaces from which women were largely excluded and as such demonstrates the deeply gendered character of the modernist experience. The adventures of the flâneur and of modernism were one of male-coded public spaces from which women were excluded (for example, the boulevards and cafés) or entered only as objects for male consumption. Thus, the flâneur's gaze was frequently erotic, and women were the objects of that gaze.

Links **Aesthetics, city, modernism, modernity, postmodernism**

Foucault, Michel (1926–1984) Foucault is a major figure in French philosophy whose work is associated with the ideas of poststructuralism and which has become a very significant influence within contemporary cultural studies. Influenced by Nietzsche, Foucault explored the varying discursive practices that exert power over human bodies but without any commitment to any underlying structural order or finally determinate power. Foucault attempts to identify the historical conditions and determining rules of the formation of discourses and the operation of power/knowledge in social practice that achieves the ordering of meaning. Much of Foucault's work is concerned with the historical investigation of power as a dispersed capillary woven into the fabric of the social order that is not simply repressive but is also productive (of, for example, subjectivity).

- **Associated concepts** Archaeology, discourse, episteme, genealogy, governmentality, power/knowledge, subject position.
- **Tradition(s)** Postmodernism, poststructuralism.
- **Reading** Foucault, M. (1979) *The History of Sexuality, Vol. 1: The Will to Truth*. London: Penguin Lane.

Foundationalism Foundationalism is the generic name given to the philosophic attempt to give absolute universal grounds or justifications for the truth of knowledge and values. Poststructuralism, pragmatism and postmodernism are anti-foundationalist philosophies that are strongly represented within cultural studies. That is, they argue that the provision of universal foundations for knowledge or values is not possible and that justifications take place within the bounds of historically and culturally specific language-games.

The adoption of a foundationalist epistemology allows thinkers to make universal truth-claims where truth is taken to be an accurate representation of an independent object world. It follows that once we know the truth about the workings of the social world then we can intervene strategically in human affairs with confidence in the outcomes. In particular, Enlightenment philosophy and the theoretical discourses of modernity have championed 'reason' as the source of progress in knowledge and society. That is, modern reason has been conceived as leading to certain and universal truths that would, through the demystification of religion, myth and superstition, lay the foundations for humanity's forward path. Enlightenment thinkers hailed human creativity, rationality and scientific exploration as underpinning the break with tradition that modernity heralds. Enlightenment philosophy is foundationalist because it sought universal propositions that would apply across time, space and cultural difference.

By contrast, anti-foundationalism holds that knowledge is specific to language-games so that we cannot found or justify our actions or beliefs in any universal truths. This argument indicates a loss of faith in the foundational schemes and universalizing epistemology that have justified the rational, scientific, technological and political projects of the modern world. Anti-foundationalism suggests that while we can describe this or that description of the world to be more or less useful and as having more or less desirable consequences, we cannot claim it to be true in the sense of correspondence with an independent reality. Further, since in this view human history has no telos, or historical end-point to which it is unfolding, then human 'development' is best understood as the outcome of numerous acts of chance and environmental adaptation which make the 'direction' of human evolution contingent. 'Progress' or 'purpose' can only be given meaning as a retrospectively told story.

Nevertheless, we do not, according to supporters of anti-foundationalism, require universal foundations to pursue a pragmatic improvement of the human condition on the basis of the values of our own tradition. Answers to the key questions about what kind of human being we want to be and/or what kind of a society we want to live in are not metaphysical or epistemological in character but rather are pragmatic and value-based. It is not possible to escape values any more than we can ground them in metaphysics so that historically and culturally specific value-based knowledge is an inevitable and inescapable condition of human existence. Subsequently, judgements are made by reference to likely or intended consequences as measured against our values rather than being founded on transcendental truth.

Links **Enlightenment, epistemology, ethnocentrism, postmodernism, poststructuralism, pragmatism, truth**

72   **Freire, Paulo (1921–1997)** The Brazilian philosopher and educator Paulo Freire spent a lifetime developing and integrating a philosophy of education and learning with empirical research. His interest in the relationship between power, class and education along with his radical pedagogy has been influential not so much in terms of cultural studies theory (though there are exceptions to this) but upon many of its practitioners, most of whom are teachers in higher education. For Freire, education involves a dialogic relationship between teachers and students both of whom learn, question, reflect and participate in making meaning. Freire stresses the development of a critical consciousness that allows people to question and explore the character of their society with a view to acting as subjects in creating a more democratic culture.
- **Associated concepts** Cultural politics, dialogic, power, praxis, resistance, writing.
- **Tradition(s)** Humanism, Marxism.
- **Reading** Freire, P. (1970) *Pedagogy of the Oppressed*. New York: Continuum.

Freud, Sigmund (1856–1939) Freud gained notoriety in the first decade of the twentieth century as the originator of psychoanalysis, which he developed in Vienna before being forced to flee in the face of the Nazis' persecution of Jews. According to Freud, the self is constituted in terms of an ego, or conscious rational mind, a superego, or social conscience, and the unconscious, the source and repository of the symbolic workings of repressed desire that is generated through the resolution of the Oedipus complex. Freud's proposition that sexuality is the key to subjectivity and culture through the active operation of the unconscious in everyday life is his most significant legacy. His work remains controversial and while a number of cultural studies writers have embraced psychoanalysis in order to explore gendered subjectivity, others have rejected it as phallocentric and mythological.

Associated concepts Identification, Oedipus complex, sex, subjectivity, unconscious.
Tradition(s) Psychoanalysis.
Reading Freud, S. (1977, orig. 1905) *Three Essays on Sexuality*. The Pelican Freud Library, Vol. 7. Harmondsworth: Penguin.

G

Geertz, Clifford (1923–) Geertz, an American-born cultural anthropologist and currently Professor of Social Science at Princeton University (USA), describes his approach to understanding culture as being semiotic but not structuralist. That is, culture is grasped through the interpretation of signs and signifying practices but does not depend on a structure or universal system of signification. Geertz explores culture as quite specific meaningful practices and interpretations situated in particular ordinary and everyday contexts. For Geertz, an understanding of lived culture requires in-depth ethnographic fieldwork that generates 'thick descriptions' of cultural life. As such, his influence within cultural studies has been most directly felt by those thinkers associated with ethnography and the exploration of lived culture.

- **Associated concepts** Constructionism, culture, difference, experience, practice, realism, signs.
- **Tradition(s)** Ethnography, hermeneutics, semiotics.
- **Reading** Geertz, C. (1973) *The Interpretation of Cultures*. New York: Basic Books.

Gender The notion of gender can be understood to be referring to the cultural assumptions and practices that govern the social construction of men, women and their social relations. The concept gains much of its force through a contrast with a conception of sex as the biological formation of the body. Thus, femininity and masculinity as forms of gender are the outcome of the cultural regulation of behaviours that are regarded as socially appropriate to a given sex. Given that gender is held to be a matter of culture rather than 'nature', so it is always a matter of how men and women are represented.

A good deal of feminist writing has sought to challenge what they take to be essentialism and biological determinism through the conceptual division between a biological sex and a culturally formed gender. Subsequently, it is argued that no fundamental sex differences exist and that those that are apparent are insignificant in relation to arguments for social equality. Rather, it is the social, cultural and political discourses and practices of gender that are held to lie at the root of women's subordination.

However, the sex–gender distinction upon which this argument is based has itself become the subject of criticism. The differentiation between sex as biology and gender as a cultural construction is broken down on the grounds that there is in principle no access to biological 'truths' that lie outside of cultural discourses and therefore no 'sex' which is not already cultural. In this view, sexed bodies are always already represented as the production of regulatory discourses. Judith **Butler** has been at the cutting edge of this argument by suggesting that the category of 'sex' is a normative and regulatory discourse that produces the bodies it governs. Thus, discourses of sex are ones that, through repetition of the acts they guide, bring sex into view as a necessary norm. Here, while sex is held to be a social construction, it is an indispensable one that forms subjects and governs the materialization of bodies.

Butler's work is emblematic of a wider body of thought produced by feminists who have been influenced by poststructuralism and postmodernism. These writers have argued that not only are sex and gender social and cultural constructions, but also that there are multiple modes of femininity (and masculinity). Here, rather than a conflict between two opposing male–female groups, sexual identity concerns the balance of masculinity and femininity within specific men and women. This argument stresses the singularity and multiplicity of persons as well as the relativity of symbolic and biological existence.

Links **Body, culture, discourse, femininity, feminism, performativity, sex, women's movement**

Genealogy In general terms the notion of genealogy is concerned with the derivation and lineage of persons, ideas or phenomena. Within cultural studies the concept has meanings associated with **Foucault**, who deploys the idea of genealogy in order to examine power and the historical continuities and discontinuities of discourses as they are brought into play under specific and irreducible historical conditions.

Foucault is said to have produced a genealogy of the modern subject. That is, he traced the derivation and lineage of subjects in and through history. Here, the subject is radically historicized, that is, the subject is understood to be wholly and only the product of history. Indeed, for Foucault genealogy's task is to explore the ways in which the body is imprinted by history as the site of disciplinary practices that bring subjects into being. These practices are the manifestation of specific historical discourses of crime, punishment, medicine, science, sexuality and so forth. Hence, power is generative; that is to say, it is productive of subjectivity.

Discourses of disciplinary and bio-power, which arise in a variety of sites including schools, prisons, hospitals and asylums, produced what Foucault called 'docile bodies' that could be subjected, used, transformed and improved. Genealogy traces these discourses and practices historically and locates particular kinds of 'regimes of the self' in specific historical and cultural conjunctures. That is, different types of subject are the outcome of particular historical and social formations.

Links **Archaeology, discourse, power, practice, subjectivity**

Genre A genre is a classification of type or kind that when applied to literature, television or film gives rise to such groups as the romance novel, the western, the gangster movie, film noir and so forth. As such, genre regulates the narrative process producing coherence and credibility through patterns of similarity and difference. Genres structure the narrative process and contain it; they regulate it in particular ways using specific elements and combinations of elements to produce unity and plausibility. Genre involves the systematic and structured repetition of problems and solutions in narratives. However, genres must also involve sufficient levels of textual difference to generate meaning and pleasure. In other words, each western or each musical has to be both the same as others and different from them.

For example, the general features of soap opera as a genre involve open-ended narrative forms, the use of core locations, the tension between the conventions of realism and melodrama and the pivotal themes of inter-personal relationships. Thus, soap opera as a long-running serial without a formal ending does not have the sense of closure to be found in the feature film or the 13-episode series. Further, most soaps establish a sense of geographical space that the audience can identify with and to which the characters return again and again. In terms of form or style, soap opera utilizes the conventions of realism and melodrama and can be differentiated in terms of the balance struck between them. Soap opera has the themes of marriage, divorce, break-ups and coming togethers, alliances, arguments, acts of revenge and acts of caring at the core of its narrative dynamic and emotional interest. Given the stress in soaps on the personal sphere it is understandable that the family forms the mythic centre of the genre.

Since the mid-1970s we have witnessed a notable collapse or blurring of genre boundaries within cultural products that has been hailed by some as the marker of postmodernism in film, television and architecture. For example, *Bladerunner* and *Blue Velvet* are frequently cited as films which mix the genres of noir, horror, sci-fi etc. Further, they are 'double-coded', allowing them to be understood both by the literati and a popular audience. Likewise, the popular television programme *The Simpsons* commonly requires us to have a self-conscious awareness of other television and film genres as it makes a range of intertextual references. For example, *The Simpsons* has made use of the road-movie format, with direct reference to *Thelma and Louise*.

Links **Narrative, postmodernism, realism, representation, soap opera, television, text**

Giddens, Anthony (1938–) Formerly Professor of Sociology at the University of Cambridge (UK), the British-born thinker Anthony Giddens was until recently the Director of the London School of Economics. Giddens has sought to legitimate the project of sociology and has sometimes been critical of the impulses of cultural studies; nevertheless, his work has exerted considerable influence amongst writers in the field. Giddens' expertise in classical sociology formed the bedrock of his structuration theory, which endeavours to overcome the dualism of agency and structure. His more contemporary work has coalesced around the themes of modernity, identity and globalization. For Giddens, globalization is a consequence of the dynamism of modernity, while that which others have labelled postmodern is for him better understood as late-modern, that is, the radicalization of the de-traditionalizing forces of modernity. In this context the self is a reflexive project freed from traditional constraints and in a state of continual re-invention.

- **Associated concepts** Agency, globalization, identity project, life-politics, modernity, reflexivity, structure, time–space geography.
- **Tradition(s)** Hermeneutics, Marxism, structuralism, structuration theory.
- **Reading** Giddens, A. (1984) *The Constitution of Society*. Cambridge: Polity Press.

Gilroy, Paul (1956–) Gilroy, who was born in Bethnal Green, London, was amongst those who studied at the Birmingham **Centre for Contemporary Cultural Studies** (CCCS). He is currently a Professor at Yale University (USA). Gilroy was critical of the 'culturalism' at CCCS for its implicit British nationalism and was a significant figure in bringing the categories of race and racialization to the fore in cultural studies, via for example his study of race in the UK – *There Ain't No Black in the Union Jack*. Gilroy has challenged essentialist notions of race or ethnicity and has written extensively about the 'changing same ' of diaspora cultural identities understood in terms of routes more than roots. Gilroy argues that black self-identities and cultural expressions utilize a plurality of histories and that we should think of identities as being in motion rather than existing as absolutes of nature or culture. He has argued against the very idea of classifying people into 'races'.

- **Associated concepts** Black Atlantic, diaspora, ethnicity, hegemony, identity, ideology, race.
- **Tradition(s)** Cultural studies, Marxism, postcolonial theory.
- **Reading** Gilroy, P. (1993) *The Black Atlantic*. London: Verso.

Globalization The concept of globalization refers us to the increasing multi-directional economic, social, cultural and political connections that are forming across the world and our awareness of them. Thus globalization involves the increased compression of the world and our growing consciousness of those processes. The compression of the world can be understood in terms of the expansionism of the institutions of modernity while the reflexive intensification of consciousness of the world can be perceived beneficially in cultural terms.

Globalization is constituted in part by planetary scale economic activity that is creating an interconnected if uneven world economy. Thus, 200 transnational corporations which produce between one-third and one-half of world output constitute 50 per cent of the world's largest economic units. In the financial sector the collapse of the European Exchange Mechanism, Black Monday on the stock exchange and the so-called 'Asian economic meltdown' of the 1990s have demonstrated that states are at the mercy of the global money markets. The emergence and growth of global economic activity are not entirely new but the current phase, dating from the early 1970s, is marked by an acceleration of time–space compression propelled by transnational companies' search for new sources of profit in the face of the crisis of Fordism. Thus, accelerated globalization refers to a set of related economic activities understood as the practices of capitalism in its 'disorganized' era.

Globalization is not just an economic matter but is also concerned with issues of cultural meaning. While the values and meanings attached to place remain significant, we are increasingly involved in networks that extend far beyond our immediate physical locations. We are not yet a part of a world-state or unitary world-culture but we can identify global cultural processes, of cultural integration and disintegration, that are independent of inter-state relations. In particular, cosmopolitanism is an aspect of day-to-day Western life as diverse and remote cultures have become accessible, as signs and commodities, via our televisions, radios, supermarkets and shopping centres. Further, patterns of population movement and settlement established during colonialism and its aftermath, combined with the more recent acceleration of globalization, particularly of electronic communications, have enabled increased cultural juxtapositioning, meeting and mixing. Indeed, all locales are now subject to the influences of distant places.

It is commonly argued that globalization is the consequence of the dynamism and inherently globalizing character of the institutions of modernity. Indeed, **Giddens** likens the institutions of modernity to an uncontrollable juggernaut of enormous power that sweeps away all that stands before it. In particular, globalization is to be grasped in terms of the expansionism of the world capitalist economy, the global information system, the nation-state system and the world military order. In this view, modernity originated in Western Europe and subsequently rolled out across the globe. However, this characterization has been subject to the criticism that it is Eurocentric, envisaging only one kind of modernity, that of the West. Instead, it can be argued that different spatial zones of the globe have become modern in a variety of ways requiring us to speak of global moderni*ties* in the plural.

Certainly, on the level of culture, globalization is far from an even process of Western expansion driven by economic imperatives. Rather, it is better characterized in terms of the disjunctive relationships between flows of money, technology, media, ideas and people. That is, globalization involves the dynamic movements of ethnic groups, technology, financial transactions, media images and ideological conflicts that are not neatly determined by one harmonious 'master plan'. Rather, the speed, scope and impact of these flows are fractured and disconnected. Metaphors of uncertainty, contingency and chaos are replacing those of order, stability and systemacity. Globalization and global cultural flows cannot be understood through neat sets of linear determinations but are better comprehended as a series of overlapping, overdetermined, complex and chaotic conditions which, at best, cluster around key 'nodal points'.

Links **City, cultural imperialism, glocalization, modernity, postcolonial theory**

Glocalization The concept of glocalization, in origin a marketing term, has been deployed to express the global production of the local and the localization of the global. The global and the local are mutually constituting, indeed, much that is considered to be local, and counterpoised to the global, is the outcome of translocal processes. For example, nation-states were forged within a global system and the contemporary rise in nationalist sentiment can be regarded as an aspect of globalization.

Further, the current direction of global consumer capitalism is such that it encourages limitless needs/wants whereby niche markets, customization and the pleasures of constant identity transformation give rise to a certain type of heterogeneity. Here the products of global forces are localized, that is, they are made pertinent to 'local' concerns. Thus, the global and the local are relative terms. The

78

idea of the local, specifically what is considered to be local, is produced within and by globalizing discourses including capitalist marketing strategies that orientate themselves to differentiated 'local' markets. Thus an emphasis on particularity and diversity can be regarded as an increasingly global discourse.

Overall, capitalist modernity involves an element of global cultural homogenization for it increases the levels and amount of global co-ordination. However, mechanisms of fragmentation, heterogenization and hybridity are also at work so that it is not so much a question of *either* the homogenization or heterogenization of global culture, but rather of the ways in which both of these two tendencies work in tandem to produce the landscape of contemporary life.

Links **Cultural imperialism, globalization, hybridity, modernity, postcolonial theory**

Governmentality The concept of governmentality derives from the work of **Foucault** for whom it designates a form of regulation throughout the social order by which a population becomes subject to bureaucratic regimes and modes of discipline. Foucault describes governmentality as involving the institutional procedures and calculations of government that allow for the exercise of power over a target population using political economy as a form of knowledge in conjunction with apparatuses of security. Thus, governmentality refers us to the institutions, procedures, analyses and calculations that form specific governmental apparatuses and forms of knowledge which are constitutive of self-reflective conduct and ethical competencies.

While governmentality is associated with the state, it is also to be understood in the broader sense of regulation throughout the social order or, to put it in Foucault's preferred manner, the 'policing' of societies by which a population becomes subject to bureaucratic regimes and modes of discipline. Governmentality is a growing aspect of the micro-capillary character of power, that is, the multiplicity of force relations that are not centralized but dispersed. This includes modes of regulation that operate through medicine, education, social reform, demography and criminology by which a population can be categorized and ordered into manageable groups. Here the state is held to be a more or less contingent collection of sometimes conflicting institutions and apparatuses with the 'bureau' an autonomous 'technology for living' organized around its own faculties and possessing its own modes of conduct of life.

The concept of governmentality stresses that processes of social regulation do not so much stand over and against the individual but are constitutive of self-reflective modes of conduct, ethical competencies and social movements. According to **Foucault** and **Bennett**, contemporary culture is increasingly understandable in terms of governmentality since culture is not just a matter of representations and consciousness but of institutional practices, administrative routines and spatial arrangements.

Links **Culture, discourse, poststructuralism, power, power/knowledge**

Gramsci, Antonio (1981–1937) Gramsci was an Italian Marxist theorist and political activist whose main contribution to cultural studies has been courtesy of his application of Marxism to modern Western societies. In particular, he developed and deployed the concepts of ideology and hegemony in ways that gained considerable currency within cultural studies during its formative years in the 1970s. Gramsci was influential in developing a non-reductionist Marxism that explored meaning and ideas as developmental forces that were not explicable in economic terms alone, hence his significance to Western Marxists such as Stuart **Hall** who were interested in culture.

- **Associated concepts** Base and superstructure, civil society, class, common sense, hegemony, ideology.
- **Tradition(s)** Marxism.
- **Reading** Gramsci, A. (1968) *Prison Notebooks*. London: Lawrence and Wishart.

Grand narrative This is a term used for an overarching story or metanarrative that claims universal validity as a foundational scheme that justifies and explains all facets of the human project. Thus grand narratives are totalizing schemes that seek to explain every aspect of life under their rubric. Examples would be Marxism, Christianity and science.

The power of modern grand narrative has been the subject of a critique by poststructuralist and postmodern writers, most notably **Lyotard**. For Lyotard modern knowledge rests on its appeal to grand narratives, whereas the postmodern, in arguing that knowledge is specific to language-games, embraces local, plural and heterogeneous knowledges. Here the postmodern condition involves a loss of faith in the foundational schemes that have justified the rational, scientific, technological and political projects of the modern world.

For example, whereas science might once have been relied upon to generate universal and certain truths, it is now better understood as generating domain-specific truths that have a certain utility in relation to specific purposes. Further, while science has brought us medicine, increased food production and global communications, it has also generated pollution and sophisticated weapons systems of mass destruction. The questioning of the certainties of modern science is a part of what Lyotard describes as 'incredulity toward metanarratives'. By this he means that there remain no viable grand narratives, or elevated standpoints, from which to pronounce universal truth. For Lyotard, we should resist the totalizing terror of such dogmas in favour of the celebration of difference and understandings located within particular knowledge regimes.

Links **Marxism, modernity, postmodernism, poststructuralism, pragmatism, truth**

Grossberg, Lawrence (1947–) Having once been a student at the **Centre for Contemporary Cultural Studies (CCCS)** Birmingham (UK), Grossberg is now one of the leading exponents of cultural studies in the United States. He is currently Morris Davis Professor of Communication Studies at the University of North Carolina at Chapel Hill. Grossberg has written extensively on cultural theory, including its relationship to Marxism, the philosophical/psychoanalytic work of **Deleuze and Guattari**, along with the modern roots of cultural studies and its continuing political implications. He has been somewhat critical of the contemporary emphasis in cultural studies on identity as difference. Grossberg's work has demonstrated a continued interest in rock and popular music both in terms of its radical potential and its ideological use by the conservative Right in the United States.

- **Associated concepts** Articulation, cultural politics, hegemony, identity, ideology, popular culture.
- **Tradition(s)** Cultural studies, Marxism, psychoanalysis.
- **Reading** Grossberg, L. (1992) *We Gotta Get Out of This Place: Popular Conservatism and Postmodern Culture*. New York and London: Routledge.

H

Habermas, Jürgen (1929–) A professor of philosophy at the University of Frankfurt (Germany), Habermas stands in the tradition of the Frankfurt School, yet, he also differs from them in important respects. Thus, rather than dismissing Enlightenment reason *per se*, as **Adorno** was inclined to do, Habermas distinguishes between instrumental reason and critical reason. The former, epitomized by scientific rationality, involves the subordination of the social-existential questions of the 'lifeworld' to the 'system imperatives' of money and administrative power. However, the Enlightenment also has a critical side that for Habermas is the basis of the emancipatory project of modernity, which remains unfinished. A critic of postmodernism, Habermas has sought universal grounds for the validation of claims to human emancipation through the exploration of communicative processes that include the 'ideal speech situation' and the 'public sphere'.

- **Associated concepts** Commodification, Enlightenment, ideal speech situation, modernity, public sphere.
- **Tradition(s)** Critical theory, Marxism.
- **Reading** Habermas, J. (1989) *The Structural Transformation of the Public Sphere.* Cambridge: MIT Press.

Habitus An idea developed by Pierre **Bourdieu** as a part of his sociology of culture wherein the habitus is understood as a set of durable values, practices and dispositions which is both structured and structuring. The habitus is the context in which we understand the world and acquire beliefs, values and knowledge through practice. Further, it is through practice that the habitus manifests itself at that moment when a specific problem is approached and 'solved' through a particular set of dispositions. Though formed within a particular field, the dispositions of the habitus are transportable into other fields.

The dispositions of the habitus are the consequence of family, class and educational background but appear to us as natural. Indeed, the universalism attributed to the values, attitudes and practices of the habitus represents for Bourdieu a misrecognition or forgetting in relation to the conditions of production of the habitus itself. However, the habitus is not simply a fixed set of phenomena as a consequence of structural conditioning but is also generative. That is, the habitus consists of the practical mastery of skills, routines, aptitudes and assumptions that can be modified and used as the basis of improvisations, especially when transported from one field to another.

The concept of the habitus represents Bourdieu's attempt to confront the paradox of structure and agency or subjectivist (from the point of view of the actor)

82

and objectivist (from the point of view of structure) accounts. Bourdieu argues that practice is always imbued with a sense of agency and subjective point of view, but needs to be understood in relation to and put in the context of the 'objective' structures of culture and society. However, the fact that Bourdieu reads the classificatory schemes of the habitus as 'ultimate values' that are more basic than consciousness or even language does seem to tip the balance of his explanations towards the structural end of the scale. Some critics would argue that the concept of habitus is thus a reductionist one, an argument reinforced, for example, by the very tight fit Bourdieu reads between class structure and cultural tastes and attitudes.

Links **Agency, cultural capital, practice, reductionism, structuration, structure,**

Hall, Stuart (1932–) If there can be any single person most identified with the development of cultural studies as a distinct domain of study it would be Stuart Hall. A West Indian-born British thinker initially associated with the 'New Left' of the late 1960s, Hall was the Director of the Birmingham **Centre for Contemporary Cultural Studies** from 1968 to 1979 and it was during this time that an identifiable and particular field called cultural studies began to emerge. Though identified with Marxism, Hall has also been critical of its reductionist tendencies and set out to study popular culture in its own right. Hall has made considerable use of the work of **Gramsci** and the concepts of ideology and hegemony, for example in his exploration and critique of Thatcherism in Britain. However, he also played a significant part in deploying the poststructuralism of **Derrida** and **Foucault** to develop a form of post-Marxism concerned with discourse, representation and the new post-1960s configuration of capitalism, identities and politics that emerged in Western cultures.

- **Associated concepts** Articulation, circuit of culture, cultural politics, encoding–decoding, ethnicity, hegemony, identity, ideology, New Times, popular culture.
- **Tradition(s)** Cultural studies, Marxism, post-Marxism, poststructuralism.
- **Reading** Hall, S. (1996) 'On Postmodernism and Articulation: An Interview with Stuart Hall' (ed. L. Grossberg), in D. Morley and D-K. Chen (eds), *Stuart Hall*. London: Routledge.

Haraway, Donna (1944–) American feminist Donna Haraway trained as a scientist and her cultural writings reflect her continued concern with the epistemological and social issues raised by science. She rejects the claims of science, and some branches of feminism, to hold the God-like neutral knowledge of a disembodied gaze. Instead she advocates 'partial perspectives' that recognize their inherent limitations and remind us that no single perspective is complete. In her 'Cyborg manifesto' Haraway suggests that the boundaries between animal, human and machine are breaking down. She also rejects the distinction between sex and gender on the grounds that biology is a partial perspective that privileges sexuality. Consequently she describes herself in terms of multiple identities that include the cyborg, a position that she argues has advantages for women.

- **Associated concepts** Constructionism, epistemology, foundationalism (anti-), multiple identities, post-feminism, post-humanism.
- **Tradition(s)** Cultural studies, Marxism, postmodernism, poststructuralism.
- **Reading** Haraway, D. (1991) *Simians, Cyborgs, and Women: The Reinvention of Nature.* London: Free Association Books.   **83**

Hartley, John (1948–) John Hartley was born in London (UK) and educated at the University of Wales and at Murdoch University (Australia). He is currently a professor and Dean of the Creative Industries Faculty at Queensland University of Technology, Australia. He was amongst the pioneer writers in cultural studies to explore the texts and institutions of television from a cultural perspective using the tools of semiotics. He has written widely on the themes of media, popular culture, democracy and modernity with a particular interest in journalism. He is the founder of the *International Journal of Cultural Studies*.

- **Associated concepts** Popular culture, reading, resistance, semiotics, television, text.
- **Tradition(s)** Cultural studies, Marxism, poststructuralism, structuralism.
- **Reading** Hartley, J. (1992) *Tele-ology: Studies in Television.* London: Routledge.

Harvey, David (1935–) British-born Harvey has worked as a professor at Johns Hopkins University (USA) and at Oxford University (UK). He is one of the leading exponents of a Marxist-inspired cultural geography and the revival of interest in issues of space and place. In Harvey's account, postmodernism is not primarily an epistemological condition or an aesthetic trend but a social and spatial condition that results from crucial changes at the level of political economy. As described by Harvey, a crisis of overproduction within Fordism, sparked by the 1973 oil crisis, prompted the development of more flexible production techniques involving new technology, the reorganization of labour and a speed-up of production/consumption turnover times. Harvey associates this move towards post-Fordism with the postmodernization of culture and in particular with forms of urban design and culture promoted by the 'new cultural intermediaries'.

- **Associated concepts** Globalization, place, political economy, post-Fordism, space, time–space geography.
- **Tradition(s)** Cultural studies, Marxism, poststructuralism.
- **Reading** Harvey, D. (1989) *The Condition of Postmodernity.* Oxford: Blackwell.

Hebdige, Dick (1951–) Hebdige's use of semiotic theory to investigate youth cultures in Britain in the 1970s formed an important part of the first wave of cultural studies as it developed within the Birmingham **Centre for Contemporary Cultural Studies**. Here Hebdige explored the idea of style in relation to spectacular youth subcultures on the level of the autonomous play of signifiers and in doing so asserted the specificity of the cultural. For Hebdige, style is a signifying practice that can act as a form of semiotic resistance to the dominant order. Hebdige is currently Director of the Interdisciplinary Humanities Center at the University of California, Santa Barbara and has continued publishing articles on music, cultural studies, art and critical theory. His current research preoccupations include mixed media pedagogy and the integration both of critical thinking into art making, and of critically inflected art practice into the mainstream.

- **Associated concepts** Bricolage, signs, style, subculture, youth culture.
- **Tradition(s)** Cultural studies, Marxism, poststructuralism, structuralism.
- **Reading** Hebdige, D. (1979) *Subculture: The Meaning of Style*. London and New York: Routledge.

Hegemony The concept of hegemony played a significant part in the development of cultural studies and was a core concept of the field during the 1970s and 1980s. According to this theory, there is a strand of meanings within any given culture that can be called governing or ascendant. The process of making, maintaining and reproducing this authoritative set of meanings, ideologies and practices has been called hegemony.

For **Gramsci**, from whom cultural studies appropriated the term, hegemony implies a situation where a 'historical bloc' of ruling class factions exercises social authority and leadership over the subordinate classes through a combination of force and, more importantly, consent. Gramscian concepts proved to be of long-lasting significance within cultural studies because of the central importance given to popular culture as a site of ideological struggle. In effect, Gramsci makes ideological struggle and conflict within civil society the central arena of cultural politics, with hegemonic analysis the mode of gauging the relevant balance of forces.

Within Gramscian analysis, a hegemonic bloc never consists of a single socio-economic category but is formed through a series of alliances in which one group takes on a position of leadership. Ideology plays a crucial part in allowing this alliance of groups (originally conceived in class terms) to overcome narrow economic-corporate interest in favour of 'National-Popular' dominance. Thus, 'a cultural–social unity' is achieved through which a multiplicity of dispersed wills and heterogeneous aims are welded together to form a common conception of the world. The building, maintenance or subversion of a common conception of the world is an aspect of ideological struggle involving a transformation of understanding through criticism of the existing popular ideologies.

Hegemony can be understood in terms of the strategies by which the world-views and power of ascendant social groups are maintained. However, this has to be seen in relational terms and as inherently unstable since hegemony is a *temporary* settlement and series of alliances between social groups that is won and not given. Further, it needs to be constantly re-won and re-negotiated so that culture is a terrain of conflict and struggle over meanings. Hegemony is not a static entity but is constituted by a series of changing discourses and practices that are intrinsically bound up with social power. Since hegemony has to be constantly re-made and re-won, it opens up the possibility of a challenge to it; that is, the making of a counter-hegemonic bloc of subordinate groups and classes.

Neo-Gramscian hegemony theory has been challenged on the grounds that Western culture no longer has a dominant centre either in terms of production or meaning. Rather, culture is heterogeneous both in terms of the different kinds of texts produced and the different meanings that compete within texts. Right across the Western world, it is argued, we have been witnessing the end of anything remotely resembling a 'common culture'. In particular, the past thirty years have seen the fragmentation of lifestyle cultures through the impact of migration, the 're-emergence' of ethnicity, the rise and segmentation of youth cultures and the impact of gender politics. Above all, the restructuring of global capitalism, niche marketing and the aestheticization of daily life through the creation of an array of lifestyles centred on the consumption of aesthetic objects and signs has fragmented the cultures of class blocs.

In their post-Marxist revision of the concept of hegemony **Laclau** and Mouffe put aside the final determination of social and cultural relations by class, which for them does not determine cultural meanings. That is, ideology has no 'class-belonging'. They stress that history has no prime agents of social change and a social formation has no one central point of antagonism. Instead, hegemonic and counter-hegemonic blocs are formed through temporary and strategic alliances of a range of discursively constructed subjects and groups of interest. Here, the 'social' is not understood to be an object but rather a field of contestation in which multiple descriptions of the self and others compete for ascendancy. For Laclau and Mouffe, it is the role of hegemonic practices to try to fix difference, to put closure around the unstable meanings of signifiers in the discursive field.

Links **Class, cultural politics, culture, ideology, Marxism, post-Marxism**

Hermeneutics A philosophical endeavour concerned with textual meaning and theories that explain interpretation as a process. It is associated in particular with a German philosophical tradition that includes Heidegger, Iser and Gadamer. A central issue for hermeneutics has been the generation of meaning and the degree to which this can be said to reside in texts and/or is produced by readers. For contemporary hermeneutic theory, understanding and meaning are realized by actual readers in a process of textual interpretation that depends on the meanings inscribed in a text and the activity of readers. The interplay that occurs between texts and readers is known as 'the hermeneutic circle'.

The influence of hermeneutics within cultural studies has largely been through a reader-reception theory that challenges the idea that there is one textual meaning associated with authorial intent. It also contests the notion that textual meanings are able to police meanings created by readers/audiences but instead stresses the interactive relationship between the text and the audience. Thus the reader approaches the text with certain expectations and anticipations which are modified in the course of reading to be replaced by new 'projections'. Understanding is always from the position and point of view of the person who understands. This involves not merely reproduction of textual meaning but the production of new meaning by the readers. The text may structure aspects of meaning by guiding the reader but it cannot fix meanings that are the outcome of the oscillations between the text and the imagination of the reader.

The premises of hermeneutics have been questioned since the rise of poststructuralism which has challenged the idea that authors and readers as unified subjects are the source of meaning. In other words, poststructuralism has disputed the implicit humanism of hermeneutics and its association of meaning with the intentionality of persons. Thus Foucault argued against interpretative or hermeneutic methods that seek to disclose the 'hidden' meanings of language, suggesting instead that we be concerned with the description and analysis of the surfaces of discourse and their effects. Further, **Barthes** famously declared 'the death of the author' in the whirlpool of intertextuality.

Links **Active audience, author, encoding–decoding, intertextuality, meaning, reading**

Hoggart, Richard (1918–) As Professor of English at Birmingham University (UK) in 1964, Richard Hoggart was instrumental in the formation of the **Centre for Contemporary Cultural Studies** (CCCS) and became its first Director. His influential book *The Uses of Literacy* explores the character of English working class culture as it developed and changed from the 1930s through to the 1950s. In the first part of his book Hoggart gives a sympathetic, humanist and detailed account of the lived culture of the working class before going on to give a rather more acid account of the development of 'commercial culture'.

Hoggart's central legacy to cultural studies is the legitimacy he accorded to the detailed study of working class culture, that is, to the meanings and practices of ordinary people as they seek to live their lives and make their own history. As such, he has often been associated with culturalism, and, though this may not be warranted, it does at least distinguish him from the Marxist and Left-leaning turn taken by cultural studies after he handed over the Directorship of CCCS to Stuart **Hall**.

- **Associated concepts** Capitalism, class, commodification, mass culture, popular culture.
- **Tradition(s)** Cultural studies, culturalism.
- **Reading** Hoggart, R. (1957) *The Uses of Literacy*. Harmondsworth: Penguin.

Holism A methodological approach that insists on the non-separability of the parts of any domain of analysis from the whole in which it rests. Further, the properties of the whole are not fully determined by the properties of its parts. The whole is always more than the sum of its parts and the designation of levels is a device for understanding that can only be used in the context of a well-defined analytic arrangement or metaphor designed to achieve particular purposes.

Methodological holism argues that the best way to study a complex system is to treat it as a whole rather than be content with analysis of the structure and 'behaviour' of its component parts. Indeed, the non-separability inherent to holism suggests that the properties of the whole are not fully determined by the properties of its parts. In this view, a society or culture always adds up to more than is stated by a description of the relationships of the parts or levels. While a methodological individualist maintains that to study society is to investigate the behaviour of individuals, a methodological holist argues that this will have limited value in illuminating the workings of the social and cultural whole.

Given the central place that language occupies in the study of culture it is worth noting that linguistic holism suggests that an understanding of language requires utterances to be put in the context of the entire network of language. Meaning is always relational and context-specific. Thus the philosophy of language espoused by those writers who have been influential in cultural studies – **Derrida**, **Bakhtin**, **Foucault**, **Wittgenstein** – emphasizes the relational character of language and the contextual nature of truth. A language-oriented study of culture must then seek to locate culture as a linguistic and cultural whole (way of life).

Culture is constitutive of other practices, that is, culture (as language or discourse) is the classificatory process that makes an act meaningful. Thus, the study of culture requires a methodological holism given that any act is multi-faceted in its meanings, partaking as it does of the multi-accentuality of the sign. For example, buying flowers for one's partner is a commercial transaction enacted within a network of economic relations. However, within the context of contemporary social relationships, buying flowers acts as a sign of affection (or apology or a strategy etc.) implicated in gender relations and the politics of the family. Of course, within the context of the whole, discourses mark out the boundaries of significance through their classificatory operations so that we need to grasp both the non-separable unity of forms of life *and* their cultural categorizing into parts.

Links **Circuit of culture, culture, discourse, ethnography, language, methodology, signs**

Homology The idea of homology within cultural studies marks the synchronic relationship by which social structures, social values and cultural symbols are said to 'fit' together. The concept is used to describe the 'accord' between a structural position in the social order, the social values of subcultural participants and the cultural symbols and styles by which they express themselves. In particular, the theory of homology connects a located lived culture as a set of constitutive relationships to the surrounding objects, artefacts, institutions and practices. Homological analysis records snapshots of social structures and cultural symbols. It involves two levels of related analysis; the examination of the social group and the investigation of their preferred cultural item. It is concerned with how far the structure and content of particular cultural items parallel and reflect the structure, style, typical concerns, attitudes and feelings of the social group.

Homological analysis is fundamentally structural in its exploration of the continuous play between the cultural group and a particular item which produces specific styles, meanings, contents and forms of consciousness. Thus **Willis** holds that the ensemble of the bike, noise and 'rider on the move' expresses the 'motorbike boys'' culture, values and identities so that the strength of the motorcycle matches the secure character of the bikers' world. Accordingly, the motorcycle underwrites the boys' commitment to tangible things, to toughness and power and to masculine assertiveness and a rough camaraderie.

Subcultural participants are not held to have cognitive understandings of

88

homologies in the way that the cultural theorist does; nevertheless, the creativity and cultural responses of groups are not random but expressive of social contradictions. Thus subcultures are said to live out important criticisms and insights into contemporary capitalism and its culture. They 'understand' in the logic of cultural action something of their own conditions of existence. Indeed, the concept of homology, crossed with that of bricolage, was to play a significant part in cultural studies' seminal work on youth cultures whereby the creative, expressive and symbolic work of subcultures was read as a form of resistance. Thus, the boots, braces, cropped hair, Stayprest shirts and Ska music of Skinheads in the late 1960s and 1970s was grasped as a stylistic symbolic bricolage that communicated the hardness of working class masculinity and resonated with the group's situated social relations in a homological unity.

Links **Bricolage, resistance, structure, style, subculture, symbolic, youth culture**

hooks, bell – aka Gloria Watkins (1952–) hooks is an African American feminist writer whose thinking is centrally concerned with the intersections of class, gender and race in culture and politics. Political engagement and a certain polemically oriented non-academic style of writing that has pedagogic and interventionist objectives mark her work. She is critical of 'white supremacist capitalist patriarchy', a phrase that echoes a concern with the abuses of male power in the context of both race and class in the contemporary United States. Thus she has been critical of both white middle class feminism and black men's oppression of black women. She is a prolific and eclectic writer whose recent work has explored rap music, film, black 'folk' culture, African American politics and the character of teaching and learning.

- **Associated concepts** Capitalism, class, gender, patriarchy, popular culture, race.
- **Tradition(s)** Cultural studies, feminism, Marxism.
- **Reading** hooks, b. (1990) *Yearning: Race, Gender and Cultural Politics* Boston, MA: South End Press.

Humanism A general term for the philosophical view that places unified human beings at the centre of any understanding of the universe. More specifically, humanism posits the existence of an 'inner core' as the source of meaning and action as theorized by Descartes in his famous phrase 'I think therefore I am'. Thus, for humanism we are understood to be unique and whole persons endowed with the capacities of reason, consciousness and agency. Here the rational, conscious individual subject is placed at the heart of Western philosophy and culture. In putting the human being at the centre of meaning and action, humanism displaces God and religion from their traditional pre-modern location at the heart of the universe. As such, humanism partakes of the Enlightenment philosophy of the seventeenth and eighteenth centuries but cannot be simply identified with it since humanism is arguably the ascendant attitude of contemporary common sense.

In placing human beings at the centre of culture, humanism could be seen as encouraging the individualism that is so much a marker of contemporary Western social life. Thus, conceiving of the person in the style of humanism is not simply a matter of philosophy but of the wider cultural processes of subject and identity formation. Indeed, it is central to the current Western account of the self to see persons as unified and capable of organizing themselves. For example, morality talk, which in Western culture seeks to make intelligible and manageable the moral and ethical dilemmas that face us, is centrally concerned with questions of individual responsibility for actions. Indeed, individual responsibility is embodied in laws that hold persons accountable for their actions.

A humanistic understanding is also manifested in the organization of academic knowledge into discrete subjects. Thus psychology is held to be about the workings of the individual mind, Western medicine treats individual ailments, and economic theory, though concerned with social processes, has the rational, self-interested, choice-making individual at its heart. Further, it is often argued that realism as a set of representational conventions upholds a humanist viewpoint through its focus on the individual person.

It is commonly suggested that, within cultural studies, humanism is represented by that strand of work known as culturalism and by ethnographic and other qualitative forms of research. This is so because the level of analysis in this approach is taken to be the whole person and their intentions, meanings and experience on a phenomenological plane. That is, culturalism has stressed the active, creative capacity of people to create cultural meanings and lived experience. By contrast, work associated with structuralism and poststructuralism has been seen as 'post-humanist' as it displaces the unified agent from the centre of analysis. Here meaning resides in discourses that are exterior to individual human beings and which constitute subjectivity as an effect.

Links **Culturalism, post-humanism, poststructuralism, realism, structuralism, subjectivity**

Hybridity The concept of the hybrid made considerable strides into the vocabulary of cultural studies during the 1990s in the context of discussions about globalization, diaspora cultures and postcolonialism. At its core, hybrdity involves the mixing together of previously discrete cultural elements to create new meanings and identities. Indeed, the notion of hybridity has played a significant part in destabilizing the very idea of an unchanging culture that has secure locations since hybrids destabilize and blur established cultural boundaries in a process of fusion or creolization. One can make a distinction between structural hybridization that refers to a variety of social and institutional *sites* of hybridity, for example border zones or cities like Miami or Singapore, and cultural hybridization that describes a range of cultural responses from separation and assimilation to hybrids that destabilize and blur cultural boundaries.

In the context of the accelerated globalization of late modernity writers have begun to talk about hybrid cultural identities rather than a homogeneous national or ethnic cultural identity. Indeed the instability of meaning leads us to think of culture, identities and identifications as always a place of borders and hybridity rather than as fixed stable entities. Globalization provides the context for an increased range of sources and resources available for identity construction. Patterns

90

of population movement and settlement established during colonialism and its aftermath, combined with the more recent acceleration of globalization, particularly of electronic communications, have enabled the increased cultural juxtapositioning, meeting and mixing that is constitutive of hybridity.

The concept of hybridity remains problematic in so far as it assumes or implies the meeting or mixing of completely separate and homogeneous cultural spheres. To think of British Asian or Mexican American hybrid forms as the mixing of two separate traditions is problematic because neither the British, Asian, Mexican nor American culture is bounded and homogeneous. Each category is always already a hybrid form which is also divided along the lines of religion, class, gender, age, nationality and so forth. Thus hybridization involves the mixing together of that which is already a hybrid. Nevertheless, the concept of hybridity has enabled us to recognize the production of new identities and cultural forms, for example 'British Asians' and British Banghra. Thus, the concept of hybridity is acceptable as a device to capture cultural change by way of a strategic cut or temporary stabilization of cultural categories.

In Britain, for example, the emergence of British-born young 'Asians' gave rise to a generation that was much more deeply involved in transactions across ethnic boundaries than were the original migrants. Young British Asians went to school with white and Afro-Caribbean Britons, shared leisure sites, watched television and were frequently bilingual. Thus as British Asian young people have become skilled operators of code switching so they developed their own home-grown hybrid cultural forms such as ragga–banghra–reggae–rap crossovers. Many of the cultural issues involved in this process have been aired in contemporary films such as *East Meets West*, *Bahji On the Beach* and *Bend It Like Beckham*.

The differences within and between diaspora communities and the surrounding cultures in the context of globalization prevent easy identification of particular subjects with a given, fixed, identity. Thus subject positions are drawn from a variety of discourses and sites and shifting identifications enact a hybrid identity that draws on multiplying global resources. Thus, identities are never either pure or fixed but formed through the articulation of age, class, gender, race and nation.

Links **Black Atlantic, culture, diaspora, globalization, glocalization, identity**

Hyperreality Hyperreality is a concept deployed within some versions of postmodern thought signifying 'more real than real'. It refers to the manner by which simulations or artificial productions of 'real life' execute their own worlds to constitute reality. As such, hyperreality is a 'reality effect' by which the real is produced according to a model and appears to be more real than the real. Consequently, the distinction between the real and a representation collapses or implodes.

For example, the world according to the postmodern philosopher **Baudrillard** is one in which a series of modern distinctions have broken down (sucked into a 'black hole' as he calls it) collapsing the real and the unreal, the public and the private, art and reality. For Baudrillard, postmodern culture is marked by an all-encompassing flow of fascinating simulations and images, a hyperreality in which we are overloaded with images and information. He argues that today it is everyday reality that is hyperrealist so that we live in an 'aesthetic hallucination' of reality.

Here, the hyperreal is the real retouched in a 'hallucinatory resemblance' with itself whereby the real implodes on itself. Implosion in Baudrillard's work describes a process leading to the collapse of boundaries between the real and simulations. This includes that between the media and the social so that 'TV is the world'. Television simulates real-life situations, not so much to represent the world as to execute its own. News re-enactments of 'real life' events blur the boundaries between the 'real' and the simulation, and between 'entertainment' and 'current affairs'.

Links **Advertising, commodification, postmodernism, representation, signs, simulacrum**

I

Ideal speech situation This is a notion specifically associated with the philosophy of Jürgen **Habermas**. Working within the tradition of critical theory, Habermas has sought universal grounds for the validation of moral judgement and claims to human emancipation. He does so by arguing that human social and cultural interactions presuppose language and that in the very structure of speech we may find the essential grounding conditions for all forms of social organization. When we speak, argues Habermas, we are making four validity claims: namely, to comprehensibility, truth, appropriateness and sincerity. These claims, he argues, imply both the logical justification of truth and the social context for their rational debate, the conditions for which Habermas calls an 'ideal speech situation'. Here competing truth-claims are subject to rational debate and argument; that is, within an ideal speech situation truth is not subject to the vested interests and power plays of truth seekers but rather emerges through the process of argumentation. For Habermas, our very ability to make truth-claims is dependent on a democratically organized public sphere that approximates an ideal speech situation.

Some postmodern critics, particularly **Lyotard**, have argued that Habermas' notion of an ideal speech situation that underpins the public sphere reproduces the totalizing discourse of 'Enlightenment reason', ignoring its repressive character. That is to say, there can be no common or ideal speech situation since language and culture are radically diverse in character and unavailable to either a single discursive ethics or to a universal set of truth-claims. It could be countered that the purpose of Habermas' work does not lie in the final determination of common needs, but centres on the possibility of intersubjective agreement concerning the very social norms that allow different needs to be articulated and realized. That is, Habermas would argue that he is stressing the importance of the democratic process rather than the outcome of that process.

Links **Communication, critical theory, Enlightenment, language, language-game, public sphere**

Identification In everyday language the concept of identification involves the processes of describing, naming and classifying. That is, to identify. Within cultural studies this concept, while retaining aspects of this meaning, has also been deployed in a more specifically psychoanalytic sense in relation to the construction of identity. More particularly, identification is at the core of the processes of fantasy and attachment that are said to partially suture or stitch together discourses and psychic forces to constitute identity. That is, the process of identification involves a form of emotional investment in the discursive descriptions of our self and others that are available to us.

In classic psychoanalytic theory gendered subjectivity is constituted through processes of identification with sexed adults. Thus it is argued that the formation of contemporary masculinity is a consequence of boys' separation from their mother via identification with the father and symbolic Phallus as the domain of social status, power and independence. From this base, Judith **Butler** reads psychoanalysis in a way that opens up a space in which to discuss how regulatory norms are invested with psychic power through processes of identification.

Butler argues that the 'assumption' (taking on) of sex involves identification with the normative phantasm (idealization) of 'sex'. Sex is a symbolic subject position assumed under threat of punishment (for example, of symbolic castration or abjection). Thus, for Butler, identification is understood as a kind of affiliation and expression of an emotional tie with an idealized fantasized object (person, body part) or normative ideal. It is grounded in fantasy, projection and idealization. However, identification is not an intentional imitation of a model or conscious investment in subject positions. Rather, it is indissoluble from the very formation of subjects and is coterminous with the emergence of the ego.

Identification constitutes an exclusionary matrix by which the processes of subject formation simultaneously produce a constitutive outside. That is, identification with one set of norms, say heterosexuality, repudiates another, say homosexuality. However, according to Butler, identifications are never complete or whole since identification is with a fantasy or idealization and so can never be coterminous with 'real' bodies or gendered practices. There is always a gap or slipping away of identification so that identity is always unstable. Further, identifications can be multiple and need not involve the repudiation of all other positions. Indeed, repudiated elements are always within the identification as that which is rejected but returns so that identifications of homosexuality are always within heterosexuality and vice versa.

Links **Emotion, femininity, gender, identity, masculinity, psychoanalysis, queer theory, sex**

Identity The concept of identity became a central category of cultural studies during the 1990s. It pertains to cultural descriptions of persons with which we emotionally identify and which concern sameness and difference, the personal and the social. For cultural studies, identity is a cultural construction because the discursive resources that form the material for identity formation are cultural in character. In particular, we are constituted as individuals in a social process that is commonly understood as acculturation without which we would not be persons. Indeed, the very notion of what it is to be a person is a cultural question (for example, individualism is a marker of specifically modern societies) and without language the very concept of identity would be unintelligible to us.

Within cultural studies, identities are understood to be discursive-performative. That is, identity is best described as a discursive practice that enacts or produces that which it names through citation and reiteration of norms or conventions. The concept of identity is further deployed in order to link the emotional 'inside' of persons with the discursive 'outside'. That is, identity represents the processes by which discursively constructed subject positions are taken up (or otherwise) by concrete persons' fantasy identifications and emotional 'investments'. The argument that identity is not a universal entity but a culturally specific discursive construction is grounded in an anti-representationalist account of language whereby discourse defines, constructs and produces objects of knowledge. Consequently, what we can say about the identity characteristics of, for example, men, is culturally circumscribed.

The popular cultural repertoire of the Western world holds that we have a true-self, an identity which we possess and which can become known to us. Here, identity is thought to be a universal and timeless core, an 'essence' of the self that is *expressed* as representations that are recognizable by ourselves and by others. That is, identity is an essence signified through signs of taste, beliefs, attitudes and lifestyles. However, cultural studies writers question the assumption that identity is a fixed 'thing' that we possess. Identity, it is argued, is not best understood as an entity but as an emotionally charged description. Rather than being a timeless essence, what it is to be a person is said to be plastic and changeable, being specific to particular social and cultural conjunctures.

The anti-essentialist position that is widely held within cultural studies stresses that identity is a process of *becoming* built from points of similarity and difference. There is no essence of identity to be discovered, rather, identity is continually being produced within the vectors of resemblance and distinction. Thus identity is not an essence but a continually shifting description of ourselves so that the meaning of identity categories – Britishness, blackness, masculinity etc. – are held to be subject to continual deferral through the never-ending processes of supplementarity or différance. Since meaning is never finished or completed, identity represents a 'cut' or a snapshot of unfolding meanings.

This argument points to the political nature of identity as a 'production' and to the possibility of multiple, shifting and fragmented identities that can be articulated together in a variety of ways. This signals to **Hall** the 'impossibility' of identity as well as its 'political significance'. It is the very plasticity of identity that makes it politically significant since contestation over the meanings of identity categories concerns the very kinds of people we are becoming.

On the whole, cultural studies has adopted the idea that identities are contradictory and cross-cut or dislocate each other. No single identity acts as an overarching, organizing identity, rather, identities shift according to how subjects are addressed or represented. Thus we are constituted by fractured multiple identities. If one accepts this argument, then the apparent 'unity' of identity is better understood in terms of the articulation of different and distinct elements which, under other historical and cultural circumstances, could be re-articulated in different ways. Thus, individuals are the unique historically specific articulation of discursive elements that are contingent but also socially determined or regulated.

Identity politics Identity politics is concerned with the making and maintenance of   **95**
cultural rights for those persons making identity claims within society and culture.
Acceptance of anti-essentialist arguments about identity within cultural studies
leads to an understanding of identity politics as the forging of 'new languages' of
identity with which to describe ourselves. This is allied to actions aimed at changing
social practices, usually through the formation of coalitions where at least some
values are shared. Identity politics is a sub-set of cultural politics and is thus also
concerned with the 'power to name' and to make particular descriptions stick. In
particular, the representation of identities is a 'political' question because they are
intrinsically bound up with questions of power as a form of social regulation that
is productive of the self and enables some kinds of identities to exist while denying
it to others.

Identity politics has been most closely identified with feminism, gay activism
and questions of ethnicity. Though these cases are clearly not the limit of identity
politics they represent the most high-profile campaigns. For example, the language
of feminism brings oppression into view and expands the logical space for moral
and political deliberation. As such feminism develops a 'new language' in which the
claims of women do not sound crazy but come to be accepted as 'true' (in the sense
of a social commendation). The emergence of such a language is not the discovery
of universal truth but part of an evolutionary struggle that has no immanent
teleology, that is, no future pre-determined destiny to which it must evolve. As
such, feminism imagines, and seeks to bring into being, an alternative form of
community by forging a moral identity for women as women by gaining linguistic
authority over themselves.

Since the meanings involved in identity categories are potentially endless, so any
sense of self, of identity or of communities of identification (nations, ethnicities,
sexualities, classes etc.) and the politics that flow from them are necessary fictions
marking a temporary, partial and arbitrary closure of meaning. That is, while it is
possible to go on re-describing what it means to be a 'woman' for ever, in order to
say anything (to mark significance), and in order to take action, a temporary closure
of meaning is required. Thus, feminist politics needs at least a momentary and
pragmatic agreement about what constitutes a woman and what is in women's
interests under particular circumstances. For post-Marxism it is the role of
hegemonic practices to try to fix difference, that is, to put closure around the
unstable meanings of signifiers in the discursive field and thereby to stabilize what,
for example, femininity, masculinity or American identity means.

The political concept of citizenship can be understood as a form of identity and
thus the politics of identity is a part of a much wider politics of citizenship and the
public sphere. Thus, a civic 'identity of citizenship' holds together a diversity of
values and lifeworlds within a democratic framework. The identity of citizenship
may be the only thing we have in common, but a commitment by diverse groups
to the procedures of democracy and to intersubjectively recognized rights and

duties of citizenship in the social, civil and political domains advances democracy and provides the conditions for particularistic identity projects. This involves the 'hegemony of democratic values' developed in the public sphere so that citizenship is a mechanism for linking the micro-politics of identity with the official macro-politics of institutional and cultural rights.

Links **Citizenship, cultural politics, hegemony, identity, ideology, post-Marxism**

Identity project The idea of identity as a project refers to the ongoing creation of narratives of self-identity relating to our perceptions of the past, present and hoped-for future. Though cultural theory now understands identities as being fractured or multiple, in everyday life we continue to describe ourselves in terms of a narrative of the self. As modernity not only breaks down the traditional forms of identity but also increases the levels of resources for identity construction, so we are all faced with the task of constructing our identities as a project.

By this is meant that identity is something we create, something always in process, a moving towards rather than an arrival. An identity project builds on what we think we are now in the light of our past and present circumstances together with what we think we would like to be, the trajectory of our desired future. Here, self-identity is constituted by the ability to sustain a narrative about the self thereby building up a consistent feeling of biographical continuity. The identity stories that form a project attempt to answer the critical questions 'What to do? How to act? Who to be?' and lead us to grasp identity as the self understood reflexively by any given person.

Links **Identity, multiple identities, narrative, performativity, self-identity, subjectivity**

Ideological state apparatus A term that was developed by **Althusser** in the late 1960s and early 1970s in the context of his structuralist Marxism. The concept entered the vocabulary of cultural studies at the moment when thinkers at the **Centre for Contemporary Cultural Studies** engaged with structuralism and the question of ideology.

For Althusser, our entry into the symbolic order, and thus our constitution as subjects, is the work of ideology which, he argues, hails or 'interpellates' concrete individuals as concrete subjects. According to Althusser, ideology exists in an apparatus and its associated practices. Thus he designates a series of institutions as 'ideological state apparatuses' (ISAs): namely, the family, the education system, the church and the mass media. While Althusser regards the church as the dominant pre-capitalist ISA, he argues that within the context of capitalism it has been replaced by the educational system. Thus schools and universities are implicated in the ideological (and physical) reproduction of labour power along with the social relations of production that pertain to capitalism.

Althusser's work was significant in elevating the debate about ideology to the forefront of thinking within cultural studies. However, his influence waned not least because the operation of ISAs as argued by Althusser is too functionalist in orientation. That is, ideology appears to operate behind people's backs in terms of the 'needs' of an agentless system. The Althusserian formulation of the question of ideology is also too coherent. The educational system, for example, is the site of contradictory ideologies and of ideological conflict rather than a place for the unproblematic and homogeneous reproduction of capitalist ideology.

Links **Agency, ideology, Marxism, nation-state, social formation, structuralism**

Ideology So influential has the concept of ideology been within cultural studies that the whole field was once dubbed 'ideological studies'. Of course, the notion of ideology has a long history and comes in various shapes and sizes. However, from a cultural studies perspective, it has been the Marxist variants of the concept that have formed the core usage and the centre of debate regarding its validity.

The concern of contemporary Western Marxism with the concept of ideology is rooted in the failure of proletarian revolutions to materialize and the inadequacy of historical materialism in relation to questions of subjectivity, meaning and cultural politics. Put simply, the concern with ideology began as an exploration into why capitalism, which was held to be an exploitative system of economic and social relations, was not being overthrown by working class revolution. In particular, the question asked was whether the working class suffered from 'false consciousness', that is, a mistakenly bourgeois world-view which served the interest of the capitalist class. There are two aspects of **Marx**'s writing that might be grounds for pursuing such a line of thought.

First, Marx argues that the dominant ideas in any society are the ideas of the ruling class. Second, he suggests that what we perceive to be the true character of social relations within capitalism are in actuality the mystifications of the market. That is, the appearance of market relations of equality obscures the deep structures of exploitation. Here ideology has a double-character, both of which function to legitimate the sectional interests of powerful classes. Namely, (a) ideas as coherent statements about the world that maintain the dominance of capitalism and (b) world-views which are the systematic outcome of the structures of capitalism which lead us to inadequate understandings of the social world.

The most long-lasting and authoritative Marxist account of ideology in the context of cultural studies has come from the writings of **Gramsci** that became especially influential within cultural studies during the late 1970s. For **Gramsci** ideology is grasped as ideas, meanings and practices which, while they purport to be universal truths, are maps of meaning that support the power of particular social classes. Here, ideology is not separate from the practical activities of life but provides people with rules of practical conduct and moral behaviour rooted in day-to-day conditions. Ideology is understood to be both lived experience and a body of systematic ideas whose role is to organize and bind together a bloc of diverse social elements, to act as social cement, in the formation of hegemonic and counter-hegemonic blocs. Though ideology can take the form of a coherent set of ideas it more often appears as the fragmented meanings of common sense inherent in a variety of representations. Within this paradigm common sense and popular culture become the crucial sites of ideological conflict.

One problem with the concept of ideology is the scope of its use. Early Marxist and sociological versions of the concept of ideology restricted its usage to ideas associated with, and maintaining the power of, the dominant class. Later, more extended versions of the concept added questions of gender, ethnicity, age etc. to that of class. In other words, ideology refers to the way meaning is used to justify the power of ascendant groups that encompasses classes but also includes social groups based on race, gender, age etc. This kind of understanding of ideology refers only to the ideas of the powerful. However, other uses of the concept grasp ideology as justifying the actions of *all* groups of people so that marginal and subordinate groups also have ideologies in the sense of organizing and justifying ideas about themselves and the world.

The second fundamental problem with the concept of ideology refers to its epistemological status, that is, the relation of ideology to truth and knowledge. In particular, it is the declaration of objective interests and the possibility of false beliefs that is the fundamental problem. In its turn to language, cultural studies espoused anti-representationalism and anti-essentialism. However, there remains a contradiction between the adoption of this argument and the common usage of the concept of ideology as being false. That is, an anti-representationalist position on language that asserts that there is no Archimedean point from which to access the adequacy of representation as universal truth, cannot deploy a concept of ideology (as falsehood) posited in contrast to an objective universal truth. There are no grounds for claiming knowledge as universal transcendental truth, rather, there are only varieties of describing and speaking about the world from within our own milieu. Truth is culture-bound, contingent and specific to the historical and cultural conditions of its production. Thus, in this view, the concept of ideology as falsity has lost its power as an explanatory concept.

Today, the notion of ideology at best implies the 'binding and justifying ideas' of all social groups. This binding function of lived ideology does not have to have any reference to a representational concept of truth. While actors no doubt hold their beliefs to be true, it is the common sharing of beliefs that binds, not the representational truth or falsity of ideas. The difference between ascendant and subordinate groups is one of degrees of power and differing substantive world-views not of ideological versus non-ideological ideas. We are all, as **Foucault** argued, implicated in power relations and in this sense the concept of ideology is virtually interchangeable with his notion of power/knowledge.

When the concept of ideology is read as power/knowledge then it suggests structures of signification that constitute social relations in and through power. If meaning is fluid – a question of difference and deferral – then ideology can be understood as the attempt to *fix meaning* for specific purposes. Ideologies are then grasped as discourses that give meaning to material objects and social practices; they define and produce the acceptable and intelligible way of understanding the world while excluding other ways of reasoning as unintelligible and unjustifiable. Ideologies are thus about binding and justification rather than being concerned with truth, falsity and objective interests. They are the 'world-views' of *any* social group that both constitute them as a group and justify their actions.

This does not mean that we are unable to distinguish between ideas in terms of their specific consequences for social groups judged against our values (that is, what we regard as a good or bad outcome). Truth understood as the values we hold to be good, that is, truth as social commendation, is a very different use of the word than truth as a universal actuality that is mirrored by forms of representation. The picture we now have before us is one of competing social groups operating with justifying ideas and values rather than coherent blocs of truth and falsity. We will certainly want to pick and choose between such ideologies and their consequences. However, we do this not because we possess the universal truth but because we are ourselves a part of such groups and hold to certain values and justifying ideas as an aspect of our acculturation.

Links **Anti-essentialism, hegemony, Marxism, power/knowledge, representation, truth**

Imagined community The concept of the 'imagined community' is most obviously associated with the work of Benedict Anderson on the 'nation'. For Anderson, the nation is an 'imagined community' and national identity a construction assembled through symbols and rituals in relation to territorial and administrative categories. National identities are intrinsically connected to, and constituted by, forms of communication. The nation is an imagined community because most of its members will never know most of the other members and yet they consider themselves to be a part of the same commonality. Despite their physical separation, members of a nation often regard themselves as sharing in a fraternity with which they identify.

An imagined community such as a nation is, according to Anderson, intrinsically connected to communication processes. Thus, it was the mechanized production and commodification of books and newspapers, the rise of 'print capitalism', that allowed vernacular languages to be standardized and disseminated. This provided the conditions for the creation of a national consciousness. In particular, the mechanization of printing and its commercial dissemination 'fixed' a vernacular language as *the* 'national' language and in so doing made a new imagined national community possible. Communication facilitates not just the construction of a common language but also a common recognition of time. For example, the media encourage us to imagine the simultaneous occurrence of events across wide tracts of time and space, which contributes to the concept of nation.

From a cultural studies perspective Anderson tends to overstate the unity of the nation and the strength of nationalist feeling and thus covers over differences of class, gender, ethnicity and so forth. Nevertheless, the whole idea of an imagined community has wider applicability than the nation. The concept can be utilized in relation to all forms of collective identity. Thus, just as national identity takes the form of identification with representations of the nation, so can ethnic groups, feminists, classes, New Social Movements and other communities of action and identity be understood as imagined.

Links **Identification, identity, modernity, national identity, nation-state, symbolic**

Intellectuals The main concern that cultural studies has had with the idea of an intellectual is to consider what kind of a cultural and political role they might play. In a sense, to ask this question is to address what the purpose of cultural studies itself is as an intellectual project.

In the context of the Gramscian cultural studies of the 1970s and 1980s, many writers within the field held the ambition of linking intellectuals with political movements in the model of the 'organic' intellectual. Organic intellectuals are said to be a constitutive part of working class (and later feminist, postcolonial, African American etc.) struggles. They are said to be the thinking and organizing elements of the counter-hegemonic class and its allies. Given that **Gramsci** has an expansive notion of the organic intellectual, this role is not played only by those situated within the educational world but by trade unionists, writers, campaigners, community organizers, teachers and so forth. By contrast, traditional intellectuals, who fill the scientific and philosophical positions in universities, the media, publishers and so forth, are said to maintain and circulate those ideologies constitutive of ruling class cultural hegemony.

In thinking of themselves in 'organic' terms, cultural studies writers sought to play a 'de-mystifying' role in the 'ideological struggle' by pointing to the constructed character of cultural texts. They aimed to highlight the myths and 'ideologies' embedded in texts in the hope of producing subject positions, and real subjects, who are enabled to oppose subordination. Indeed, as a political theory cultural studies has hoped to organize disparate oppositional groups into a politico-cultural alliance. However, there is little evidence to suggest that cultural studies writers have ever been 'organically' connected with political movements in any significant way. Rather, cultural studies intellectuals acted 'as if' they were organic intellectuals or in the hope that one day they could be.

It is questionable whether cultural studies has ever been conceivable in terms of organic intellectuals. In particular, the prime institutional sites for cultural studies are those of higher education. Consequently, though individuals and groups identified with cultural studies may try to forge connections outside of the academy with social and political movements, workers in cultural institutions, and cultural management, cultural studies shares its relative isolation from popular culture with most other academic disciplines.

In this context the main purpose of cultural studies' intellectuals as enacted through teaching and writing is restricted to intellectual clarification and legitimization (which might for Gramscians be seen as a part of ideological conflict). As such, cultural studies is a potential tool for activists and policy makers rather more than a form of 'direct' or 'organic' political activity. Cultural studies is no less valuable for that; storytellers have had an important role in human history. Thus, though the activists of New Social Movements do not need cultural studies *per se,* nevertheless, theorizing may be of assistance in 'clearing the way' for activists through re-definition and re-description of the world. As such, 'doing cultural studies' is an intellectual activity rather more than it is political activism.

Links **Cultural policy, cultural studies, hegemony, ideology, writing**

Intertextuality On one level the idea of intertextuality refers to the self-conscious citation of one text within another as an expression of enlarged cultural self-consciousness. Increased awareness of intertextuality is argued to be a sign of the postmodern condition. Hence the intertextual historical blurring encountered within postmodernism by which representations of the past and present are displayed together in a bricolage that juxtaposes previously unconnected signs to produce new codes of meaning. For example, shopping centres have made the mixing of styles from different times and places a particular 'trade mark' while MTV is noted for the blending of pop music from a variety of periods and locations.

There has also been a notable collapse or blurring of genre boundaries since the late 1970s within cultural products that is a facet of intertextuality. Thus *Bladerunner* and *Blue Velvet* are frequently cited as films that mix the genres of noir, horror, sci-fi., etc. Likewise, conventions of film noir and the road movies are re-worked and re-cycled in *Pulp Fiction* and *True Romance*. In television, intertextuality involves explicit allusion to particular programmes and oblique references to other genre conventions and styles. For example, reference to *Goodfellows* in *The Sopranos* or to *Thelma and Louise* in *The Simpsons*. This intertextuality is an aspect of enlarged cultural self-consciousness about the history and functions of cultural products.

More philosophically, and as argued by **Kristeva** in the context of her discussion of **Bakhtin** and the notion of the dialogic, the concept of intertextuality refers to the accumulation and generation of meaning across texts where all meanings depend on other meanings generated and/or deployed in alternative contexts. This is also the contention of the 'later' **Barthes** when he announces the 'death of the author', arguing that a text has no single meaning that stems from a unified agent but is made up of a set of already existing cultural quotations. In other words, textual meaning is unstable and cannot be confined to single words, sentences or particular texts. Meaning has no single originatory source, but is the outcome of relationships between texts, that is, intertextuality.

The idea that there are no clear and stable denotative meanings, because all meaning contains traces of other meanings from other places, has been mined most consistently by **Derrida**, for whom meaning is always already deferred and in process. In particular, Derrida critiques what he calls the 'logocentrism' of Western philosophy. That is, Derrida investigates and deconstructs the idea that meaning has a fixed *a priori* transcendental form that exists within human reason before any other kinds of thinking occur. Here, words carry multiple meanings, including the echoes or traces of other meanings from other related words in other contexts. Language is non-representational and meaning is inherently unstable so that it constantly slides away.

Cultural studies has taken from Derrida the key notions of deconstruction, différance, trace and supplement all of which, along with the concept of intertextuality, stress the instability of meaning, its deferral through the interplay of texts, writing and traces. Consequently, no categories have essential universal meanings but are social constructions of an inherently intertextual language. This is the core of the anti-essentialism prevalent in cultural studies.

Links Anti-essentialism, author, deconstruction, dialogic, différance, postmodernism, poststructuralism

102   **Irigaray, Luce (1932–)** Irigaray was born and educated in Belgium though she has spent a considerable period of her working life in France. She engages in philosophy, linguistics and psychoanalysis to explore the operations of patriarchy and the exclusions of women. For Irigaray, woman is outside the specular (visual) economy of the Oedipal moment and thus outside of representation (that is, of the symbolic order) so that 'woman' is not an essence *per se* but rather that which is excluded. Irigaray proceeds by way of deconstructing Western philosophy which she critiques for its exclusions while 'miming' the discourse of philosophy; that is, she talks its language but in ways that question the capacity of philosophy to ground its own claims. Her style varies from the lyrical and poetic to the political and didactic.

- **Associated concepts** Différance, *écriture feminine*, Oedipus complex, Other, patriarchy, phallocentric, sex, subjectivity.
- **Tradition(s)** Feminism, poststructuralism, psychoanalysis.
- **Reading** Irigaray, L. (1985) *This Sex Which Is Not One* (trans. C. Porter and C. Burke). Ithaca, NY: Cornell University Press.

Irony It is pertinent to note that the increased popularity of the concept of irony is coterminous with the decline of the certainties of Marxism, science, progress and other grand narratives of modernity. In other words, cultural theory is moving away from a sense of surety in its foundations towards awareness of its own contingency. In that sense, irony refers to a reflexive understanding of the contingency or lack of foundations of one's own values and culture. This mode of thinking, both in cultural theory and in everyday life, is said by a number of writers to be a feature of the postmodern condition.

Speaking philosophically, the foremost proponent of the concept of irony in social and cultural theory is Richard **Rorty**. For Rorty, recognition of the contingency of language leads us to irony where the concept means holding to beliefs and attitudes that one knows are contingent and could be otherwise, that is, they have no universal foundations. This condition directs us to ask about what kind of a person we want to be (for no transcendental truth and no transcendental God can answer this question for us) and how we should relate to fellow human beings – how shall we treat others?

For Rorty, these are pragmatic questions requiring political-value responses and not metaphysical or epistemological issues. Rorty goes on to argue that we do not require certain and universal foundations in order to pursue a pragmatic improvement of the human condition. Rather, we do so on the basis of the values of 'our' own tradition even though we are aware that our values are not the only defendable ones. In this sense, irony underpins social, cultural and political pluralism for it cuts away the idea that 'we' and only we know how to proceed for the best.

In more everyday usage, the concept of irony can refer to the self-knowledge that what is being said or done has been said and done before. Eco gives us a nice example when he points to the lover who offers his partner red roses and the statement 'as Barbara Cartland would say, I love you.' Thus, the necessary romantic gesture is made but with recognition that red roses and I love you has been said and done before. This is the doubleness of a self-undermining statement by which the already known is spoken in inverted commas.

Increased cultural reflexivity is the social force that has encouraged the growing use of irony in culture. For example, a widespread awareness of the history of film, television, music and literature promotes this feeling. Thus, television has a history and repeats it within and across channels to produce the conditions of an ironic knowingness. For example, *The Simpsons* has made a 'dysfunctional' American family the ironic heroes of a series that is both entertainment and a subtle reflection on American cultural life. In accordance with contemporary culture, not only is the television set at the heart of *The Simpsons'* life and that of its audience but we are required to have a self-conscious awareness of other television and film genres as it makes a range of intertextual references. For example, *Itchy and Scratchy*, *The Simpsons'* children's favourite cartoon, parodies *Tom and Jerry* mocking the double standard by which television violence is simultaneously condemned and enjoyed.

Links **Epistemology, foundationalism, intertextuality, postmodernism, pragmatism, truth**

J

Jameson, Frederic (1934–) Jameson is a leading American cultural critic and *the* Marxist theorist of postmodernism as the cultural logic of late capitalism. For Jameson, postmodernism is implicated in a depthless sense of the present and a loss of historical understanding marked by fragmentation, instability and disorientation. Postmodern aesthetics involves the cannibalization of styles from past and present with a consequent loss of authentic artistic style in favour of pastiche that breaks down any firm distinction between high and low culture. However, unlike some postmodernists, Jameson argues that postmodern cultural practices are not superficial but expressive of developments and experiences in a deep 'reality' of global late capitalism. In particular, late capitalism extends commodification to all realms of personal and social life transforming the real into the image and simulacrum.

- **Associated concepts** Aesthetics, capitalism, cultural materialism, hyperreality, postmodernism, simulacrum.
- **Tradition(s)** Critical theory, hermeneutics, Marxism.
- **Reading** Jameson, F. (1991) *Postmodernism or The Cultural Logic of Late Capitalism.* London and New York: Verso.

K

Kellner, Douglas (1943–) Kellner is an American theorist who is currently Chair of the Philosophy of Education at the University of California, Los Angeles. Kellner has been a prolific writer and many of his books deal with the critical theory of the Frankfurt School and the contemporary emergence of postmodernism and poststructuralism. He has been a leading advocate for cultural studies in the United States, arguing for a multi-perspectival approach that combines political economy and cultural analysis. He has applied this perspective to an understanding of media and globalization amongst others. In his recent work, *The Postmodern Adventure*, he argues that massive geopolitical shifts and dramatic developments in computerization and biotechnology are heralding the transformation from the modern to the postmodern age.

- **Associated concepts** Cultural politics, culture industry, identity, ideology, political economy, popular culture.
- **Tradition(s)** Critical theory, Marxism, postmodernism.
- **Reading** Kellner, D. (with S. Best) (2001) *The Postmodern Adventure: Science, Technology and Cultural Studies in the Third Millennium.* New York and London: The Guilford Press.

Kristeva, Julia (1941–) Born in Bulgaria, and schooled in Marxism and Russian formalism (see **Bakhtin**), Kristeva emigrated to France where she initially studied with Roland **Barthes** and wrote for the avant-garde journal *Tel Quel*. Working as a professor at both the universities of Pairs and Columbia (New York), she developed a critique of structuralism and a methodology she calls 'semanalysis' that seeks to explore signification and 'set categories and concepts ablaze'. She argues that transgression of the dominant symbolic order is marked in certain kinds of (modernist) literary and artistic practice through the rhythms, breaks and absences in texts that develop a new language. A practising psychoanalyst in the tradition of **Lacan**, her work is particularly concerned with gender and subjectivity, which are critical issues for cultural studies.

- **Associated concepts** Avant-garde, intertextuality, semiotics, subject position, subjectivity, symbolic order.
- **Tradition(s)** Feminism, Marxism, poststructuralism, psychoanalysis.
- **Reading** Kristeva, J. (1986) 'Revolution in Poetic Language', in T. Moi (ed.), *The Kristeva Reader.* Oxford: Blackwell.

L

Lacan, Jacques (1901–1981) Lacan was a French psychoanalyst whose work has been particularly influential within feminism and on a number of theories of subjectivity and identity. Through this body of work Lacan's writings have become the most prominent form of psychoanalysis within cultural studies. Lacan's value to cultural theory has been in his revision of Freudian principles using structuralism and poststructuralism in ways that give particular attention to the place of language in the structuring of the unconscious and of subjectivity. That is, for Lacan entry into the subject positions of the symbolic order is the very condition of subjectivity. Further, the unconscious is said to be structured 'like a language' and is thus a site of signification and meaningfulness.

- **Associated concepts** Mirror phase, Oedipus complex, subject position, subjectivity, symbolic order, unconscious.
- **Tradition(s)** Psychoanalysis, poststructuralism, structuralism.
- **Reading** Lacan, J. (1977) *Écrits: A Selection.* London: Tavistock.

Laclau, Ernesto (1935–) Laclau was born in Argentina and educated at the University of Buenos Aires and the University of Essex (UK) where he has also worked as a Professor of Political Philosophy. His anti-foundationalist philosophy of radical contingency is aimed at the dissolution of concepts and the weakening of the project of modernity. In particular he argues that there are no necessary links between discursive concepts, and that those links that are forged are temporary articulations bound together by hegemonic practice. With Chantal Mouffe, he has developed a form of post-Marxism that has been very influential within cultural studies, especially through the work of Stuart **Hall**. For Laclau and Mouffe, radical politics cannot be premised on any particular political project (for example, the proletariat of Marxism) but must instead be constructed in terms of the recognition of difference and the identification and development of points of common interest. The central purpose is to further the project of radical democracy.

- **Associated concepts** Anti-essentialism, articulation, différance, foundationalism (anti-), hegemony.
- **Tradition(s)** Marxism, post-Marxism, poststructuralism.
- **Reading** Laclau, E. and Mouffe, C. (1985) *Hegemony and Socialist Strategy: Toward a Radical Democratic Politics.* London: Verso.

Language Issues of language are central to culture and thus to cultural studies.

Language is important to an understanding of culture for two central and related reasons: first, language is the privileged medium in which cultural meanings are formed and communicated; and second, language is the primary means and medium through which we form knowledge about ourselves and the social world. Language forms the network by which we classify the world and make it meaningful, that is, cultural.

Following the influence of structuralism within cultural studies, the investigation of culture has often been regarded as virtually interchangeable with the exploration of meaning produced symbolically through signifying systems that work 'like a language'. To hold that culture works 'like a language' is to argue that all meaningful representations are assembled and generate meaning with essentially the same mechanisms as a language. That is, the selection and organization of signs into texts which are constituted through a form of grammar.

An essentialist or referential understanding of language argues that signs have stable meanings that derive from their enduring referents in the real. In that way, words refer to the essence of an object or category which they are said to reflect. Thus the metaphor of the mirror is to the fore in this conception of language. However, for the anti-essentialist (anti-representationalism) view of language that informs cultural studies, language is a system of differential signs that generate meaning through phonetic and conceptual difference. That is to say, meaning is relational and unstable rather than referential and fixed. Here meaning derives from the *use* of signs so that language is better understood with the metaphor of the tool rather than that of the mirror.

For cultural studies, language is not a neutral medium for the formation and transfer of values, meanings and forms of knowledge that exist independently beyond its boundaries. Rather, language is *constitutive* of those very values, meanings and knowledges. That is, language gives meaning to material objects and social practices that are brought into view and made intelligible to us in terms which language delimits.

Within those philosophies of language that have been deployed by cultural studies there is a division between those who think there is something called 'a language' that has a structure and those who do not. In the former camp lies **Saussure** and structuralism (semiotics) which has been concerned with the 'systems of relations' of the underlying structure of sign systems and the grammar that makes meaning possible. Meaning production is held to be the effect of the 'deep structures' of language that are manifested in specific cultural phenomena or human speakers but which are not the outcome of the intentions of actors *per se*.

However, thinkers in the latter camp see the concept of 'language' as itself a tool or metaphor for understanding the marks and noises that human beings deploy to achieve their purposes but which does not itself have any underlying structure or 'existence'. Thus, **Derrida** undermines the notion of the stable structures of language. Meaning, it is argued, cannot be confined to single words, sentences or particular texts but is the outcome of relationships between texts, that is, intertextuality. For Derrida, meaning can never be 'fixed', rather words carry multiple meanings including the echoes or traces of meanings from related words in different contexts.

This instability of meaning is only a 'problem' if we think that there is something called language whose job it is to originate a fixed entity called 'representational meaning'. If we think of language as constituted by the use of marks and noises that have temporarily stabilized uses related to the achievement of purposes, then words 'mean' what we use them to do in the context of social practice. The endless play of signification that Derrida explores is regulated and partially stabilized through pragmatic narratives and social action so that the meaning of any given word is stabilized by social knowledge of what it is used for, when, under what circumstances and so forth.

Within cultural studies this stress on language as a practice derives from both **Bakhtin** and **Wittgenstein**. For the latter, language is not best understood as a metaphysical presence nor a coherent system but as a tool used by human animals to coordinate their actions in the context of social relationships. The meaning of a word lies in its use by living human beings in the context of a specific form of life. Signification does not occur in a separate domain from other practices and all practices signify. Meaning is the product of the indistinguishability of signs and social practice. The metaphor of the 'tool' captures the idea that we do things with language. That said, the concept of 'using a tool' should not be read as implying the intentionality of a pre-existent subject. Rather, 'use' is acquired through our acculturation and habituation into social practices and their associated justifications.

Links **Anti-essentialism, dialogic, discourse, holism, language-game, meaning, poststructuralism, pragmatism, representation, semiotics, signs, structuralism**

Language-game The concept of a language-game is strongly associated with the ordinary language philosophy of the 'later' **Wittgenstein**, for whom the meaning of words derives from their usage in a complex network of relationships between signs, and not from some essential characteristic or referent. Thus meaning is contextual and relational; it depends on the relationships between words that have 'family resemblances' and on specific utterances in the context of pragmatic narratives.

Wittgenstein argues that seeking out universal theoretical explanations for language is not a useful way to proceed. Language is not a metaphysical presence or structure but a tool used by human animals to coordinate their actions in the context of social relationships. Thus the meaning of a word is said to be its use in the language, so what matters is the particular circumstances under which a word or sentence is actually used. Hence for Wittgenstein, a meaningful expression is one that can be given a use by living human beings as a form of life.

The anti-essentialism at the core of the concept of the language-game is apparent in Wittgenstein's discussion of the word 'game' itself. Thus, the meaning of the word 'game' does not derive from some special or essential characteristic of a game but through a complex network of relationships and characteristics only some of which are ever present in a specific game. Hence, games are constituted by a set of 'family resemblances'. Members of a family may share characteristics with one another without necessarily sharing any specific feature in common. In this sense the word game is relational; the meaning of card-game depends on its relations to board-game and ball-game.

Nevertheless, as Wittgenstein argues, when it comes to explaining the word game to others we are likely to show them different games and to say this is what games are. In a sense, to know what games are is to be able to play games. Thus, while language-games are rule-bound activities, those rules are not abstract components of language (as in structuralism) but *constitutive rules*, rules that are such by dint of their enactment in social practice. The rules of language constitute our pragmatic understandings of 'how to go on' in society.

One of the better known 'uses' of Wittgenstein's concept of the language-game within cultural studies is that of the postmodern philosopher **Lyotard**. He argues that Wittgenstein has shown that there is no unity of language and that languages are untranslatable and incommensurable. From this follows the celebration of difference and 'local' knowledge regimes. However, **Rorty**, who is also influenced by Wittgenstein, argues that we should see language as a practice that utilizes skills so that, though exact translation of languages is not feasible, we can learn the skills of language to make cross-cultural communication pragmatically possible.

There are similarities between the concept of différance in the writings of **Derrida** and that of language-game in the work of Wittgenstein. For example, both writers stress the non-representational character of language, the arbitrary relationship between signs and referents and the contextual character of truth. However, Wittgenstein more than Derrida underlines the pragmatic and social character of language. While meaning may formally proliferate in the rarefied world of texts, this is not so in social practice where meaning is regulated and stabilized for pragmatic purposes.

Links **Anti-essentialism, deconstruction, language, meaning, pragmatism, signs**

Liberalism Classical Liberal philosophy is founded on the work of John Locke and J.S. Mill and involves consideration of the principles of individual freedom of action and an equality of rights. Here the purpose of government is to protect individual liberty while not itself transgressing that freedom. Thus Liberalism addresses what it sees as the inherent tension between the spheres of liberty and authority, between individual freedom of thought and collective opinion. Thus Liberalism is a political and cultural philosophy concerned with the balancing act between individual freedom and the reduction of suffering through community action.

For Liberals, a 'better' culture is often taken to be one that fosters individuality and individual freedom provided that this does not violate the freedom and rights of others. Thus in the more contemporary formulations of Rawls and **Rorty**, Liberalism is also connected to notions of cultural pluralism, diversity and justice. Here the hope of Liberalism is to find ways for human beings to be freer, less cruel, more leisured and richer in goods and experiences while trying to maximize people's opportunities to live their lives as they see fit. That is, to pursue a private project founded on their own values and beliefs while not causing suffering to others.

Within the domain of cultural studies writers have demonstrated a range of attitudes towards Liberalism. Thus Marxism is generally opposed to the political views of Liberalism on the grounds that a stress on individuality is an ideological obscuring of the collective grounds of inequality and injustice. That is, the inequalities generated by structures of capitalist society are such that the vast majority of individuals cannot be free. Here social inequality is understood to be to the detriment of equal citizenship and thus capitalism is argued to be in conflict with the central concern of Liberalism to treat all persons as free and equal. On the other hand, Liberals have criticized Marxism for its tendency towards epistemological authoritarianism and political totalitarianism.

Critics influenced by poststructuralism have been critical of the humanism that they see as inherent to the Liberal stress on individuality. While such a reading of Locke and Mill is entirely plausible, it is not valid in relation to Rorty, who explicitly adopts the idea of the fragmented self. For Rorty, one cannot *have* an identity; rather one *is* a centreless weave of beliefs, attitudes and identifications. The fact that one might describe subjects as fragmented and acculturated for analytic purposes does not for him negate the agency and culturally ascribed individuality that Liberalism deploys nor the usefulness of Liberalism as a political and cultural philosophy. Rorty is saying that Liberalism is a culturally specific rather than universal way of looking at the world that happens to be the best option currently available. In other words, a commitment to liberal democracy has no universal foundation that is grounded in a philosophical account of human nature etc. – nor does it need one.

Liberalism appears to be compatible with the stress on diversity and difference within postmodernism. The postmodern conception of the public sphere as involving diversity and the desirability of multiple 'publics' while working to reduce social inequality is entirely harmonious with Liberalism. Similarly, the post-Marxist project of 'radical democracy' seeks to appropriate and extend key principles of the liberal democratic polity. The values of justice, tolerance, solidarity and difference, formed on the historically contingent grounds of a Western democratic political tradition, are those which drive **Laclau** and Mouffe's vision with its stress on equality, non-discrimination and self-management.

A commitment to Liberalism does not mean that any particular institution of liberal democracy could not be reformed or that any specific cultural and political direction could not be improved on. Thus, it is entirely acceptable to Liberals to critique those aspects of our societies and cultures that restrict freedoms and cause suffering. As such, cultural studies could be understood as a critical wing of liberal societies drawing attention to the continuation of suffering without rejecting the fundamental viability of liberal democracy. However, those schooled in Marxism, and to some degree poststructuralism, and who tend to envisage a more revolutionary overthrow of the institutions and practices of liberal societies would disagree. They would see cultural studies as a more radical and marginalized project with more far-reaching revolutionary implications.

Links **Citizenship, humanism, Marxism, post-Marxism, poststructuralism, pragmatism**

Life-politics Life-politics is concerned with reflexivity, self-actualization, choice and lifestyle in pursuit of qualitatively better ways to live. Life-politics revolves around the creation of justifiable forms of life involving less emphasis on economic accumulation and more on the need to re-moralize social life and adopt new lifestyles. The account given below is essentially that of Anthony **Giddens** in the early 1990s.

The 'emancipatory' politics of modernity is concerned with liberation from the constraints that limit life-chances. That is, 'emancipatory' politics directs its attention to the exploitative relations of class and the freeing of social life from the fixities of tradition. This includes an ethics of justice, equality and participation. In contrast, given a degree of release from material deprivation, 'life-politics' is more concerned with self-actualization, choice and lifestyle. Life-politics revolves around the creation of justifiable forms of life that will promote self-actualization in a global context. They are centred on the ethics of 'How shall we live?'.

The more we 'make ourselves', the more the questions of 'what a person is' and 'who I want to be' are raised. This takes place in the context of global circumstances that no one can escape. For example, the recognition of the finite character of global resources and the limits of science and technology may lead to a de-emphasis on economic accumulation and to the need to adopt new lifestyles. Likewise, developments in biological science lead us to ask questions about how to understand the nature of life, the rights of the unborn, and the ethics of genetic research.

Links **Cultural politics, identity, identity politics, New Social Movements, politics**

Logocentricism The concept of logocentricism entered the vocabulary of cultural studies courtesy of **Derrida**, who critiques its pre-eminence within Western philosophy. By logocentricism Derrida means the reliance on fixed *a priori* transcendental meanings. That is, universal meanings, concepts and forms of logic that exist within human reason before any other kinds of thinking can occur. This would include a universal conception of reason or beauty. The idea is closely tied to the notion of phonocentrism by which Derrida means the priority given to sounds and speech over writing in explaining the generation of meaning. This is so because it is in the directness of speech rather than in the metaphorical nature of writing that Western philosophy is said by Derrida to find transcendental meaning.

According to Derrida, Socrates held speech to come directly from the heart of truth and the self whereas writing was regarded as a form of sophistry and rhetoric. For Derrida this signals Socrates' attempt to find wisdom and truth through reason unmediated by signification. That is, the priority given to speech as a form of unmediated meaning is the search for a universal transcendental truth that grounds itself. The idea that there is direct access to truth and stable meaning is untenable because in representing a truth that 'exists' outside of representation one must be re-representing it. That is, there can be no truth or meaning outside of representation. There is nothing but signs and writing is a permanent trace that exists *always already* before perception is aware or conscious of itself. Thus, Derrida deconstructs the idea that speech provides an identity between signs and meaning.

This argument is a part of the wider anti-representationalist point that signs do

112

not possess clear and fixed meanings. For example, in his discussion of the opposition between nature and culture Derrida points out that nature is already a concept in language (that is, culture) and not a pure state of being beyond signs. Likewise, while Christianity claims to be based on the transcendental truth of the word of God, that word is available only through the unstable signs of writing, that is, through the Bible. Ultimately, Derrida argues, literal meaning is always already underpinned by metaphor – its apparent opposite.

Links **Deconstruction, meaning, poststructuralism, representation, truth, writing**

Lyotard, Jean-François (1924–1998) The French-born thinker Jean-François Lyotard was Professor of Philosophy at the Universities of Paris – vii and California, Irvine. His early thinking was within the bounds of Marxism but he later broke away from it and gained international recognition for his theorizing of the postmodern condition. For Lyotard, the postmodern condition is not a historical epoch or a set of institutional parameters but rather the condition of knowledge of post-industrial societies. While modern knowledge rests on its appeal to grand narratives, the postmodern condition involves an 'incredulity toward metanarratives' and embraces local, plural and heterogeneous knowledges that are specific to language-games. Lyotard also addresses the implications of this for notions of justice through the concept of a 'differend', that is, a conflict between parties where there is no common ground of arbitration.

- **Associated concepts** Epistemology, foundationalism (anti-), grand narrative, irony, language-game, post-industrial society.
- **Tradition(s)** Marxism, postmodernism.
- **Reading** Lyotard, J-F. (1984) *The Postmodern Condition.* Minneapolis, MN: University of Minnesota Press.

M

Marx, Karl (1818–1883) Karl Marx was a German philosopher, economist and revolutionary of Jewish lineage whose work spawned Marxism as a stream of thought. The key influences on his work were German philosophy, notably that of Hegel, and English political economy, including the writings of Adam Smith. Marx is most closely associated with an analysis of capitalism as a class-based system of exploitation and the need to transcend it with an egalitarian socialist/communist society. Marx argued in favour of a philosophy of historical materialism that could grasp the historical specificity of human affairs in the context of the material conditions of existence. Thus human consciousness and culture were to be explained in the context of the primary influence of economic and class structures.

- **Associated concepts** Alienation, base and superstructure, capitalism, class, commodification, cultural materialism, ideology, political economy.
- **Tradition(s)** Marxism.
- **Reading** Marx, K. (1954) *Capital, Vols* 1–3. London: Lawrence and Wishart.

Marxism Marxism can make a strong claim to being the most important theoretical paradigm within cultural studies at the moment of its institutional foundation though its pre-eminence has arguably been superseded by that of poststructuralism. Cultural studies writers have had a long, ambiguous but productive relationship with Marxism so that, while cultural studies is not a Marxist domain *per se,* it has drawn succour from it while also subjecting it to critique. Indeed, many of the leading figures associated with the 'origins' of cultural studies – **Williams**, Thompson, **Hall** – all engaged with Marxism as an economic, social, cultural and political theory of immense importance. Stuart Hall, perhaps the most significant figure in contemporary cultural studies, still makes claims to be 'a Marxist' though post-Marxism is perhaps a more prudent designation.

As its name implies, Marxism is a body of though derived from the work of Karl **Marx** which dates from the mid-nineteenth century and stresses the determining role of the material conditions of existence, the development and dynamics of capitalism and the historical specificity of human affairs. The central place of class conflict in Marxist theory and the promise of a classless society supply Marxism with its claim to be an emancipatory philosophy of social equality. Marxism is, above all, a form of historical materialism that stresses the changeable character of social formations whose core features are located in the material conditions of existence.

Marx argued that the first priority of human beings is the production of their means of subsistence through labour power and the use of tools. Thus the means of production (tools), and the relations of production constituted by the social organization of labour, form a mode of production, which is a central category of Marxism. The organization of a mode of production is not simply a matter of coordinating objects, rather, it is inherently tied up with relations between people which, while social, that is, cooperative and coordinated, are also matters of power and conflict. Marxists regard social antagonisms, which are an intrinsic part of a mode of production, as the motor of historical change. Further, given the priority accorded to production, other aspects of human relations, for example, consciousness, culture, and politics are said to be structured by economic relations.

For Marxism, history is not a smooth evolutionary process but is marked by significant breaks and discontinuities. Thus, Marx discusses the transformations from an ancient mode of production to a feudal mode of production and thence to the capitalist mode of production. Different forms of material organization and different social relations characterize a mode of production and each is superseded by another as internal contradictions, particularly those of class conflict, lead to its transformation and replacement.

The centrepiece of Marx's work was an analysis of the dynamics of capitalism, a mode of production premised on the private ownership of the means of production. The fundamental class division of capitalism is between those who own the means of production, the bourgeoisie, and those who, being a propertyless proletariat, must sell their labour to survive. The central driving force of capitalism is the endless search for profit that is achieved through the extraction of surplus value from the workforce. The realization of surplus value in monetary form is achieved by the selling of goods as commodities. By commodity fetishism Marx means that the surface appearance of goods sold in the market place obscures the origins of those commodities in an exploitative relationship. At the same time, the fact that workers are faced with the products of their own labour that are now separated from them means that they are alienated from the core human activity of labour and indeed from themselves.

Capitalism is a dynamic system whose profit-driven mechanisms lead to the continual revolutionizing of the means of production and the forging of new markets. Indeed, for Marx this was its great merit in relation to feudalism. However, the mechanisms of capitalism also lead to perennial crises and ultimately, or so Marx argued, to its superseding by socialism. Notably, Marx hoped that capitalism would be rift asunder by class conflict with the proletariat's organizations of defence, trade unions and political parties, overthrowing and replacing it with a mode of production based on communal ownership, equitable distribution and ultimately the end of class division.

For Marxism, culture is a material force tied into the socially organized production of the conditions of human existence and refers to the forms assumed by social existence under determinate historical conditions. This idea is expressed in the metaphor of the base and the superstructure wherein the cultural superstructure is shaped or determined by the organization of the economic mode of production. This is a form of cultural materialism. Amongst the criticisms of Marxism to have emerged are:

- The apparent teleology intrinsic to it, that is, the positing of an inevitable point to which history is moving (that is, the demise of capitalism and the arrival of a classless society).
- The determinism and reductionism inherent in some readings of Marxism by which culture is to be explained by reference to the workings of the economy.
- The apparent success of capitalism, not merely its survival but its transformation and expansion.
- The failure of proletarian revolutions to occur on a widespread scale and to generate classless societies where they have transpired.

Links **Base and superstructure, capitalism, class, cultural materialism, ideology, post-Marxism, reductionism**

Masculinity An identity category that refers to the cultural characteristics associated with being a man. That is, masculinity is a discursive-performative construction that describes and disciplines the cultural meaning of being a man. Masculinity is not an essential quality of embodied subjects but a matter of representation, that is, masculinity is constituted by ways of speaking about and disciplining bodies. As such, masculinity is a site of continual political struggle over meaning in the context of multiple modes of being a man.

In Western culture the current period may be the first time in which some men are seeing themselves as possessing a problematic 'masculinity'. The sense that masculinity is not an unchanging given of nature has sparked a growing research interest into men and masculinity. This work has focused on cultural representations of men and masculinity, the character of men's lives as they experience them and the problems that men face in contemporary culture. Traditional masculinity has encompassed the values of strength, power, stoicism, action, control, independence, self-sufficiency, camaraderie and work amongst others. Devalued were relationships, verbal ability, domestic life, tenderness, communication, women and children. In particular, the contemporary male concern with metaphors of reason, control and distance is an instantiation of wider discourses of masculinity circulated in the context of modernity.

These traditional values of masculinity may no longer be serving men well and a number of critics now talk about a 'crisis of masculinity'. A very substantial number of men in the West are at some point in their lives implicated in depression, suicide, alcoholism, drug abuse, violence and crime. Some of the problems men face can be understood to be an outcome of the incompatibility between ascendant notions of masculinity and that which is required to live contentedly in the contemporary social world. It has been argued that the central problems of men's lives are rooted in the adoption of impossible images of masculinity that men try, but fail, to live up to.

Links **Identity, femininity, gender, men's movement, representation, sex, subjectivity**

Mass culture Mass culture is a pejorative term developed by both conservative literary critics and Marxist theorists from the 1930s onwards to suggest the inferiority of commodity-based capitalist culture as being inauthentic, manipulative and unsatisfying. This inauthentic mass culture is contrasted to the authenticity claimed for high culture (as well as to an imagined people's culture). In this context high culture is understood to be the peak of civilization and the concern of an educated minority. Further, both the authentic culture of the people and the minority culture of the educated elite are said to have been lost to the standardization processes of industrialized 'mass culture'.

For traditional cultural and literary criticism the romantic idea of the 'artistic object', produced by the 'artistic soul', is allied to a sense of the complexity and authenticity of the work of art. It is argued that the quality work is distinctive in the subtlety, complexity and adequacy of its formal expression of content. This in turn requires the necessary skills and work by readers in order to access a genuine aesthetic experience. By contrast, mass culture is seen as superficial and unsatisfying as a consequence of both its formal inadequacy and its production by capitalist corporations seeking to maximize their profits by selling to the lowest common denominator. Thus, 'mass culture' is held to be inauthentic because it is not produced by 'the people', manipulative because its primary purpose is to be purchased and unsatisfying because it requires little work to consume and thus fails to enrich its consumers.

These are the views of conservative critics like F.R. Leavis but they are not dissimilar from those of the Marxist-inspired Frankfurt School on this issue. Thus, **Adorno** and Horkheimer coined the term 'the culture industry' to suggest that culture is now a production of capitalist corporations who produce commodities that purport to be democratic, individualistic and diversified, but are in actuality authoritarian, conformist and highly standardized. Thus mass culture is mass deception. This involves not just 'meanings' but the structuring of the human psyche into the conformist ways of the 'authoritarian personality'.

On the whole, cultural studies has argued against seeing culture as 'mass culture' and has adopted the more sympathetic concept of 'popular culture'. This is in part because the judgements of quality on which the idea of mass culture is founded are derived from an institutionalized and class-based hierarchy of cultural taste. Indeed, judgements about aesthetic quality are always open to contestation so that universal evaluations are not sustainable. The concepts of beauty, harmony, form and quality can be applied as much to a machine as to a novel or a painting and are thus culturally relative. Elite cultural critics have commonly by-passed popular cultural forms for social as much as 'creative' reasons.

Rather than be in the business of aesthetic judgement, cultural studies has tended to develop arguments that revolve around the social and political consequences of constructing and disseminating specific discursive constructions of the world. Nevertheless, the relativity of 'value' within cultural studies leads to a dilemma. On the one hand, there is a desire to legitimize popular and non-Western culture as valuable in the face of a traditional Western high cultural aesthetic disdain. On the other hand, there is a reluctance to sanction a position in which we are disbarred from making judgements about the products of the culture industries. Of course, cultural studies does make value judgements about cultural products. However, these conclusions tend to be based on political rather than aesthetic criteria.

The critics of mass culture tend to over-emphasize aesthetics and the internal construction of cultural products assuming audience reaction from an analysis of texts. This is a position challenged by cultural studies research into cultural consumption which argues that meanings are produced, altered and managed at the level of use by people who are active producers of meaning. That is, rather than being inherent in the commodity, meaning and value are constructed through actual usage. In general, critics who stress the production of culture talk of 'mass culture' while writers who stress consumption prefer to call it 'popular culture'.

Links **Commodification, common culture, consumption, culture industry, popular culture**

Mass media The mass media are those institutions of communication such as newspapers, magazines, television and the film industry that produce and distribute texts on a large scale in the context of capitalist modernity. The functions of the mass media might be seen as those of providing information, entertainment and education. In general the mass media can be understood in terms of texts (e.g. programmes), the relationship between texts and audiences (audience research), political economy (organizations/industry) and the wider patterns of cultural meaning that they contribute to and are constituted by.

The mass media are at the centre of public life and culture within contemporary Western societies. Indeed, the public sphere is now arguably a media-saturated one in which the visual has gained in prominence over the verbal and mediated relationships are more conspicuous than face-to-face encounters. In this mediated sphere, not only does 'the public' enter the domestic sphere via the television set but also the boundaries between the public and privates spheres are blurred. The mass media are implicated in the selective provision of social knowledge and imagery through which we grasp our own world as well as that of others and as such are a significant global resource for the construction of identity.

Cultural studies has paid particular attention to the 'ideologies' constructed and disseminated by the mass media and their role in the fabrication of cultural hegemony. However, it has also been argued that mass media texts are polysemic, that is, they contain many meanings that audiences can explore as active producers of significance. Thus, the identification of ideology in texts is no guarantee that they will be taken up by readers. Nor is the significance of the mass media confined to textual meanings for it is situated and sustained within the activities of everyday life and thus contributes to our cultural patterns of time, space and routine.

The first sociological studies of the mass media were in the context of 'mass society theory' of the 1930s to 1950s and attributed a large degree of unwholesome power to the media. Here the prefix 'mass' is a pejorative one in line with the negative characteristics attached to the idea of 'mass culture'. The mass media were seen as catering to the lowest common denominator of standards in pursuit of ratings maximization while the audience was understood to be a mass of passive recipients of media messages. However, this view has been continuously modified over the years, first by the 'uses and gratification' approach that explored the various uses that audiences had for the media and later, in the context of cultural studies, by the active audience paradigm which emerged during the 1980s. In both cases there is less stress on the power of the media to affect the audience and more on the way in which the media are a resource for audience members in the manufacture of meaning.

Links **Active audience, circuit of culture, ideology, mass culture, polysemy, television, text**

McRobbie, Angela (1951–) A former postgraduate student at the Birmingham **Centre for Contemporary Cultural Studies** (CCCS), Angela McRobbie is currently Professor of Communications at Goldsmiths' College, University of London. Her early research work on the relationship between teenage girls and magazines in the 1970s involved textual analysis and a fairly straightforward model of how ideology is absorbed by readers. She later produced sophisticated readings of magazines for women and girls that put a greater stress on their active meaning-making and consuming practices. In that sense her work has epitomized the broader trajectory of cultural studies as it has moved from a central concern with ideology in the tradition of **Gramsci**, to an engagement with consuming practices and postmodernism. More recently she explored many other areas of contemporary culture including fashion, modern art and pop music.

- **Associated concepts** Bricolage, consumption, gender, hegemony, ideology, youth culture.
- **Tradition(s)** Cultural studies, feminism, post-feminism, post-Marxism, postmodernism.
- **Reading** McRobbie, A. (1991) *Feminism and Youth Culture*. London: Macmillan.

Meaning The idea of meaning is an important one to cultural studies in so far as the concept of culture is based on the notions of 'maps of meaning' and shared or contested meaning. Indeed, cultural studies' particular take on the concept of culture has stressed the intersection of power and meaning. Thus key ideas such as ideology, hegemony and discourse depend on some notion of meaning.

The problems begin with the idea of meaning when one asks the obvious question, what does meaning mean? Or, to put it another way, where does meaning reside? For some purposes a simple everyday language-use answer will be sufficient. That is, meaning lies in the attitudes, beliefs, purposes, justifications and reasons deployed by people in day-to-day life. Meaning indicates that something matters to us; hence signification is to do with significance. As such, meaning guides our actions or more often is a *post hoc* explanation and justification for them. However, this style of answer may not satisfy a more philosophical form of inquiry since all the crucial concepts being deployed in such an explanation – attitude, belief, purpose, etc. – are subject to deconstruction by asking the question, what does belief, attitude, purpose etc. mean?

The source of the problem lies in the implicit assumption that words derive meaning by reference to items in an independent object world. That is, the meaning of the word chair derives from an object that contains the essence of chair or that the word love refers to an identifiable quality that is essential love or that meaning is a thing that is represented by the sign 'meaning'. Philosophically speaking, this form of explanation is known as nomenclaturism whose basic idea is that the meaning of a name is the object that it stands for. To ask the question 'what does meaning mean' indicates the absurdity and non-workability of nomenclaturism since the essence of meaning – what meaning means – cannot be found.

Cultural studies has adopted, at least ostensibly, anti-essentialist theories of language that are designated with terms like 'holism' and 'nominalism'. Linguistic holism suggests that the meaning of words depends on their place in the entire whole of language or at least on their place in a specific language-game. Likewise, nominalism argues that concepts cannot be conceived as having 'existence' in the way that objects do but are instead part of a system of names whose significance lies in the relations between themselves.

The most influential theories of meaning within cultural studies have been those of **Saussure** (structuralism) and **Derrida** (poststructuralism) and to some extent **Wittgenstein** and **Bakhtin**. Both Saussure and Derrida hold that meaning is generated through the differences between signs rather than by reference to objects. However, structuralism is concerned with the stable 'systems of relations' that form an underlying structure of sign systems and the grammar that makes meaning possible. By contrast, Derrida undermines the notion of the stable structures of language when he argues that meaning cannot be confined to single words, sentences or particular texts but is the outcome of relationships between texts, that is, intertextuality.

For Derrida, meaning can never be 'fixed', but rather is continually supplemented by other words including the echoes or traces of meanings from related words in different contexts. For Derrida, there is no original meaning circulating outside of 'representation', that is, there is no primary source of signification and no self-present transparent meaning. Rather, meaning slides down a chain of signifiers abolishing a stable signified. Thus does Derrida seek to expose the undecidability of meaning.

For Wittgenstein the 'undecidability' of meaning is put in the context of the pragmatic activities of human beings. He argues that language is best understood as a tool used by human animals to coordinate their actions in the context of social relationships. For Wittgenstein meaning is not a matter of 'representationalism' (i.e. the assumption that words mirror objects) but rather the *use* of words in the context of a language-game. Thus, a meaningful expression is one that can be given a use by living human beings and the rules of language constitute our pragmatic understandings of 'how to go on' in society. Here, to ask what meaning means is like asking 'how big is the colour blue'? It makes no sense. Instead we must inquire about the complex of uses to which we put the word meaning.

Links **Culture, deconstruction, dialogic, language-game, poststructuralism, representation, semiotics, structuralism**

Meme The idea of a meme was originally coined by the evolutionary biologist Richard Dawkins in the 1970s to act as a conceptual bridge between genetic theory and cultural theory. Subsequently the term has been taken up widely by other writers and one can now reasonably talk about 'meme theory'. A meme is said to be the smallest cultural element that is replicated by means of the human capacity for imitation. Memes are cultural instructions for carrying out behaviour stored in the brain and passed on through being copied. Human consciousness itself is a product of memes so that each of us can be described as a massive memeplex (group of memes) running on the physical machinery of the human brain. The broad implication of meme theory is that cultural change takes place as a consequence of memes doing their own thing independently of human 'will'.

Examples of memes would include the wheel, the alphabet, particular tunes or musical phrases, clothing fashions, books and ideas like 'God is dead'. The reproduction of a particular meme is not necessarily best for human beings, rather, memes are replicated simply because they can be. That is, a successful meme is one that is continuously imitated. This reproduction is advantageous to memes rather than to human beings *per se*. Memes replicate independently of genes so that meme theory is not best understood as a form of genetic reductionism. The general development of language and our capacity for endless talk may be an outcome of the explosion of memes rather than of biological advantage. This suggests that the massive expansion of the human brain was the outcome of meme replication and is an example of meme–gene co-evolution.

There are more memes than there are host brain processing power and retention capacity so that memetic selection must be taking place. The reason why some memes succeed and others fail is a consequence of the properties of our sensory systems and mechanisms of attention. That is, the most significant single element determining which memes proliferate lies in the parameters set by our evolved psychological mechanisms. This explains why some ideas, practices and emotional states, and not others, are passed from generation to generation and neighbour to neighbour. The more ways there are to spread memes, and the faster they can go, the less constrained they will be by genes. The development of mass communications on a global scale, from the printing press through television and on to the Internet, has been a major contemporary mechanism for this process.

Links **Culture, determinism, discourse, evolutionary psychology, language**

Men's movement Since the 1970s there has been an identifiable 'men's movement', albeit one that operates on a fairly limited scale. The initial perspective of this movement was as a sympathetic counterpart to feminism, indeed, one aspect of the movement was a self-effacing wish to make amends to women. Another trend was fuelled by the psychotherapeutic idea of 'working-on-oneself' to become a better person. However, by the 1990s a trend had emerged in the movement that was less sympathetic to feminism so that men were urged to 'get in touch' with a lost masculinity that was more vital than the 'softer' feminized man of the contemporary world.

Robert Bly's 'mytho-poetic' reading of this 'lost masculinity' puts a lot of stress on initiation rites and myths that express the male journey away from the mother towards male identity. However, despite his nostalgia, Bly continues to have some sympathy for feminism. Other writers have been somewhat more antagonistic and have sought to reassert traditional masculine roles. Of particular concern to them has been the loss of the traditional place of the father and their grievances regarding the role of the courts in child custody and maintenance payment issues. They bemoan what they see as an emergent matriarchy and reassert the need for traditional masculinity.

The differences of analysis and prescription put forward by various men suggest that there is no coherent and identifiable men's movement as such. Rather there are a series of overlapping groups, ideas, themes and practices that form a heterogeneous 'men's movement' rather in the manner of set theory or a language-game. In this the men's movement has characteristics in common with New Social Movements. There is no doubt that men and boys are facing significant personal and cultural problems at this moment in history. However, the countercultural model of confrontation that revolved around an 'enemy' that could be identified and defeated is unlikely to be successful. Rather, men need to find new ways to be human that bestow masculinity as a side effect of doing and living in a manner that brings respect, esteem and self-worth.

Links **Cultural politics, feminism, gender, masculinity, New Social Movements**

Metaphor The concept of metaphor is derived from the Greek word *metaphora* that means 'transfer' or 'carry over'. Thus, in general terms, a metaphor involves the application of a signifier to a referent to which it does not normally or literally apply. Thus a metaphor entails the replacement of one signifier by another. For example, the idea of the Panopticon in the work of **Foucault** acts as a metaphor for a continuous, anonymous and all-pervading power and surveillance operating at all levels of social organization. Or we might consider understanding 'culture' as 'like a language', 'conversation' or 'performance' as examples of metaphor in use.

However, this use of the concept of the metaphor implies a valid distinction between metaphorical and literal meaning. This is something denied by a number of philosophers of language who have been influential within cultural studies; namely, Nietzsche, **Foucault**, **Wittgenstein**, **Derrida** and **Rorty**. Thus Nietzsche, in rejecting the idea of an objective and universal knowledge, famously described truth as a 'mobile army of metaphors and metonyms'. Here the idea of a 'literal truth' is displaced by understanding the distinction between metaphor and literal meaning to be one of time and use so that literal meanings are simply metaphors that have become naturalized (that is, so familiar that we do not see their metaphorical character).

Thus language is metaphorical 'all the way down', by which is meant that all language is metaphorical. Here truth is the literalization (or temporary fixing through social convention) of metaphors within a language-game into what Rorty calls a 'final vocabulary' – one without current challenge whose metaphoric condition is invisible to us in the normal day-to-day conduct of life. By contrast, the power and value of a new metaphor lies in its strangeness and thus in the ability to help us look at the world in new ways. Ultimately, argues Derrida, the very idea of literal meaning is based on the idea of the 'letter', that is, writing, and as such, literal meaning is always underpinned by its apparent opposite – metaphor.

Links **Language, meaning, poststructuralism, pragmatism, truth, writing**

Methodology There are two ways in which to grasp the concept of methodology. The first and technically more sound route is to understand the term as referring to the philosophical investigation of the techniques of inquiry adopted by any given discipline. As such, methodology is a branch of epistemology. However, it is common place, if somewhat misguided, to also use the term methodology to refer to the specific techniques employed by a discipline to acquire and manage data. Here, the concept is being used to refer to research methods.

The main methodological/epistemological debate within cultural studies has been between representationalism (realism) and anti-representationalism (poststructuralism, postmodernism and pragmatism). The realist argument is that a degree of certain knowledge about an independent object world (a real world) is possible even though methodological vigilance and reflexivity need to be maintained. In contrast, writers influenced by poststructuralism, postmodernism and pragmatism do not think that an objective and accurate picture of an independent object world is possible. Here, knowledge is not a question of discovering objective and accurate truth but of the construction of interpretations about the world which are 'taken to be true'.

The standard methodological distinction regarding research methods is between quantitative and qualitative approaches. That is, between, respectively, methods that centre on numbers and the counting of things (for example, statistics and surveys) and those that concentrate on the meanings generated by actors gathered through participant observation, interviews, focus groups and textual analysis. Cultural studies has not paid much attention to the classical questions of research methods but has for practical purposes favoured qualitative methods with their focus on cultural meaning. Thus, work in cultural studies has centred on three kinds of research methods:

(a) Ethnography, which has often been linked with culturalism and a stress on the investigation of 'lived experience'.
(b) A range of textual approaches which have tended to draw from semiotics, poststructuralism and deconstructionism.
(c) A series of audience reception studies which are eclectic in their theoretical roots but for whom hermeneutic theory has been of significance.

Links **Deconstruction, epistemology, ethnography, hermeneutics, signs, truth**

Mirror phase A term connected to the psychoanalytic work of **Lacan** for whom the resolution of the Oedipus complex marks the formation of the unconscious as the realm of the repressed. This establishes the very possibility of gendered subjects through entry into the symbolic order. Prior to the resolution of the Oedipus complex, infants are said to be unable to differentiate themselves from the surrounding world of objects, including other persons. Pre-Oedipal infants experience the world in terms of sensory exploration and autoeroticism so that the primary focus at this stage is the mother's breast as a source of warmth, comfort and food. This is a relationship that the child cannot control. Infants begin to regard themselves as individuated persons during what Lacan calls the 'mirror phase'. This involves identification with another person, primarily the mother, as being 'One' and/or recognition of themselves in a mirror as 'One'.

However, since **Freud** and Lacan argue that we are fragmented subjects, such recognition of wholeness is understood by them to be a form of 'misrecognition' and part of the infant's 'imaginary relations'. The staging of the mirror phase thus marks the manifestation of the *lack* that Lacan sees at the core of subjects. Specifically, this is the lack of the mother as a result of separation at the mirror phase. More generally, it is the lack that human subjects experience by virtue of the prior existence of a symbolic order that they cannot control. Here language is understood to be the symbolization of desire in a never-ending search for control that has its source at the moment of the mirror phase.

Links **Identification, Other, psychoanalysis, subjectivity, symbolic order, unconscious**

Modernism There are three primary uses of the term modernism within cultural studies: namely, (i) the cultural experience of modernity; (ii) an artistic style associated with being modern; and (iii) a philosophical position that asserts the possibility of universal knowledge.

The central cultural experience of modernism is that of change, ambiguity, doubt, risk, uncertainty and fragmentation. The social and cultural processes of individualization, differentiation, commodification, urbanization, rationalization and bureaucratization underpin these characteristics. As industry, technology and communications systems have transformed the human world at a breathless pace so they have also dissolved the certainties of tradition so that, to paraphrase **Marx**, 'All that is solid melts into air'. While such transformations hold out the promise of the end of material scarcity, they also carry dangers of alienation, disaffection and self-destruction.

The ambiguity, doubt, risk and continual change that are markers of modernism are manifested in the constitution of the self. 'Tradition' values stability and the place of persons in a normatively ordered and immutable cosmos, a firmness of parameters in which things are as they are because that is how they should be. By contrast, modernism values change, life planning and reflexivity. In the context of tradition, self-identity is primarily a question of social position, while for the modern person it is a 'reflexive project' wherein identity is not fixed but created. For modernism, the self is not a question of surface appearance but of the workings of deeper structures so that metaphors of depth predominate (e.g. the unconscious).

Faust is one of the emblematic modern figures because he was determined to make himself and his world, even at the cost of a deal with the devil. Just as Faust was a troubled, destructive and tragic figure so the poverty and squalor of industrial cities, two destructive world wars, death camps and the threat of global annihilation mark the culture of moderns. On a more optimistic note, another crucial figure of modernism is the flâneur who walks the anonymous spaces of the modern city experiencing the aesthetic pleasures of shops, displays, images and persons.

The concept of modernism also refers to the aesthetic forms associated with artistic movements dating from the nineteenth century. Key modernist figures include Joyce, Wolff, Kafka and Eliot in literature along with Picasso, Kandinsky and Miro in painting. While it would be better to talk of modernisms rather than modernism, general themes of artistic modernism include:

- Aesthetic self-consciousness.
- An interest in language and questions of representation.
- A rejection of realism in favour of an exploration of the uncertain character of the 'real'.
- A jettisoning of linear narrative structures in favour of montage and simultaneity.
- An emphasis on the value of aesthetic experience drawn from romanticism.
- An acceptance of the idea of depth and universal mytho-poetic meaning.
- The exploration and exploitation of fragmentation.
- The value and role of avant-garde high culture.

Modernism rejects the idea that it is possible to adequately represent the 'real' so that representation is not an act of mimesis or copying but an aesthetic expression or conventionalized construction of the 'real'. In the context of an uncertain and changing world, modernist literature saw its task as finding the means of expression with which to capture the 'deep reality' of cultural life. Hence the concern with the place of form, and particularly language, in constructing meaning. This is manifested in the experimental approach to aesthetic style characteristic of modernist work that seeks to express depth through fragmentation. Modernists have been interested in practices that reveal their own techniques and allow for reflection upon the processes of signification. If any one style can be said to encapsulate modernism it is the use of montage. That is, the selection and assemblage of shots or representations to form a composite of jutaxposed ideas and images that are not 'held together' by realist notions of time and motivation.

Joyce's *Ulysses* is regarded as archetypal of high modernist novels because of its stream of consciousness, non-realist, narrative style. In doing so, Joyce attempts to represent the real in new ways using language to capture the fragmented character of the self. Yet, while Joyce would have agreed with Nietzsche that 'God is dead', and that there can be no cosmic universals, there is nevertheless a sense in his work that Art can draw on, and re-configure, universal mythic-poetic meanings. Thus, a day in the life of one Dubliner is framed in terms of the universalist Ulysses of Greek myth. For their supporters, such as **Adorno**, the modernist works of Kafka, Beckett and Schoenberg are amongst the most radical of art forms. In particular, it is the 'negativity' of modernism, its refusal to be incorporated by the dominant language of contemporary culture, which allows it to stand as a beacon of hope and a symbol of non-accommodation.

As a philosophy of knowledge, modernism has been associated with an emancipatory project through which Enlightenment reason would lead to certain and universal truths that would lay the foundations for humanity's path of progress. That is, Enlightenment philosophy and the theoretical discourses of modernity have confidence in reason and modern science to find the truth that heralds progress. Yet, modernism is ambiguous for it is far from clear that science does proceed through laws of certainty. Thus, for Popper science proceeds through experimentation and the principle of falsification; the Einsteinian paradigm which predominates in contemporary science is one of relativity and Kuhn has explored the way in which science periodically overthrows its own paradigms. Consequently, modern science can be understood as premised on the methodological principle of doubt and the chronic revision of knowledge. Enlightenment science may have begun with the search for certain laws but it is now beset with doubt and chaos.

125

Links **Aesthetics, avant-garde, Enlightenment, flâneur, modernity, paradigm, postmodernism, truth**

Modernity Modernity can be understood as a post-traditional historical period marked by industrialism, capitalism, the nation-state and increasingly sophisticated forms of social surveillance. The institutions of modernity are said by **Giddens** to consist of capitalism, industrialism, military power (of the nation-state) and surveillance. The institutions of modernity are inherently dynamic and expansionist.

Britain was transformed by the *industrial* revolution from a pre-industrial society with low productivity and zero growth rates into a society with high productivity and increased growth. Between 1780 and 1840 there were significant changes to British economy and society, including a shift from domestic production for immediate use to mass consumer goods production for exchange, and from simple family-centred production to a strict impersonal division of labour deploying capital equipment. The population trebled and the value of economic activity quadrupled. Changes also occurred in personal, social and political life, including alterations in working habits, time organization, family life, leisure activity, housing and the shift from rural to urban living.

The industrial organizations of modernity have been organized along *capitalist* lines, a mode of production premised on the private ownership of property and the pursuit of profit. In the *Communist Manifesto*, first published in 1848, **Marx** characterized the processes of inquiry and innovation that marked capitalist modernity as involving the subjection of nature to the forces of man and machine. Subsequently, the productive dynamism of capitalism has spawned not just coal but nuclear power, not just trains but rockets, not just filing cabinets but computers and e-mail. Capitalism is restless in its search for new markets, new raw materials and new sources of profit and capital accumulation.

The emergence of an industrial labour process included an increase in the size and division of labour, mechanization and the intensification of work. The workshop and factory were utilized as a means of exerting discipline and the creation of new work habits. That is, they marked new forms of *surveillance*, a concept that refers to the collection, storage and retrieval of information, the direct supervision of activities and the use of information to monitor subject populations. Though surveillance is not the invention of modernity *per se*, it did introduce new, more complex and extensive forms including a shift from personal to impersonal control so that bureaucratization, rationalization and professionalization become core institutional configurations of modernity.

Today we understand the world as divided into discrete nation-states. However, the *nation-state* is a relatively recent modern contrivance which most of the human species has not participated nor identified with. The modern nation-state is a political apparatus recognized to have sovereign rights within the borders of a demarcated territorial area and possessing the ability to back these claims with military power within the context of a world-wide nation-state system. The state specializes in the maintenance of order through the rule of law and the monopoly of legitimate violence. The combination of state military power, political ambition and the emotional investments of national identity have underpinned modern twentieth-century warfare that is now fought with industrialized modern armies. Thus soldiers are trained, disciplined and bureaucratized and arms are produced in factories owned by capitalist corporations engaging in international arms trading.

Links **Capitalism, globalization, modernism, nation-state, postmodernity, surveillance**

Moral panic The concept of a moral panic came into the cultural studies vocabulary in the early 1970s through its engagement with deviancy theory and the investigation of youth subcultures. A moral panic is a social process by which the media latch onto a culturally identified group and label their behaviour as troublesome and likely to re-occur. The groups so labelled have been characterized as contemporary 'folk devils'. The public response to the new witchcraft is a moral panic that involves the tracking down and punishment of the deviant culture. The recipients of a moral panic, for example the more visible and spectacular youth cultures including Mods, Punks and Skinheads, respond with increased deviancy so that a cycle of labelling, amplification and deviancy is set in motion.

In this model it is assumed that the media work on previously existing subcultural activities where youth cultures are held to exist in authentic distinct and pristine form prior to media intervention. That is, subculture theory perceived youth culture to be 'outside' of the media and opposed to it. In contrast, many contemporary theorists suggest that youth cultures are always 'inside' the media and even are dependent on it. Thus, while studies of 'moral panics' tend to position youth cultures as innocent victims of negative stigmatization, media 'misunderstanding' can be an objective of subcultural industries where 'moral panic' can act as a form of marketing hype.

Hall and others applied the concept of a 'moral panic' to the British press treatment of street robbery. These authors explore the articulation of 'mugging' with race and the alleged black threat to law, order and the British way of life. Specifically, they give an account of the political, economic, ideological and racial crisis of Britain that formed the context of the moral panic and explicate the argument that the moral panic around mugging facilitated the move into the 'exceptional state' of an authoritarian 'law and order' society.

Links **Mass media, New Social Movements, race, subculture, youth culture**

Morley, David (1949–) Currently a Professor at Goldsmiths College, University of London, and a former member of the Birmingham **Centre for Contemporary Cultural Studies**, Morley was a key figure in the development of the 'active audience' paradigm within cultural studies. His early work on television audiences during the 1980s combined a theoretical justification of ethnographic methods with empirical studies of audience readings within the broad parameters of an encoding–decoding model. Within this context he also developed work relating to the gendered character of television viewing and the linkages between globalizing media and cultural identity. In addition, Morley's writing contains a long-running concern with the absorption of technology into everyday cultural life.

- **Associated concepts** Active audience, consumption, encoding–decoding, gender, ideology, television.
- **Tradition(s)** Cultural studies, ethnography, hermeneutics, Marxism.
- **Reading** Morley, D. (1992) *Television, Audiences and Cultural Studies*. London and New York: Routledge.

Multiculturalism The idea of a multicultural society has become official policy in many Western cultures and represents a liberal democratic attempt to promote ethnic/racial equality. It is premised on the idea of displaying tolerance towards a range of cultural practices within the contexts of the nation-state. As a policy approach it has been influential in the education and cultural spheres where it has underpinned attempts to introduce people to a range of different beliefs, values, customs and cultural practices. For example, the teaching of multi-faith religious education, the performance of rituals and the promotion of ethnic food became facets of educational policy. As such, multiculturalism aims to express respect for and indeed celebration of difference.

While multiculturalism as a strategy has much to commend it, some commentators argue that the process of relativizing cultures can, in the context of institutionally racist social orders, overlook the dimension of power. That is, the day-to-day experiences of racism in relation to housing, employment and physical violence may slip from view. Critics of multiculturalism from within cultural studies have argued that we would be better served by an anti-racist approach that highlights the operations of power and challenges the ideological and structural practices that constituted racist societies. This includes contesting racist language in school textbooks and the over-representation of black pupils in school exclusions and suspensions. It has also been suggested that the philosophy and strategies of multiculturalism rest on essentialist versions of 'ethnic' identity and thus homogenize cultural experience rather than recognizing the hybridity inherent to contemporary cultural identities.

Links **Cultural policy, cultural politics, ethnicity, hybridity, identity, postcolonial theory, race**

Multimedia corporation A multimedia corporation is a communications-oriented organization that operates across a range of media outlets. It is widely held that the ownership of communications by private capital is subject to a general process of concentration via conglomeration. This produces multimedia corporations which are part of a wider process of capital conglomeration. Three basic kinds of conglomerate operating in the communications field can be identified: industrial conglomerates, service conglomerates and communications conglomerates. These operate in the context of changes in the communications industries centred on the processes of synergy, convergence and deregulation.

Diversification by financial, computer and data processing companies into telecommunications has created multimedia giants that dominate sectors of the market. For example, between April 1997 and March 1998 there were at least 333 mergers involving media and communications companies world-wide. Of these, 133 were identified as 100 per cent acquisitions and 106 involved 'foreign' investors. Corporations based in the United States (139) and the United Kingdom (42) were responsible for the largest part of the mergers and acquisitions noted (*Screen Digest*, April 1998). For example, in 2000 the major Internet company America On-Line (AOL) took over Time Warner which was already the world's largest media group having itself emerged from the merger of Time and Warner and the subsequent acquisition of Turner Broadcasting (CNN). Other multimedia corporations operating on a global scale include Disney, News Corporation, Bertelsmann and Paramount–Viacom.

Links **Capitalism, convergence, deregulation, mass media, synergy, television**

Multiple identities This idea refers to the assumption of different and potentially contradictory identities at different times and places and which do not form a unified coherent self. That is, persons are best understood as being composed not of one but of several identities that are not integrated into a cohesive 'self'. In so far as we feel that we have a consistent identity from birth to death this is because we construct a unifying story or narrative of the self.

Here identity does not involve an essence of the self but rather a set of continually shifting subject positions where the points of difference around which cultural identities could form are multiple and proliferating. They include, to name but a few, identifications of class, gender, sexuality, age, ethnicity, nationality, political position (on numerous issues), morality, religion etc. and each of these discursive positions are themselves unstable. No single identity can, it is argued, act as an overarching organizing identity, rather, identities shift according to how subjects are addressed or represented. Thus we are constituted as fractured, with multiple identities articulated into a new unity.

Multiple narratives of the self are arguably not the outcome of the shifting meanings of language alone but are also the consequence of the proliferation and diversification of social relationships, contexts and sites of interaction (albeit constituted in and through discourse). The proliferation and diversification of contexts and sites of interaction prevent easy identification of particular subjects with a given, fixed, identity so that the same person is able to shift across subject positions according to circumstances. Thus do discourse, identities and social practice in time–space form a mutually constituting set.

In a sense one does not *have* an identity or even identities; rather, one is described as being constituted by a centre-less weave of beliefs, attitudes and identifications. Since we cannot see our identities as objects of our own vision or understanding, we cannot say what a person is; rather, we have to decide how people are best described for particular purposes. Amongst the advantages of describing identity as the weaving together of patterns of discourse into a centre-less web, and not as a set of attributes that are possessed by a unified core self, is that it offers the possibility of an enlargement of the self through the addition of new beliefs, attitudes and desires phrased in new vocabularies.

Links **Articulation, discourse, identity, postmodernism, subjectivity**

Myth In general terms a myth is a story or fable that acts as a symbolic guide or map of meaning and significance in the cosmos. In cultural studies, the concept of a myth refers more to the naturalization of the connotative level of meaning, a use that is somewhat similar to the notion of ideology. Thus myth makes particular world-views appear to be unchallengeable because they are natural or God-given. This argument is taken from the work of Roland **Barthes** in the late 1960s and early 1970s for whom myth has the task of giving historical contingency an eternal justification.

According to Barthes, we can talk of two systems of signification; that is, denotation and connotation. Denotation is the descriptive and 'literal' level of meaning shared by virtually all members of a culture. Thus, 'pig' denotes the concept of a useful pink farm animal with a snout and curly tail etc. At the second level of signification, that is, connotation, meanings are generated by connecting signifiers to wider cultural concerns, that is the beliefs, attitudes, frameworks and ideologies of a social formation. Meaning becomes a matter of the association of signs with other cultural codes of meaning. Thus, 'pig' may connote nasty police officer or male chauvinist according to the sub-codes or lexicons at work.

Meaning is said to multiply up from a given sign until a single sign is loaded with manifold meanings. This connotation carries expressive value arising from the cumulative force of a sequence (syntagmatically) or, more usually, by comparison with absent alternatives (paradigmatically). Where connotations have become naturalized as hegemonic, that is, accepted as 'normal' and 'natural', they act as conceptual maps of meaning by which to make sense of the world. These are myths, a second-order semiological system or metalanguage that speaks about a first-level language. The sign of the first system (signifier and signified) which generates denotative meaning becomes a signifier for a second order of connotative mythological meaning.

Barthes gives an often-quoted example of the work of signification and myth that refers to the cover of the French magazine *Paris-Match*. This features a young black soldier in French military uniform saluting the tricolour with his eyes cast upward towards the French flag. On a denotative level this can be read as 'a black soldier salutes the French flag'. However, the repertoire of cultural codes available to Barthes and his contemporaries (which included French colonial history and their military involvement in Algeria) allowed him to interpret the image in a more mythological way. That is, the connotations of the image suggest the loyalty of black French subjects to the French flag in a way that undermines criticism of French imperial activity.

Links **Code, ideology, semiotics, signs, structuralism**

N

Narrative A narrative is a story or ordered sequential account of events. However, narratives are more than a simple record of occurrences for they offer us frameworks of understanding and rules of reference about the way the social order is constructed. That is, narratives supply answers to the question, how shall we live? Narrative theory concerns the form, pattern or structure by which stories are constructed and told. Since texts tell stories, whether that is Einstein's theory of relativity, **Hall**'s theory of identity or the latest episode of *The Simpsons,* narrative theory plays a part in cultural studies.

Though stories take different forms and utilize a variety of characters, subject matters and narrative structures (or ways of telling a story), structuralist theory has concerned itself with the common features of story formation. According to structuralism, narrative minimally concerns the disruption of equilibrium and the tracing of the consequences of the said disruption until a new equilibrium is achieved. For example, an established soap opera couple is shown in a loving embrace as a prelude to the later revelation that one of them is having an affair. The question posed is, will this spell the end of the relationship?

Not only can one generate theory about narratives, but also theory can itself be understood in narrative terms. That is, theory can be grasped as narratives that seek to account for perceived occurrences. Since knowledge is not merely a matter of collecting facts from which theory can be deduced or against which it can be tested, so no amount of stacking up of empirical data produces a story about our lives without theory, that is, narrative form.

While narratives are rationales for courses of action and meaning they are also at the heart of self-identity. That is, identity is understood as a story of and about the self. Given the fractured or multiple character of identity, what we think of as our self – the 'I' of dialogue – can be grasped as a *post hoc* narrative we construct for and about ourselves. Further, though we may feel our personal narratives to be highly particular, they are not simply matters of individual interpretation. Rather, they are always already a part of the wider cultural repertoire of narratives, discursive explanations, resources and maps of meaning available to members of cultures. The requirements for telling an intelligible story about us are culturally moulded; that is, to possess an intelligible self requires a borrowing from a cultural repository of narrative forms.

Links **Identity, meaning, multiple identities, soap opera, structuralism, theory**

National identity A national identity is a form of imaginative identification with the nation-state as expressed through symbols and discourses. Thus, nations are not only political formations but also systems of cultural representation whereby national identity is continually re-produced through discursive action. Since cultures are not static entities but are constituted by changing practices and meanings that operate at different social levels so any given national culture is understood and acted upon by different social groups. That is, governments, ethnic groups and classes may perceive national identity in divergent ways. Representations of national culture are snapshots of the symbols and practices that have been foregrounded at specific historical conjunctures for particular purposes by distinct groups of people.

National identity is a way of unifying cultural diversity so that, rather than thinking of nations and national cultures as a 'whole', we should understand unity or identity to be the consequence of discursive power that covers over difference. Nations are marked by deep internal divisions and differences so that a unified national identity has to be constructed through the narrative of the nation by which stories, images, symbols and rituals represent 'shared' meanings of nationhood. Thus national identity involves identification with representations of shared experiences and history as told through stories, literature, popular culture and the media.

Narratives of nationhood emphasize the traditions and continuity of the nation as being 'in the nature of things' along with a foundational myth of collective origin. This in turn both assumes and produces the linkage between national identity and a pure, original people or 'folk' tradition. As such the 'nation' can be grasped as an 'imagined community' and national identity as a construction assembled through symbols and rituals in relation to territorial and administrative categories. Thus national identities are intrinsically connected to, and constituted by, forms of communication.

Links **Globalization, identification, identity, imagined community, narrative, nation-state**

Nation-state The modern nation-state is a relatively recent historical invention so that most of the human species have never participated in any kind of state nor identified with one. Though we speak of the nation-state it is necessary to disentangle the couplet since national cultural identities are not necessarily coterminous with state borders. Various global diaspora – African, Jewish, Indian, Chinese, Polish, English, Irish etc. – attest to the existence of national and ethnic cultural identities that span the borders of nation-states.

The nation-state is a political concept that refers to an administrative apparatus deemed to have sovereignty over a specific space or territory within the nation-state system. The requirement to defend their territory and to control their population has led modern nation-states to develop increasingly sophisticated forms of surveillance and military power. As a political apparatus and a symbolic form the nation-state has a temporal dimension in that political structures endure and change while the symbolic and discursive dimensions of national identity narrate and create the idea of origins, continuity and tradition. The modern nation-state can be seen to have three critical functions: namely, external defence, internal surveillance and the maintenance of citizenship rights. According to some commentators, aspects of these nation-state functions are in decline.

In particular, the nation-state is embroiled in the multi-faceted processes of globalization that can be argued to be compromising four critical aspects of the modern nation-state: namely its competence, form, autonomy and legitimacy. Thus, nation-state's are increasingly unable to manage and control their own economic policy or to protect citizens from global events such as environmental disasters. That is, the state's *competence* is undermined which, in turn, leads to the development of inter-governmental or supra-governmental agencies that alter the *form* and scope of the state. The globalization of economic and political processes means that the nation-state is increasingly unable to maintain direct control of policy formation, but must be an actor on the international stage of compromise and capitulation. That is, the *autonomy* of the state is increasingly restricted. If the competence and autonomy of the state is being slowly undermined and at least some of its powers are transferred to supra-state bodies, then the state cannot fully carry out its modern functions. It may then suffer a crisis of *legitimation*. That is, since the state cannot do what it is expected to do people may lose faith in it.

Other writers do not accept that the nation-state is being eroded and argue that international cooperation between states and trans-state agencies *increases* the state's ability to direct its own fate. Further, nationalism and state military power play significant roles in international relations and show little sign of withering away as is evidenced by a series of military conflicts including those involving US and British forces in the Middle East during 1991 and 2003. International diplomacy still operates through states rather than by-passing them. The position regarding the internal powers of the state is also ambiguous. On the one hand, states like Britain have privatized and de-regulated in a process of de-centralization, but, on the other hand, have taken increased authoritarian powers over questions of law and order, morality and internal surveillance. Though the state is changing its form, transferring some of its powers to supra-state bodies and undergoing a degree of 'legitimation crisis', this is far from total and there seems to be little prospect of the nation-state disappearing in the immediate future.

Links **Diaspora, ethnicity, globalization, modernity, national identity, surveillance**

New Social Movements New Social Movements (NSMs) are commonly seen as encompassing civil rights struggles, feminism, ecology politics, peace movements, youth movements and the politics of cultural identity. Significantly it has often been the 'new' social and political movements of identity politics (that often have their origins in the 1960s and have proliferated and grown since then) that have provided cultural studies with its alleged constituency.

New Social Movements are increasingly strident social and political collectivities based outside of the workplace. Orthodox class identifications and political strategies do not lie at the heart of NSMs, rather their rise appears to correlate with a reduction in trust for the major political parties and an interest in more direct forms of political action. Though it would be mistaken to see New Social

Movements as entirely replacing class politics, conflict since the 1960s has been somewhat displaced from the opposition of manager and worker to a wider struggle for control over the direction of social, economic and cultural development. In particular, the axis of conflict for NSMs has shifted to questions of identity, self-actualization and 'post-materialist' values.

New Social Movements tend to be more preoccupied with direct democracy and member participation than with representative democracy. Though the achievement of specific instrumental goals does form a part of their agenda, NSMs are more concerned with their own autonomy and the value orientation of wider social developments. Indeed, they can be understood as having a 'spiritual' component centred on the body and the 'natural' world that acts as a source of moral authority.

NSMs are commonly marked out by their anti-authoritarian, anti-bureaucratic and even anti-industrial stance alongside their loose, democratic and activist-oriented organizational modes. Consequently, the boundaries between particular movements are often blurred in terms of value-orientation, specific goals and overlapping flexible and shifting 'membership'. Though New Social Movements often engage in 'direct action' this is not usually aimed at the authority and personnel of orthodox representative politics (for example, Members of Parliament or Congress) in the first instance. Rather, the initial symbolic protest commonly revolves around other actors or institutions in civil society such as corporations, research establishments, military bases, oil rigs, road building projects and so forth.

The politics of NSMs challenge the cultural codes of institutionalized power relations through symbolic events and evocative language that lend them coherent form as an 'imagined community'. Hence the images generated by New Social Movements are core to their activities and act to blur the boundaries between their form and content. Indeed, many of the activities of NSMs are media events designed to give themselves popular appeal. Here, the symbolic languages of these movements are polysemic and thus broad enough to suit the imprecision of their aims while forming the basis of an alliance constituted by a range of otherwise disparate people. In this sense, more than traditional modern party politics, NSMs are expressly a form of cultural politics with which most cultural studies writers have felt an affinity. For example, Greenpeace is one of the most successful of today's social and political organizations and whatever the merits of their arguments, their tactics are often exemplary in their use of media imagery, consumer campaigns and direct action.

Links **Cultural politics, identity, imagined community, life-politics, postmaterialism**

New Times The idea of 'New Times' was proposed by Stuart **Hall**, Martin Jacques and others in a book of the same name (published in 1989) and was a significant moment in the development of post-Marxism. In its themes and approach the book departed from the orthodox Marxist view of the day and can be read as part of the turn of cultural studies towards postmodernism in that it suggested there had been a significant change in social and cultural patterns. Thus, in these new times culture and society were marked by a fresh configuration of production, politics, consumption, lifestyles, identities and everyday private life.

The 'New Times' approach explored a wide-ranging set of cultural, social and economic issues and the connections between them. Thus it was suggested that flexible manufacturing systems supported the customization of design and quality for niche markets that in turn were connected to consumer lifestyles and the cultural configurations of postmodernism. At the same time the state was involved in the deregulation and privatization of welfare in the context of the reconfiguration of the class structure and the emergence of new social and political movements. Thus, within the backdrop of globalization, the old certainties that linked economy, culture and politics together were being put into doubt.

It was argued that Western Capitalist countries were witnessing a decline in the manual working class, a rise in service and white-collar work, and an increase in part-time and 'flexible' labour all of which was contributing to new social divisions expressed as the 'two-thirds: one-third society'. That is, two-thirds of the population are relatively well-off while one-third is either engaged in de-skilled part-time work or forms a new 'underclass' of the unemployed and unemployable. Congruent with these changes in the economy and class relations, the cultural identities and political allegiances of class factions were said to be increasingly unpredictable.

Links **Disorganized capitalism, post-industrial society, post-Marxism, postmodernism**

News The production of news holds a strategic position in debates about the mass media for its presumed, and often feared, influence on public life. News is not a reflection of reality so much as 'the putting together of reality'. That is, news is not an unmediated 'window-on-the world' but a selected and constructed representation constitutive of 'reality'. The selection of items for inclusion as news and the specific ways in which, once selected, a story is constructed are never neutral. They are always a particular version of events. It follows that news selection criteria tell us about the 'world-view' that is being assembled and disseminated.

The first selective process in the manufacture of news concerns the topics that it covers, which, for most news formats in the Western media, can be grasped as politics, the economy, foreign affairs, domestic affairs, sport and 'occasional' stories. These topics define the news paradigm, the significant omission being the domain of the personal/sexual. A second moment of selection concerns the constitution of the topic so that politics is defined as being about government and mainstream political parties with a stress on personalities. The economy is circumscribed as being about the stock exchange, trade figures, government policy, inflation, money supply and so forth. Foreign affairs means inter-governmental relations while domestic news is sub-divided into 'hard' stories – conflict, violence, industrial disputes – and 'soft' human interest stories. The category of 'sport' has traditionally been constituted by male professional sport.

The construction of a story within a topic involves news values that guide the selection processes. These include four prime news values of the Western world:

namely, reference to elite nations, reference to elite persons, personalization and negativity. Thus, while the unexpected is a significant news value, it is even more so if it has negative consequences involving elite persons of an elite nation. Thus a scandal about the private life of the President of the United States is more 'news-worthy' than successful crop figures in Mali.

Within cultural studies a hegemonic model of news has been popular. Here the ideological character of news is not held to be the result of direct intervention by owners or even a conscious attempt at manipulation by journalists, but as an outcome of the routine attitudes and working practices of staff. News journalists learn the conventions and codes of 'how things should be done' reproducing ideology as common sense. It is argued that reliance on 'authoritative sources' leads to the media reproducing 'primary definers'' accounts as news. Primary definers are taken to be politicians, judges, industrialists, the police and so forth, that is, official agencies involved in the making of news events. In translating the primary definitions of news, the media, as secondary definers, reproduce the hegemonic ideologies associated with the powerful, translating them into popular idioms.

In the hegemonic model of news the media draw off and constitute consensual assumptions about the world in a process of agenda setting. They define what constitutes news and thus that which is constituted as socially and culturally important. Though many current affairs programmes do offer balance in terms of the time given to different political views, the very field of 'politics' has already been set up as concerning established political procedures, that is, Parliament or Congress. Consequently, a balance of 'protagonists' and 'respondents' encompasses only those political discourses favouring the field of politics as currently structured.

News, especially in its televised form, is constituted not only by its choice of topics and stories but by its verbal and visual idioms or modes of address. Presentational styles have been subject to a tension between an informational-educational purpose and the need to engage us entertainingly. While current affairs programmes are often 'serious' in tone with adherence to the 'rules' of balance, more popular programmes adopt a friendly, lighter, idiom in which we are invited to consider the impact of particular news items from the perspective of the 'average person in the street'. Indeed, contemporary news construction has come to rely on an increased use of faster editing tempos and 'flashier' presentational styles including the use of logos, sound-bites, rapid visual cuts and the 'star quality' of news readers. Popular formats can be said to enhance understanding by engaging an audience unwilling to endure the longer verbal orientation of older news formats. However, they arguably work to reduce understanding by failing to provide the structural contexts for news events.

News is now one of the principal texts of the contemporary media and appears on just about every television network across the globe. Indeed it is the subject of entire globally distributed channels, including *Cable News Network (CNN)* and *BBC News 24*. The production and distribution of news is a global phenomenon that rests on the establishment of news exchange arrangements whereby subscribing news organizations have organized a reciprocal trade in news material with a particular emphasis on the sharing of visual footage. Indeed, the availability of common news footage and a shared professional culture has led to substantial convergence of news stories that may reflect a drift towards an international standardization of basic journalistic discourses and the domination of global news agendas by Western news agencies. However, the fact that Western news agencies tend to supply 'spot news' and visual reports without commentary still allows different verbal interpretations of events to be dubbed over the pictures. This has led to what one may call the localization of global news and can be regarded as a countervailing force to the pull of globalization.

Links **Hegemony, ideology, mass media, realism, representation, television**

Norm (alization) The concept of a norm refers to a social and cultural rule that governs patterns of activity. This would include such things as moral and ethical imperatives, the customs and practices of a culture and the law. On the one hand a norm can be understood as the statistically common or 'normal', while on the other hand it represents a prescribed form of behaviour upheld by the use of sanctions. Although analytically distinct, cultural practice frequently blurs the boundaries between these two uses of the term. Classical sociology has understood norms to be acquired through the process of social learning or socialization that enables actors to be competent and accepted agents. Structuralist perspectives regard norms as existing outside of individual agents in the structures of society. However 'action theory' holds them to be carried by actors and developed through the processes of symbolic negotiation.

Many writers within cultural studies deploy the idea of 'normalization' derived from Foucault rather than the more sociologically located concept of a norm. For Foucault the processes of normalization form part of the 'disciplinary' character of modern institutions, practices and discourses by which 'docile bodies' are subjected, used, transformed and improved. Here 'normalization' refers to processes by which individual subjects can be distributed around a system of graded and measurable categories and intervals which constitute the norm. Thus, discipline involves the organization of the subject in space through dividing practices, training and standardization in order to produce subjects by categorizing and naming them in a hierarchical order through a rationality of efficiency, productivity and 'normalization'.

For example, Western medicine and judiciary systems have increasingly appealed to statistical measures and distributions to judge what is normal. This leads, for example, not only to classifications of what is sane and mad but also to degrees of 'mental illness'. Classificatory systems are essential to the processes of normalization and thus to the creation of a range of subjects so that normalization forms a part of the productivity of power in the generation of subjects.

Links **Acculturation, agency, discourse, power, structure, subjectivity**

O

Oedipus complex The idea of the Oedipus complex was developed by **Freud** during the nineteenth century in the context of psychoanalysis and is thus pertinent to cultural studies in so far as psychoanalysis itself is held to make a contribution. An Oedipal complex is said to involve a boy's desire for his mother as the primary love object. This desire is prohibited by the symbolic order in the form of the incest taboo. Specifically, the father represents to a boy the threat of castration that such prohibited desire brings forth. Consequently, boys shift their identification from the mother to the father, who is identified with the symbolic position of power and control (the Phallus). For girls, this involves the acceptance that they have already been castrated. This is said to lead to fury and partial identification with the mother as a gendered role together with the association of fathers with authority, domination and mastery.

According to Freud, the resolution of the Oedipus complex achieves the ordering of an otherwise polymorphously perverse libido into the norm of heterosexual gendered relationships. That is, while the libidinal drive does not have any pre-given fixed aim or object it becomes regulated and repressed by the resolution of the Oedipus complex. For **Lacan**, the resolution of the Oedipus complex marks the formation of the unconscious as the realm of the repressed and the very possibility of gendered subjects is established through entry into the symbolic order.

Kristeva, Chodorow, Mitchell and other writers supportive of psychoanalysis suggest that the theory of the Oedipus complex marks the formation of particular styles of masculinity and femininity. It is argued that, in the context of patriarchy, mothers treat boys as independent and outgoing persons while girls are loved more narcissistically as being like the mother. Thus boys' individuation involves identification with the father and the symbolic Phallus as the domain of social status, power and independence so that a form of masculinity is produced which stresses external orientation. In contrast, girls have acquired a greater surety with the communicative skills of intimacy through introjection of, and identification with, aspects of their mothers' own narratives but suffer the traditional cost of a greater difficulty with autonomy.

Links **Gender, identification, identity, mirror phase, psychoanalysis, sex, symbolic order**

Orientalism The concept of Orientalism is associated with the work of Edward **Said**, who argued that cultural-geographical entities such as the 'Orient' are not inert facts of nature, but rather should be grasped as historically specific discursive constructions that have a particular history and tradition. Thus, 'The Orient' has been constituted by an imagery and vocabulary that have given it a specific kind of reality and presence within Western culture. In particular, the idea of Orientalism suggests that racism is not simply a matter of individual psychology or pathology, but rather is constituted through patterns of cultural representation deeply ingrained within the practices, discourses and subjectivities of Western societies.

Orientalism is a set of Western discourses of power that have constructed an Orient – have Orientalized the Orient – in ways that depend on and reproduce the positional superiority and hegemony of the West. For Said, Orientalism was a general group of ideas impregnated with European superiority, racism and imperialism that are elaborated and distributed through a variety of texts and practices. Orientalism is argued to be a system of representations that brought the Orient into Western learning. These include Flaubert's encounter with an Egyptian courtesan that produced an influential image of the Oriental woman who never spoke for herself, never showed her emotions and lacked agency or history. That is, the sexually beguiling dark maiden of male power-fantasies. In contrast, the Oriental male is seen as wily, fanatical, cruel and despotic.

In this respect, the contemporary elevation of 'Islam' to the role of chief bogeyman in Western news follows a well-worn path. Long before the current twenty-first-century crisis of relations between the West and Islam, Said argued that the Western media represented Islamic peoples as irrational fanatics led by messianic and authoritarian leaders. In recent years, a great deal of news coverage in the West has been devoted to such matters as the states of Afghanistan, Iran, Iraq and Libya (with a special emphasis on their alleged sponsoring of terrorism), the *fatwa* declared by Ayatollah Khomeini against Salman Rushdie, the US-led conflicts between the West and Iraq including the 2003 war, and, of course, Osama Bin Laden and the tragedy of 11 September 2001.

Thus we may note a certain imbalance in the cultural representation of Islam within the West. There is a concentration on the violence of some Islamic fundamentalists but little exploration of the reasons for this hostility towards the West and the part played by Western cultural and political actions in fuelling conflict. Nor is it often reported that Islam is seen by most of its adherents as a philosophy and religion of love and peaceful cooperation.

Links **Cultural imperialism, discourse, globalization, power, representation**

Other (the) The notion of the Other is closely linked to those of identity and difference in that identity is understood to be defined in part by its difference from the Other. I am male because I am not female, I am heterosexual because I am not homosexual, I am white because I am not black and so forth. Such binaries of difference usually involve a relationship of power, of inclusion and exclusion, in that one of the pair is empowered with a positive identity and the other side of the equation becomes the subordinated Other.

One theoretical source for this idea is the master–slave discussion staged by the philosopher Hegel and another is the deconstruction of the binaries of Western philosophy found in the work of **Derrida**. In both cases the identities of each side of the relationship of the binary are forged together. The master is inseparable from the slave, the identities of men are interlocked with those of women and the subjectivity of the colonial ruler is forged in tandem with the colonized subject. Indeed, the discussion of Orientalism presented by **Said** contains one of the better known uses of the concept of the Other. Here what constitutes the Orient is a projection by Western powers onto the empty subject position of the Other.

The idea of the Other also appears in the psychoanalytic work of **Lacan**, where it appears as a symbolic place and the site on which the subject is constituted. For Lacan the unconscious is the discourse of the Other formed at the moment of the subject's constitution via entry into the symbolic order. The Other is 'the lack' (loss of pre-Oedipal oneness) experienced as a consequence of the formation of the subject and is thus the source of desire. An uncapitalized use of 'the other' also appears in Lacan's work as the figure of wholeness or oneness that a child encounters during the mirror phase.

Links **Difference, identity, Oedipus complex, Orientalism, psychoanalysis, subjectivity**

P

Paradigm In general terms a paradigm can be understood as a field or domain of knowledge that embraces a specific vocabulary and set of practices. In the philosophy of science the concept of a paradigm is associated with the writing of Thomas Kuhn, for whom a paradigm is a widely recognized field of understanding or achievement in science that provides model problems and solutions to the community of practitioners. Here a paradigm lays down the guiding principles and conceptual achievements of a working model that attracts adherents and enables 'normal science' to proceed.

Kuhn argues that science periodically overthrows its own paradigms so that a period of stable 'normal science' is commonly preceded by the overthrow of the existing paradigmatic wisdom. This revolutionary process is known as a paradigm shift. An example would be the substitution of Copernican science by a Newtonian paradigm or the subsequent displacement of classical physics by quantum mechanics. Having said this, the concept of a paradigm may also be deployed in the context of the humanities and social sciences where various 'perspectives' (functionalism, symbolic interactionism, structuralism, poststructuralism etc.) might be grasped as paradigms. Thus, Stuart **Hall** describes culturalism and structuralism as key paradigms in the development of cultural studies.

The idea of the paradigmatic also forms a part of semiotics in that, for **Saussure**, meaning is produced through the selection and combination of signs along the syntagmatic and paradigmatic axes. The syntagmatic axis is constituted by the linear combination of signs that form sentences while paradigmatic refers to the field of signs (i.e., synonyms) from which any given sign is selected. Meaning is accumulated along the syntagmatic axis, while selection from the paradigmatic field alters meaning at any given point in the sentence. For example, in Figure 2 on the paradigmatic axis, the selection of freedom fighter or terrorist is of meaningful significance. It alters what we understand the character of the participants to be. Further it will influence the combination along the syntagmatic axis, since it is by convention unlikely, though grammatically acceptable, to combine terrorist with liberated.

(Paradigmatic)
Freedom fighters
Terrorists

                    Attacked *(Syntagmatic)*
                    Liberated

Figure 2

Links Cultural studies, episteme, epistemology, semiotics, truth

Patriarchy The idea of patriarchy refers to a social order in which there is recurrent and systematic domination of men over subordinated women across a wide range of social institutions and practices. The term, which is connected to feminist theory and gained currency during the second wave of the women's movement dating from the 1960s, clearly carries the connotations of the male-headed family, mastery and superiority. As such, the concept of patriarchy asserts that sex is a central organizing principle of social life where gender relations are thoroughly saturated with power.

Many feminists have argued that contemporary sexed subjectivities are not universals but rather the consequence of the relations between men and women that are formed in the context of patriarchal family arrangements which, if challenged, could be changed. From a psychoanalytic point of view, patriarchy provides the context in which through identification with the father and symbolic Phallus as the domain of social status, power and independence boys take on a form of externally oriented masculinity achieved at the price of emotional dependence on women. In contrast, while girls acquire a greater surety with the communicative skills of intimacy through introjection of, and identification with, aspects of their mothers' own narratives, they have greater difficulty with externally oriented autonomy.

A criticism of the concept of patriarchy is its treatment of the category of woman as an undifferentiated one. That is, all women are taken to share something fundamental in common in contrast to all men. Thus it can be argued that the concept obscures the differences between individual women and their particularities in favour of an all-embracing universal form of oppression. Not only do all women appear to be oppressed in the same way but also there is a tendency to represent them as helpless and powerless. This stress on difference is shared by feminists influenced by poststructuralism and postmodernism whose anti-essentialist stance suggests that femininity and masculinity are not essential universal categories of either biology or culture but discursive constructions.

Links Anti-essentialism, feminism, gender, identification, psychoanalysis, subjectivity, women's movement

Performativity A 'performative' is a linguistic statement that puts into effect (brings into being) the relation that it names, for example, within a marriage ceremony 'I pronounce you . . .' is a performative statement. Similarly, performativity is a discursive practice that enacts or produces that which it names through citation and reiteration of the norms or conventions of the 'law'. Thus, the discursive production of identities through repetition and recitation of regulated ways of speaking about identity categories (for example, masculinity).

Performativity is not a singular act but rather is always a citation and reiteration of a set of existent norms and conventions. For example, judges in criminal and civil law do not originate the law or its authority but cite the conventions of the law that is consulted and invoked. This is an appeal to an authority that has no origin or universal foundations. Indeed, the very practice of citation produces the authority that is cited and reconstitutes the law. The maintenance of the law is a matter of re-working a set of already operative conventions and involves iterability, repetition and citationality.

Though Austin originated the idea of a performative in 1962, it was Judith **Butler** who popularized the concept of performativity within cultural studies during the 1990s. In particular, Butler conceives of sex and gender in terms of citational performativity. For Butler, 'sex' is produced as a reiteration of hegemonic norms, a performativity that is always derivative. The 'assumption' of sex, which is not a singular act or event but an iterable practice, is secured through being repeatedly performed. Thus gender is *performative* in the sense that it constitutes as an effect the very subject it appears to express.

Butler combines this reworking of discourse and speech act theory with psychoanalysis to argue that the 'assumption' (taking on) of sex involves identification with the normative phantasm (idealization) of 'sex'. Sex is a symbolic subject position assumed under threat of punishment (for example, of symbolic castration or abjection). The symbolic is a series of normative injunctions that secure the borders of sex (what shall constitute a sex) through the threat of psychosis and abjection (an exclusion, throwing out or rejection). Butler goes on to argue that drag can destabilize and recast gender norms through a re-signification of the ideals of gender. Through a miming of gender norms, drag can be subversive to the extent that it reflects on the performative character of gender. Drag suggests that all gender is performativity and as such destabilizes the claims of hegemonic heterosexual masculinity as the origin that is imitated. That is, hegemonic heterosexuality is itself an imitative performance which is forced to repeat its own idealizations.

Links **Discourse, identification, identity, psychoanalysis, sex, speech act**

Phallocentric In a general sense, the concept of phallocentric refers to male-centred discourse or from the perspective of a privileged masculinity. More particularly, the idea has been deployed in reference to the use of the term Phallus within psychoanalytic theory where the Phallus is held to be a symbolic transcendental universal signifier of the source, self-origination and unifying agency of the subject. This is argued to be especially the case in relation to psychoanalysis as developed by **Lacan**.

For its critics, the phallocentric character of psychoanalysis follows from **Freud**'s assertion that women would 'naturally' see their genitals as inferior in tandem with the claim that genital heterosexual activity that stresses masculine power and feminine passivity is the normal form of sexuality. Further, in Lacan's reworking of Freud, the Oedipal moment marks the formation of the subject into the Law of the Father, and thus entry into the symbolic order itself. That is, the power of the Phallus is understood to be necessary to the very existence of subjects. For Lacan, the symbolic Phallus:

- Acts as the 'transcendental signifier' of the power of the symbolic order.
- Serves to split the subject away from desire for the mother thus enabling subject formation.
- Marks the necessary interruption of the mother–child dyad and the subject's entry into the symbolic (without which there is only psychosis).
- Allows the subject to experience itself as a unity by covering over a sense of lack.

For critics such as **Irigaray**, the centrality of the Phallus within Lacan's argument renders 'woman' an adjunct term so that the feminine is always repressed and entry into the symbolic continually tied to the father/Phallus. Indeed, for Irigaray the whole of Western philosophy is phallocentric so that the very idea of 'woman' is not an essence *per se* but rather that which is excluded. Here the feminine is understood to be the unthinkable and the unrepresentable 'Other' of phallocentric discourses.

Links **Écriture feminine, feminism, Other, psychoanalysis, sex, subjectivity**

Place Since the 1980s cultural studies has shown a growing interest in questions of space and place influenced in particular by **Foucault** and his exploration of the intersections of discourse, space and power. In this context, a place is understood to be a site or location in space constituted and made meaningful by social relations of power and marked by identifications or emotional investments. As such, a place can be understood to be a bounded manifestation of the production of meaning in space.

The organization of human activities and interactions within space, that is, in places, is fundamental to social and cultural life. For example, a 'home' is divided into different living spaces – front rooms, kitchens, dining rooms, bedrooms etc. These spaces are used in diverse ways and are the arena for a range of activities with different social meanings. Accordingly, bedrooms are intimate spaces into which we would rarely invite strangers; instead, a front room or parlour is deemed to be the appropriate space for such an encounter.

Space and place are sometimes distinguished in terms of absence–presence. That is, place is marked by face-to-face encounters and space by the relations between absent others. Thus, home is a place where I meet my family with regularity and is the product of physical presence and social rituals, whereas e-mail or letters establish contact between absent persons across space. Significantly then, a place is the focus of human experience, memory, desire and identity (which can themselves be understood as discursive constructions) which are the targets of emotional identification or investment.

The concepts of 'front' and 'back' regions (derived from the work of Erving Goffman) illustrate a fundamental divergence in social-spatial activity. Front space is constituted by those places in which we put on a public 'on-stage' performance and act out stylized, formal and socially acceptable activities. Back regions are those spaces where we are 'behind the scenes' and in which we prepare for public performance or relax into less formal modes of behaviour and speech. The social division of space into front and back regions or into the appropriate uses of kitchens, bedrooms and parlours is of course *cultural*. Thus distinct cultures design homes in different ways, allocating contrasting meanings or modes of appropriate behaviour.

Links **Discourse, emotion, identification, meaning, power, space**

Political economy Political economy is a domain of study that is concerned with power and the distribution of economic resources. Thus, political economy explores the questions of who owns and controls the institutions of economy, society and culture. Within cultural studies the main interest in political economy has been related to the scope and mechanisms by which corporate ownership and control of the culture industries shape the contours of culture.

For example, the institutions of television have been of interest to cultural studies because of their central place in the communicative practices of modern societies. These concerns have become increasingly acute as public service broadcasting has been seriously challenged by commercial television in the context of a broadcasting landscape dominated by multimedia corporations. In particular, since the mid-1980s media organizations have undergone processes of convergence and synergy that has created multimedia giants such as AOL–Time Warner and Walt Disney as governments have relaxed the regulations restricting cross-media ownership.

These are the global trends in the political economy of television that have underpinned a change in programming strategies and thus a change to the patterns of cultures. Thus, contemporary developments in television organization and funding across our world have placed visual-based advertising and consumerism at the forefront of culture. Television is pivotal to the production and reproduction of a promotional culture focused on the use of visual imagery to create value-added brands or commodity-signs. Thus has the political economy of television helped to shape the contours of contemporary culture.

However, one of the central tenets of cultural studies is its non-reductionism so that culture is understood to have its own specific meanings, rules and practices which are not reducible to another category or level of a social formation. In particular, cultural studies has waged a battle against economic reductionism, that is, the attempt to explain what a cultural text means by reference to its place in the production process. For cultural studies, the processes of political economy do not determine the meanings of texts or their appropriation by audiences. Rather, political economy, social relationships and culture must be understood in terms of their own specific logics and modes of development. Each of these domains are 'articulated' or related together in context-specific ways.

This argument has been expressed via the metaphor of the 'circuit of culture'. Here, meanings embedded at the moments of production may or may not be taken up at the levels of representation or consumption where new meanings are again produced. Indeed, meanings generated at the level of representation and consumption shape production itself through, for example, design and marketing.

Accordingly a full analysis of any cultural practice requires the analysis of both 'economy' and 'culture', including the articulation of the relations between them.

Links **Articulation, circuit of culture, cultural materialism, Marxism, reductionism, social formation**

Politics Politics is concerned with the numerous manifestations and relations of power that occur at all levels of human interaction. Since cultural studies is a field of study centred on the examination of the relations of culture and power, then it follows that the concept of politics is a core concern. However, politics as understood in the context of cultural studies is not simply a matter of electoral parties and governments but of power as it pervades every plane of social relationships. Power is not simply a coercive and constraining force that subordinates one set of people to another, though it certainly is this, but it also generates and enables social action and relationships. In this sense, power, while certainly constraining, is also enabling. Thus, politics is a central activity in the generation, organization, reproduction and alteration of any social and cultural order.

Cultural studies has been particularly concerned with the 'politics of representation', that is, the way that power is implicated in the construction and regulation of cultural classifications. A politics of representation concerns questions of discourse, image, language, reality and meaning and is 'political' because these issues are intrinsically bound up with questions of power. This is so because representation involves questions of inclusion and exclusion, that is, the issue of what is recorded in a representation and what is left out. This involves the enactment of power. For example, to represent the category of African Americans as constituted by full human beings and citizens with equal social rights and obligations is quite a different matter from representing them as a group of sub-human criminals and/or social problems.

Representations infused with power are the very building bricks that constitute culture and thus they guide our behaviour as 'maps of meaning'. In particular, cultural studies has explored popular culture as the political ground on which consent to a cultural order is won or lost through the play of power and representation. The forms of power that cultural studies explores are diverse but include the formation and performance of gender, race, class, colonialism etc. Further, cultural studies has sought to explore the connections between these forms of power and to develop ways of thinking about culture and power that can be utilized by agents in the pursuit of change. That is, cultural studies as a discipline has been predominantly concerned with issues of cultural politics.

Links **Cultural politics, hegemony, ideology, power, power/knowledge, representation**

Polysemy In the context of cultural studies the concept of polysemy highlights the notion that signs carry many potential meanings. Signs do not signify only one thing but are polysemic, that is, they are ambiguous in terms of their sense and significance. This is so because signs do not have transparent and authoritative meaning by dint of reference to an independent object world but rather generate meaning through a series of conceptual and phonic differences that are interpreted in specific contexts. Thus, red is red because it is not green rather than because the sign red is generated by the light spectrum as such, and while it may signify 'stop' in the context of traffic signs it may mean 'doctor' or 'brothel' elsewhere.

Since signs and their arrangement into texts can be interpreted in a number of different ways the generation of meaning requires the active involvement of readers. It is the readers of texts using the cultural competencies they bring to bear who temporally 'fix' meaning for particular purposes. Thus, interpretation of texts depends on readers' cultural repertoire and knowledge of social codes that are differentially distributed along the lines of class, gender, race, nationality etc.

The idea that signs have more than one meaning is also expressed by the concept of the 'multi-accentuality' of the sign (and the dialogic) that is associated with Volosinov (see **Bakhtin**). He suggests that signs possess an 'inner dialectical quality' and an 'evaluative accent' that makes them capable of signifying a range of meanings. The significance of signs changes as social conventions and social struggles seek to fix meaning, so that which meanings 'stick' is dependent on the social and cultural context in which signification occurs. That is, because the meanings of signs are not fixed but negotiable, they are fought over so that meaning is the outcome of politics and the play of power. The 'ideological struggle' can then be understood as the contest over the significance of signs as power attempts to regulate and 'fix' the otherwise shifting meanings of signs. In particular, post-Marxist writers such as **Laclau** and Mouffe understand the role of hegemonic practices to be one of trying to fix difference, that is, to put closure around the unstable meanings of signifiers in the discursive field.

The political significance of polysemic signs can be understood if we ask the question, 'what does black mean in the context of contemporary Western cultures?' Is black a term of abuse or a term of solidarity? Are the connotations of the sign black those of civil rights or criminality? Is black bad or is it beautiful? Indeed, why does black have any racial meanings at all? In short, the sign black does not have an essentialist meaning but is struggled over. Indeed, all the key cultural categories such as 'women', 'class', 'society', 'identities', 'interests' etc., cannot be conceived of as single unitary objects with fixed meanings or single underlying structures and determinations but instead need to be understood as discursive constructs. The notion that signs have many meanings that are subject to the play of power is crucial to an understanding cultural politics.

Links **Cultural politics, dialogic, hegemony, ideology, post-Marxism, power, semiotics, signs**

Popular culture Traditionally, the idea of popular culture has referred to that which remains after the canon of high culture has been established and/or as the mass-produced commodity culture of consumer capitalism. Here popular culture has been regarded as inferior both to the elevated cultures of Art or classical music on the one hand and to an imagined authentic folk culture on the other. Apologists for maintaining the distinction between high and popular culture do so on the grounds of alleged aesthetic quality arguing that high cultural forms are more subtle, complex and adequate in their formal expression of content than those of popular culture. Popular culture is accused of standardization and a levelling down that encourages, and indeed demands, conformity.

However, the criteria that are used to police the boundaries of' 'good works' are, from the standpoint of cultural studies, derived from an institutionalized and class-based hierarchy of cultural tastes. Equally, the argument that draws a contrast between popular culture and an authentic non-commodity culture cannot be sustained since there is no longer, and probably never was, any authentic folk culture against which to measure the 'inauthentic' character of commodity culture.

While contemporary popular culture is primarily a commercially produced one, many writers in cultural studies have argued that audiences make their own meanings with the texts of a commodity culture. That is, readers or audiences of cultural texts bring to bear their own cultural competencies and discursive resources to the consumption of commodities. Thus, popular culture can be regarded as the meanings and practices produced by popular audiences at the moment of consumption. This argument reverses the traditional question of 'how does the culture industry turn people into commodities that serve its interests?' in favour of exploring how people turn the products of industry into their popular culture serving their interests.

Cultural studies understands popular culture to be an arena of consent and resistance in the struggle over cultural meanings. In this sense, cultural studies holds a *political* conception of popular culture as a site for the struggle over significance; that is, an arena where cultural hegemony is secured or challenged. Understood in this way, judgements about popular culture are not concerned with questions of cultural or aesthetic value *per se*, but concern issues of classification and power.

Links Aesthetics, carnivalesque, commodification, cultural politics, culture, hegemony, ideology

Postcolonial theory A critical theory that explores the condition of postcoloniality, that is, colonial relations and their aftermath. The term 'postcolonial' might be understood to refer only to a time period since the colonization processes of the eighteenth and nineteenth centuries. However, within cultural studies it is commonly taken also to include the colonial discourse itself. Thus, the concept 'postcolonial' alludes to the world both during and after European colonization and as such postcolonial theory explores the discursive condition of postcoloniality. That is, the way colonial relations and their aftermath have been constituted through representation. Postcolonial theory explores postcolonial discourses and their subject positions in relation to the themes of race, nation, subjectivity, power, subalterns, hybridity and creolization. The two key concerns of postcolonial theory are those of domination–subordination and hybridity–creolization.

Questions of domination and subordination surface most directly through colonial military control and the structured subordination of racialized groups. In more cultural terms, questions arise about the denigration and subordination of 'native' culture by colonial and imperial powers along with the relationship between place and diaspora identities. Thus, postcolonial theory is concerned with the representation of race, ethnicity and nationhood. This includes questions about using the very language of English in forms of writing; namely, is English, the language of a major colonial power, a suitable tool for postcolonial writers? On the one hand, the English language can be said to carry within itself the very assumptions and concepts of colonial power, but on the other hand English has a variety of global forms. Depending on which side of the above equation is stressed, a postcolonial writer might choose either to abrogate or appropriate English.

The theoretical critique of essentialism combined with the physical meeting and mixing of peoples has thrown the categories of nation or ethnicity into doubt. That is, it is no longer clear that 'national' or 'ethnic' concepts like Indian or English have any kind of clear or stable meanings. Consequently, the hybridization and creolization of language, literature and cultural identities is a common theme of postcolonial literature and theory. The theme of hybridity or creolization points to the fact that neither the colonial nor colonized cultures and languages can be presented in 'pure' form but are inseparable from each other. For example, the idea of the 'Creole continuum' highlights the overlapping language uses and code-switching common to the Caribbean and involves the creation of new modes of expression particular to itself. Here dialogue with the values and customs of the past allows traditions to be transformed and bring forth the new so that the meanings of old words are changed and new words brought into being.

In metropolitan cultures like the United States and Britain, postcolonial theory has drawn attention to the hybrid cultures produced by, for example, Latino-Americans and British Asians. This process of cultural hybridity challenges not only the centrality of colonial culture and the marginalization of the colonized, but also the very idea of centre and margin as being anything other than 'representational effects'. In Britain, the 'place' and cultures of Asians in relation to Anglo-Saxon and Afro-Caribbean Britons has raised issues of purity and hybridity. In particular, the emergence of British-born young 'Asians' gave rise to a generation that was much more deeply involved in transactions across ethnic boundaries than were the original migrants. British Asian young people have developed their own home-grown syncretic or hybrid cultural forms, including increasingly popular forms of modern dance bhangra music.

Links **Diaspora, ethnicity, ethnocentrism, hybridity, national identity, Orientalism, Other**

Post-feminism The fundamental argument of post-feminism is that the central tenets of feminism have been absorbed into Western culture and surpassed. Since the 1960s, feminism has argued that women are oppressed and subjugated by men as a consequence of being women so that all men oppress all women. Feminism pointed to structural inequalities in the economy and in the institutions of social and cultural power. Further, it was suggested that certain forms of male attitudes and behaviour (contempt, violence, sexual harassment) could oppress women. Finally, despite decades of feminist action it was said that even today little or nothing has changed for women within Western culture.

However, during the 1990s post-feminist writers have suggested that women are not *necessarily* oppressed by dint of being women. Thus not all men are oppressors and it is unhelpful to understand gender relations in terms of 'women versus men'. Instead, what is required is constructive dialogue and structural change where necessary. Thus Rosalind Coward has described feminism as a movement blind to its own effectiveness. This is not to say that gender inequality and injustice are not still in evidence, rather it is to argue that there have been significant gains for women in the economy and increased visibility for women in the cultural sphere. In addition, there have been changes in sexual attitudes and behaviour and reform of pay and divorce laws so that that women can wield sexual power. Finally there has been the recognition of male loss and vulnerability that undermines the simple sense of male oppressor and female oppressed.

Links **Feminism, femininity, gender, masculinity, men's movement, patriarchy, sex**

Post-Fordism In order to understand what is meant by the concept of post-Fordism we need to have a sense of what is meant by the idea of Fordism itself, that is, that which post-Fordism is said to have superseded. Thus Fordism is a name for the post-1945 social formation of the United States and Western Europe that was founded on the large-scale industrial production of standardized goods in the context of mass consumption. It required relatively high wages in order to sustain the purchasing of large volume production and a culture of promotion and advertising to support the selling process. In a broader context, Fordism worked in tandem with Keynesian economic policies. These were marked by a corporate state that played an interventionist role as the manager of social welfare provisions, as an arbitrator of industrial conflict and as a significant direct employer.

In the account of **Harvey**, this Fordist regime began to experience problems that came to a head during the early 1970s. In particular, a system geared towards mass production and consumption faced the difficulties of saturated Western markets with a consequent crisis of over-production. In addition, Western economies were facing increased price competition from Japan and the Newly Industrialized Countries (NICs) including Taiwan, Korea and Singapore. This, combined with the success of the Oil Producing and Exporting Countries (OPEC) in pushing up world oil prices, and the failure to stabilize the world financial markets as US ascendancy weakened, led to economies blighted by stagflation (economies with nil growth but high inflation levels).

Post-Fordism marks the successful re-organization of capitalism as a way out of the global recession of the 1970s. In particular, corporations sought to re-introduce growth and increase the rate of profit through more flexible production techniques that involved the use of new technology, the re-organization of labour and a speed-up of production/consumption turnover times. On the level of production, the move from Fordism to post-Fordism involved a shift from the mass production of homogeneous goods to small batch customization. That is, economic production was transformed from a basic concern with uniformity and standardization to more flexible and variable manufacture for niche markets. This was enabled by just-in-time (JIT) stock management, the use of information technology to manage variable production runs and the large-scale sub-contracting out of domains of manufacture to horizontally related 'independent' companies.

Post-Fordism involves a re-organization of the labour process that includes multi-skilling and the elimination of rigid job demarcation lines to create a more horizontally organized workforce. For example, quality control shifts from post-production testing into the very process of manufacturing. This demands that the labour force take greater responsibility for quality and 'continuous improvement' as one of their central tasks. In theory, the expensive labour training required for multi-skilling leads companies to offer the core workforce greater long-term job security rather than waste their investment through high worker turnover. However, even if this is the case for the core workforce, about which there is considerable doubt, such privileges do not extend to the large periphery workforce upon which post-Fordism depends.

The concept of post-Fordism does not just refer to the working practices of flexible specialization but also to a new 'regime of accumulation' and an associated mode of social and political regulation. That is, a stabilizing of the relationship between consumption and accumulation, or how much companies retain and how much consumers spend. Such an analysis implies an affinity between the conditions of production and social/political relations and lifestyles so that post-Fordism marks not just an economic restructuring but also changes in everyday culture. These included the customization of design and quality to support niche markets within the framework of consumer lifestyles. Politically, post-Fordism has been associated with the rise of new social and political movements and the de-regulation and privatization of welfare provision against a background of reconfigured class relations, notably a decline in the traditional manual working class and its political allies.

Links **Capitalism, consumption, disorganized capitalism, New Times, post-industrial society, postmodernity**

Post-humanism Humanism is the philosophical view that understands persons to be the unique and unified source of meaning and agency. By contrast, post-humanism is that form of thinking that displaces the idea of the whole person as being the most significant level of analysis and understanding. In the context of cultural studies, post-humanism is most associated with structuralism, poststructuralism and psychoanalysis.

As an approach concerned with structures or predictable regularities that lie outside of any given person, structuralism is post-humanist in its de-centring of human agents from the heart of inquiry. For example, in proposing a form of structuralist Marxism, **Althusser** argued that human beings were not to be understood as agents of their own destiny but rather as the products of social structures and relations as epitomized by **Marx**'s book *Das Kapital* (in Althusser's reading). In particular, he argues that ideology hails or interpellates concrete individuals as concrete subjects and thus has the function of constituting concrete individuals as subjects. This argument is an aspect of Althusser's anti-humanism in that the subject is not grasped as a self-constituting agent but rather as the 'effect' of the structures of ideology.

The poststructuralist work of **Derrida** and **Foucault** can also be understood as post-humanist. Thus Foucault asserts that discourse constructs subject positions that we are obliged to take up so that subjects are the 'effects' of discourse. Here being a person is constituted by those positions that discourse obliges us to take up and not by our own individual acts of self-grounding agency. Discourse constitutes the 'I' through the processes of signification and the speaking subject is dependent on the prior existence of discursive positions. Thus, what it is to be a person is held to be wholly and only the product of language, culture and history.

Derrida's critique of what he calls 'logocentrism' and 'phonocentrism' in Western philosophy is also a form of post-humanism because he is undermining the idea that the individual human being is the source of stable meanings. For Derrida any reliance on fixed *a priori* transcendental meanings (logocentricism) or on the priority given to sounds and speech over writing (phonocentricism) is an untenable attempt to find truth and subjectivity through reason unmediated by signification. The privileging of speech, argues Derrida, allows philosophers to regard the formation of subjectivity as unmediated agency in a way that would involve the unique experience of the signified producing itself spontaneously from within itself.

Finally, psychoanalysis is post-humanist in that the self is conceived of in terms of an ego, superego and the unconscious. This view of personhood immediately fractures the unified humanist subject and suggests that what we do and what we think are the outcome not of a rational integrated self but of the workings of the unconscious that is normally unavailable to the conscious mind in any straightforward fashion. Here the humanist unified narrative of the self is understood to be something we acquire over time through entry into the symbolic order of language and culture.

Links Agency, humanism, identity, ideology, logocentrism, subject position, subjectivity

Post-industrial society This is a concept that emerged in the early 1970s and has gained ground ever since. It suggests that contemporary Western societies are shifting their central processes from industrial manufacturing to service industries and information exchange. The pre-eminence of information technology to the social formation, along with a relative shift of emphasis from production to consumption, is said to mark the post-industrial society. Pivotal to conceptions of the post-industrial society are (a) the critical place of knowledge in the economy and culture, (b) the shifts taking place in the kinds of work people do and (c) the related changes in the occupational structure.

Theorists of the post-industrial society give a key role in their schema to knowledge production and planning. In particular, information exchange and cultural production are seen to displace heavy industry at the heart of the economy. This, together with the emergence of new production processes, makes information technology and communications *the* industries of the future. Central to these developments are the role and capabilities of computers in managing the increase in volume, speed and distance with which increasingly complex information is generated and transferred. In this view, technological change is the driving force of social change.

The post-industrial society is said to be the site of a new class structure that is emerging as a consequence of the growing importance of knowledge and technical skills in the economy. In particular, it is said that manual jobs are giving way to white-collar, service and professional ones. The new service class is based on the possession of knowledge rather than property and is increasingly organized on craft rather than industrial lines. The professional end of the service class is not primarily involved in the direct production of commodities, but rather they sell their skills and depend on their market power. Such people usually have a high degree of autonomy, working either as professional 'experts' or in directing the labour of others. Though they do not own the means of production, they may be shareholders and/or possess the ability, at least at the top of the spectrum, to manage the strategic direction of powerful companies.

Writers describe a class structure constituted by (i) a professional class, (ii) a technician and semi-professional class, (iii) a clerical/sales class and (iv) a class of semi-skilled and craft workers. Noticeably absent from this list is the manual working class. The claim is that the majority of the population has been removed from working class manual jobs and their associated class identity. Instead of *a* working class, we now have a new cash-oriented post-industrial 'working' class, a secure and privileged labour 'aristocracy' and an unemployed underclass. As a consequence we no longer live in a society marked by class conflict of the traditional type involving a property owning 'ruling class' and a wage-earning 'working class'. Rather, what we are now experiencing are the tensions between technocrats and bureaucrats on one side and workers, students and consumers on the other.

Theories of the post-industrial society have proved to be useful in pointing to key changes in Western economies and societies since the early 1970s. However, they are also problematic in a number of respects. For many commentators, the scale, scope and range of the changes described are overstated geographically (different regions and countries experience change differently) and in absolute terms. Critics suggest that the changes described are confined to specific sectors of the economy and are not as widespread as they have been purported to be. For example, while there has been a shift towards information and service work, the standard capitalist patterns of labour organization still hold sway.

There is little doubt that the Western world has seen a decline in the industrial manufacturing sectors of its economies and a rise in the service sectors with a comparable alteration in employment patterns. However, critics argue, this category homogenizes a very diverse set of workers from office clerks and shop workers through to lawyers and the chief executive officers of major multinational corporations. This seems too heterogeneous a set of occupational and cultural modes to be regarded as one class. Indeed, increased fragmentation and stratification are markers of the new class formations.

Finally, post-industrial society theorists often seem to rely on forms of technological determinism. That is, cultural changes are explained by prioritizing technology as the motor of transformation without considering that the development and deployment of technology must be understood within a social and economic context. Not only is the very desire to develop technology cultural, but its deployment is dictated as much by questions of profit and loss as by the technology *per se*.

Links **Capitalism, class, disorganized capitalism, post-Fordism, postmodernity**

Positionality The concept of positionality is used by cultural studies writers to indicate that knowledge and 'voice' are always located within the vectors of time, space and social power. Thus, the notion of positionality expresses epistemological concerns regarding the who, where, when and why of speaking, judgement and comprehension. That is, specific acculturated persons make truth-claims at an exact and distinct time and place with particular reasons in mind. Consequently, knowledge is not to be understood as a neutral or objective phenomenon but as a social and cultural production since the 'position' from which knowledge is enunciated will shape the very character of that knowledge.

The concept of positionality acknowledges that a correspondence theory of truth is untenable. Correspondence theory claims that truth is to be understood as the accurate mirroring of an independent object world by forms of representation. However, this is not possible since there is no Archimedean place from where one could independently verify the truth of a particular description of the world. That is, there is no God-like vantage point from which to survey the world and forms of representation separately in order to establish the relationship between them. This is so because we cannot escape using representations when we try to establish such a relationship.

It follows from this argument that we cannot ground or justify our actions and beliefs by means of any universal truths. We can describe this or that discourse as being more or less useful and as having more or less desirable consequences. However, we cannot claim it to be true in the sense of correspondence with an independent object world. This is why cultural studies writers commonly regard the production of theoretical knowledge as a political practice-knowledge with consequences – rather than as neutral and independent knowing.

These arguments turn our attention away from the search for universal truth and towards justification as the giving of reasons. This reason-giving is a social practice so that to justify a belief is to give reasons in the context of a tradition and a community. Here, justification itself is a part of an ongoing 'conversation' of humanity and however we characterize 'truth' we have no reliable source for it other than our ongoing conversation with each other.

Links **Epistemology, ethnocentrism, power/knowledge, representation, truth**

Post-Marxism In a literal sense the idea of post-Marxism implies 'after Marxism' and as such might suggest that cultural studies has abandoned all the concepts and ways of thinking associated with Marxist theory. Indeed, the idea of post-Marxism does imply the superseding of the tenets of classical Marxism and suggests that Marxism is no longer the primary explanatory narrative of our time. However, the 'superseding' involved here entails the selective retention and transformation of key concepts drawn from Marxism rather than a complete jettisoning of them all.

Post-Marxism has involved the critique and reconstitution of Marxism through the application and addition of poststructuralist theory to it. This is an aspect of the wider rejection of grand narratives (including Marxism) and totalizing fields of inquiry by postmodernism. Of particular importance to post-Marxism has been the poststructuralist stress on the constitutive place of language and discourse within culture and the anti-essentialist character of all social categories. Post-Marxism has also adopted the poststructuralist view of the dispersed character of power and thus given greater credence to the micro-fields of political power and resistance than Marxism has traditionally done.

The project of post-Marxism has been particularly associated with Ernesto **Laclau**, Chantal Mouffe and Stuart **Hall**, who are critical of the essentialism, foundationalism and reductionism of Marxism. Thus, concepts such as class, history, mode of production etc. are understood to be discursive constructs rather than essential, universal concepts. Indeed, all the key cultural categories such as 'women', 'class', 'society', 'identities', 'interests' etc. are no longer conceived of as single unitary objects with fixed meanings or single underlying structures and determinations.

Within Marxism the concept of class is conceived of as an essential unified identity between a signifier and a specific group of people who share socio-economic conditions. Here a class has an objective existence. By contrast, class is understood by post-Marxism to be the effect of discourse rather than a simple objective economic fact. That is, 'class' is constituted by how we speak about and deploy the notion of class. Further, class consciousness is a discursively formed collective subject position that is neither an inevitability nor a unified phenomenon. Indeed, classes are cross-cut by conflicting interests, including those of gender, race and age. Classes may share common economic conditions of existence but do not automatically form a core, unified class consciousness.

For post-Marxist writers, discursive concepts are not to be reduced to or explained solely in terms of the economic base as in reductionist forms of Marxism. Thus, for post-Marxist writers any notion of the 'final determination' of cultural phenomena by the mode of production or class relations has to be put aside. Instead the field of the 'social' involves multiple points of power and antagonism that do not cohere around class conflict as Marxism understands them to do. Rather, post-Marxists argue that the multiple forms of power, subordination and antagonism that occur within a society are not reducible to any single site or contradiction.

It follows that post-Marxists regard the account of hegemony as read through **Gramsci** as being mistakenly centred on class. Instead, they stress that history has no prime agent of social change nor does ideology belong to particular classes. Instead, hegemonic and counter-hegemonic blocs are formed through temporary and strategic alliances of a range of discursively constructed subjects and groups of interest. Consequently, any radical politics cannot be premised on the domination of any particular political project (for example, the proletariat of Marxism). Instead it must be constructed in terms of the recognition of difference and the identification and development of points of common interest.

Here there can be no appeal to absolute standards of legitimation or to the laws of history, as orthodox Marxism has tended to do. Rather, all progressive values must be defended within the pragmatic context of particular moral traditions including modern political ideas about democracy, justice, tolerance, solidarity and freedom. Further, the prime agents of social change are held not so much to be classes (though they play a part) as social and cultural movements that have developed from a proliferation of new social antagonisms in the spaces of consumption, welfare and habitat.

Links **Anti-essentialism, foundationalism, hegemony, Marxism, poststructuralism, reductionism**

Postmaterialism The politics of the modern Western world have largely been concerned with questions of material scarcity and the unequal distribution of goods and power. In this context, the values of equality, liberty and solidarity have fuelled an emancipatory concern with an ethics of justice, parity and participation. However, given a degree of release from material deprivation within Western culture, contemporary politics has, at least for some sections of the population, become somewhat less centred on questions of economic inequality and the injustices that flow from this and more concerned with questions of justifiable self-actualization, identity, choice and lifestyle. This involves a shift of emphasis from quantity to quality, from an obsession with economic growth to a concern with the environment, health, relationships, emotional 'intelligence', spirituality and happiness. This represents a significant cultural and political shift in some quarters of Western culture. However, it arguably remains overshadowed by the continued predominance of a materialist consumer culture.

Links **Commodification, cultural politics, identity project, life-politics, values**

Postmodernism The contemporary emergence of the concept of postmodernism is not simply an academic fashion but also, and more significantly, it marks a response to substantive changes in the organization and enactment of our social worlds. However, a degree of perplexity surrounds the notion of postmodernism because it has become confused with the concept of postmodernity as well as having acquired a number of different uses of its own. We may understand postmodernism to be a notion that refers us to questions of culture and knowledge while the idea of postmodernity relates to historical patterns of social organization.

The concept of postmodernism may be comprehended thus:

● *A cultural style marked by intertextuality, irony, pastiche, genre blurring and bricolage.*

There have been significant cultural changes in contemporary life that have been described in the language of the postmodern. Core to the postmodern 'structure of feeling' is a sense of the fragmentary, ambiguous and uncertain nature of living in the context of a speed-up in its apparent pace. This feeling operates in tandem with an awareness of the centrality of contingency in contemporary life. These social and cultural changes are at the leading edge of Western societies but do not necessarily represent a sharp break with the modern.

Postmodern culture is often argued to be a more visual culture than previously encountered and is connected to a general aestheticization of everyday life. It is also distinguished by a blurring of modern historical, aesthetic and cultural boundaries, including those between culture and art, high and low culture, commerce and art, culture and commerce. Bricolage is the central cultural style of the postmodern and is observable in architecture, film and popular music video. For example, MTV is noted for the blending of pop music from a variety of periods and locations, and the film *Bladerunner* is frequently cited as a movie that mixes the genres of film noir, horror, sci-fi, romance etc.

Postmodern culture is marked by a self-conscious intertextuality, that is, citation of one text within another. This involves explicit allusion to particular cultural products and oblique references to other genre conventions and styles. This intertextuality is an aspect of enlarged cultural self-consciousness about the history and functions of cultural products. Stylistically, the markers of postmodernism in Art, film and television include aesthetic self-consciousness, self-reflexiveness, juxtaposition/montage, paradox, ambiguity and the blurring of the boundaries of genre, style and history.

The significance or in-significance of postmodern culture has been hotly debated. For some critics (for example, **Baudrillard** and **Jameson**), contemporary culture is constituted through a continual flow of images that establishes no connotational hierarchy. It is not only depthless and meaningless but also the modern distinctions between the real and the unreal, the public and the private, art and reality have broken down. This is a hyperreality in which we are overloaded with images and information.

However, other writers (for example, **Hebdige**, **McRobbie**, **Kellner**) have claimed a transgressive and progressive role for postmodern culture and its collapsing of boundaries. It is said that postmodernism makes the whole idea of representation problematic even as it is complicit with it. That is, postmodernism is marked by an ironic knowingness that explores the limitations and conditions of its own knowing. Further, in the context of a consumer culture, we act as self-conscious bricoleurs selecting and arranging elements of material commodities and meaningful signs into a personal style. Thus, the postmodern can be read as the democratization of culture and of new individual and political possibilities.

Links **Aesthetics, bricolage, hyperreality, intertextuality, irony, modernism, postmodernity**

● *A philosophical movement that rejects 'grand-narratives' (that is, universal explanations of human history and activity) in favour of irony and forms of local knowledge.*

158

Most thinkers who have been characterized as postmodern argue that knowledge is not metaphysical, transcendental or universal but rather is specific to particular times, spaces and language-games. Thus, knowledge is perspectival in character and there can be no one totalizing knowledge that is able to grasp the 'objective' character of the world. Instead, we both have and require multiple viewpoints or truths by which to interpret a complex heterogeneous human existence. In addition, knowledge is not regarded as a pure or neutral way of understanding but rather as being implicated in regimes of power.

Postmodernism rejects the Enlightenment philosophy of universal reason and progress and understands truth as a construction of language valid only within the language-game of its formation. Knowledge is not a question of 'discovering' that which already exists, rather it involves the construction of interpretations about the world that are taken to be true. In so far as the idea of truth has a historical purchase, it is the consequence of power, that is, of whose interpretations count as truth. Since postmodern philosophy argues that knowledge is specific to language-games, it embraces local, plural and heterogeneous knowledges. Consequently the postmodern condition is said to involve a loss of faith in the foundational schemes or grand narratives that have justified the rational, scientific, technological and political projects of the modern world.

Thus, while Enlightenment philosophy and the theoretical discourses of modernity championed 'reason' as the source of certain and universal truths that would lead to social progress, writers associated with postmodernism, such as **Foucault**, **Lyotard** and **Rorty** have criticized the impulses of modernity for heralding not universal progress but oppression in its search for an impossible set of metaphysical truths.

For some commentators, the assertion by postmodernism that no universalizing epistemology is possible is a form of relativism. That is, truth-claims are said to be of equal epistemological status so that we are unable to make judgements between forms of knowledge. However, Rorty has argued that what is being asserted is not relativism but the culturally specific character of truth. Indeed, there is no standpoint from which one can see across different forms of knowledge and regard them as of equal value. Rather, we are always positioned within acculturated knowledge so that judgements can only be made by reference to 'our' values and not to a transcendental truth.

Links **Enlightenment, epistemology, Grand narrative, irony, modernism, positionality, truth**

Postmodernity The concept of postmodernism refers to aesthetic, cultural and philosophical questions. However, the notion of postmodernity is more obviously a periodizing concept founded on broadly defined institutional parameters of social formations. As such, the term postmodernity is an abstraction that refers to a historical period after modernity.

Modernity is marked by the post-medieval rise of industrialization, capitalism, surveillance and the nation-state system. Consequently, postmodernity ought logically to be a post-industrial, post-capitalist and stateless society. However, no one seriously argues that contemporary Western societies are 'after-the-modern' in this clear-cut institutional way. Rather, the concept of postmodernity when used to describe institutional questions refers to a social formation in which information exchange has replaced industrial production, and in particular heavy industries, as the primary economic driver. Needless to say, information technology is a vital component of this process.

Postmodernity is also said to involve a general shift from production to consumption as the central set of social and economic processes of a social formation. In this sense, the concept of postmodernity is somewhat similar to that of the 'post-industrial society', a concept suggesting that industrialized societies are witnessing a shift of locus from industrial manufacturing to service industries with an emphasis on information technology.

However, some commentators do use the concept of postmodernity to refer not to an institutional configuration but to a condition of knowledge. Thus Bauman has argued that the circumstances of postmodernity are those of the modern mind reflecting upon itself from a distance and sensing the urge to change. The uncertainty, ambivalence and ambiguity of the postmodern condition enable, or so it is said, the possibility of grasping contingency as destiny in order to create our own futures. However, there are neither guarantees nor universal foundations for such a project, rather it appears only as a possibility inherent in the condition of postmodernity. This is one in which the postmodern mentality demands that modernity fulfil the promises of its, albeit distorted, reason. Similarly, for **Lyotard**, 'the postmodern condition' is to be understood as the condition of knowledge in the most highly developed societies. Lyotard expresses his 'incredulity toward metanarratives' and celebrates difference and understandings located within particular local knowledge regimes.

The argument that we are living in a socio-historical formation of 'post-modernity' has not gone unchallenged. Thus, **Giddens** argues that we are clearly not witnessing a post-capitalist world or one without nation-states. Further, the doubt and uncertainty that characterize contemporary knowledge are seen by him not as the condition of postmodernity but of a 'radicalized modernity'. In his view, relativity, uncertainty, doubt and risk are core characteristics of late or high modernity. Similarly, **Haberma**s sees the Enlightenment project of modernity as ongoing and unfinished with critical reason forming the basis of its continued emancipatory possibilities.

Links **Grand narrative, modernism, modernity, post-industrial society, postmodernism**

Poststructuralism Poststructuralism is a stream of thought identified with a number of different thinkers (amongst who are **Derrida**, **Foucault** and **Kristeva**), few of whom have actually adopted the term. The prefix 'post ' clearly suggests 'after', thus poststructuralism is after structuralism in that the terms of this philosophical stream are ones that involve both the absorption of key ideas from structuralism and a critique and transformation of them.

Structuralism has been concerned with the 'systems of relations' of the underlying structure of sign systems and the grammar that makes meaning possible. Here the process of selection and combination of signs, which are organized into a signifying system, is said to produce meaning. Crucially, signs do not make sense by virtue of reference to entities in an independent object world, but rather they generate meaning by reference to each other. Thus meaning is generated through the organization of signs that are held together by cultural convention.

Poststructuralism deconstructs the very notion of the stable structures of language that structuralism assumes. Meaning, it is argued, cannot be confined to single words, sentences or particular texts but is the outcome of relationships between texts, that is, intertextuality. Derrida accepts the argument that meaning is generated by relations of difference between signifiers rather than by reference to an independent object world. However, he argues that the consequence of this play of signifiers is that meaning can never be fixed. Words carry many meanings, including the echoes or traces of other meanings from other related words in other contexts.

Here, the production of meaning in the process of signification is continually deferred and supplemented, an idea encapsulated in the concept of 'différance' – 'difference and deferral' – by which the continual substitution and adding of meanings through the play of signifiers challenges the identity of noises and marks with fixed meaning. For example, if we look up the meaning of a word in a dictionary we are referred to other words in an infinite process of deferral whereby meaning slides down a chain of signifiers abolishing a stable signified. For Derrida, there is no original meaning circulating outside of representation nor a primary source of signification and self-present transparent meaning that could eternally fix the relation between signifiers and signifieds.

The other key figure of poststructuralism for cultural studies is Foucault, who also argues against structuralist theories of language that conceive of it as an autonomous rule-governed system with an underlying structure. Instead, he is concerned with the description, analysis and effects of the regulated 'surface' of language (that is, discourse) under determinate material and historical conditions. For Foucault, discourse constructs, defines and produces the objects of knowledge in an intelligible way while at the same time excluding other ways of reasoning as unintelligible. However, meaning does not proliferate in an endless deferral but is regulated by power which governs not only what can be said under determinate social and cultural conditions but who can speak, when and where.

Poststructuralism is anti-humanist in its de-centring of the unified, coherent human subject as the origin of stable meanings. For poststructuralism, a person or subject is not a stable universal entity but an effect of language that constructs an 'I' in grammar. Thus, for Foucault the subject is radically historicized, that is, persons are understood to be wholly and only the product of history. The speaking subject is dependent on the prior existence of discursive subject positions, that is, empty spaces or functions in discourse from which to comprehend the world. Living persons are required to 'take up' subject positions in discourse in order to make sense of the world and to appear coherent to others.

In sum, poststructuralism absorbs the argument of structuralism regarding the relational character of language and the production of significance through difference. However, poststructuralism rejects the idea of a stable structure of binary pairs; rather, meaning is always deferred, in process and intertextual. Poststructuralism abandons the search for origins, stable meaning, universal truth and the 'direction' of history. Truth is not so much found as made and identities are discursive constructions. That is, truth and identity are not fixed objects but are regulated ways that we speak about the world or ourselves. Instead of the scientific certainty of structuralism, poststructuralism offers us irony. That is, an awareness of the contingent constructed character of our beliefs and understandings that lack firm universal foundations.

Poststructuralism has become an extremely influential stance within cultural studies. For example, the concept of 'différance' is at the heart of **Hall**'s important conceptualization of identity as a discursive construction. Indeed, the post-structuralist inspired 'linguistic turn' within cultural studies, including the widespread adoption of the concept of discourse, is core to the anti-essentialism and social constructionism that mark the field.

Links **Anti-essentialism, différance, discourse, semiotics, structuralism, subject position**

Power The concept of power is an important one within cultural studies, indeed a concern for its mechanisms and consequences forms a central part of what makes cultural studies the way that it is. Thus, for **Bennett**, cultural studies is 'defined', at least in part, as an interdisciplinary field in which perspectives from different disciplines can be selectively drawn on to examine the relations of culture and power. Likewise, for **Hall** what marks out the pursuit of cultural studies from other related disciplines is the connection that it seeks to make to matters of power and cultural change. Hence the centrality of cultural politics to cultural studies, since questions of power and politics go hand in hand; indeed they constitute and define each other.

Cultural studies is centrally concerned with culture as constituted by the meanings and representations that are generated by signifying mechanisms in the context of human practices. The construction of representation is necessarily a matter of power since any representation involves the selection and organization of signs and meanings. For example, whether one describes a particular armed person as a 'terrorist' or a 'freedom fighter' is the practice of cultural power. Further, it is the organization of signs according to cultural conventions within a particular context that regulates meaning. Regulation is by definition a matter of power even though the apparent transparency of meaning achieved through cultural habituation may conceal its practices. Indeed, the very act of concealment and thus the naturalization of meaning is an expression of power.

Many cultural studies writers have approached questions of power through the concept of ideology, a term that refers to the organizing and justifying ideas that groups of people hold about themselves and the world. Traditionally within cultural studies the notion of ideology has been deployed to refer to ideas that justify the power of ascendant groups, though it can be used to suggest the justifying ideas of all social groups. The related concept of hegemony can be understood in terms of the strategies by which the ideologies or world-views of powerful social groups are maintained. Here culture is understood as a terrain of conflict and struggle over meanings and thus the concept of hegemony necessarily 'contains' or connotes issues of power.

In this context, power is being conceptualized as a force by which individuals or groups are able to achieve their aims or interests over and against the will of others. Power here is constraining (power over) in the context of a zero sum model (you have it or you do not) and organized into binary power blocs. Thus the idea of hegemony commonly infers the exercise of constraint by the powerful over the subordinate and connotes an undesirable 'imposition' disguised as widespread consent. However, where cultural studies has been influenced by poststructuralism it has, after **Foucault**, stressed that power is also productive and enabling (power to), circulating through all levels of society and within all social relationships. Foucault likens the circulation of power through human societies to a capillary system and argues that it is vital to the generation of subjectivity. Further, Foucault regards all knowledge as implicated with power in a mutually constituting relationship by which knowledge is indissociable from regimes of power and discipline.

Thus far the idea of power has been explored in relation to questions of representation. However, some critics have argued that a concentration on signification and texts as the repository of power ignores the institutional dimensions of cultural authority. That is, culture is caught up in, and functions as a part of, cultural technologies that organize and shape social life and human conduct. Culture is not just a matter of representations and consciousness but of institutional practices, administrative routines and spatial arrangements that are manifestations of power.

Foucault has been a prominent theorist of the 'disciplinary' character of modern institutions, practices and discourses where discipline involves the organization of the subject in space through dividing practices, training and standardization. Discipline produces subjects by categorizing and naming them in a hierarchical order through a rationality of efficiency, productivity and normalization. Disciplinary technologies are said to have arisen in a variety of sites, including schools, prisons, hospitals and asylums, producing what Foucault called 'docile bodies' that could be subjected, used, transformed and improved.

The metaphor of disciplinary power commonly associated with Foucault is the Panopticon, a prison design consisting of a courtyard with a tower in the centre capable of overlooking the surrounding buildings and cells. The inmates of the cells are visible to the observer in the tower but the onlooker is unable to be seen by the prisoners. The idea of the Panopticon is a metaphor (it is doubtful that the design was materialized) for a continuous, anonymous and all-pervading power and surveillance operating at all levels of social organization.

Links **Cultural politics, governmentality, hegemony, ideology, politics, poststructuralism, power/knowledge**

Power/knowledge After **Foucault**, the concept of power/ knowledge concerns the mutually constituting relationship between power and knowledge so that the production of knowledge is understood to be intertwined with regimes of power. That is, knowledge is formed within the context of the relationships and practices of power and subsequently contributes to the development, refinement and proliferation of new techniques of power. Consequently, theory is not neutral but always implicated in questions of social power since power and knowledge are mutually constitutive. However, no simple uncontaminated 'truth' can be counterposed to power/knowledge for there is no truth outside of or beyond power/knowledge itself.

The concept of power/knowledge can be understood by contrasting it to the predominant Enlightenment idea of a universal and objective truth. For Foucault, truth and knowledge do not possess metaphysical, transcendental or universal properties as they do for Enlightenment thinkers. Rather they are the products of socially located human beings that are specific to particular times and spaces. Since knowledge is not neutral, universal or objective but always a human product so it is also always implicated in questions of social authority.

The concept of discourse is important to Foucault's understanding of power/knowledge since discourse constructs, defines and produces the objects of knowledge in an intelligible way while excluding other forms of reasoning as unintelligible. Here knowledge as discourse is a product of the way statements are combined and regulated, that is, subject to power, under particular and determinate historical conditions. Thus power forms and defines a distinct field of knowledge/ objects constituted by a particular set of concepts. This ordered domain of language delimits a specific 'regime of truth' (that is, what counts as truth).

Links **Discourse, Enlightenment, episteme, epistemology, ideology, power, truth**

Practice A practice is a way of doing things, an action, application or performance that occurs as a consequence of intention, habit or routine. Within cultural studies the significance of the concept derives from its implicit and explicit contrast with notions of a disembodied language, text or discourse.

From within cultural studies, 'culture' has commonly been understood to work 'like a language' in that representations are assembled and generate meaning with essentially the same mechanisms as a language. That is, the formation of meaningful representations involves the selection and organization of signs into texts that are constituted through a form of grammar. Further, language endows material objects and social practices with meanings that are brought into view and made intelligible to us in terms which language delimits. While the metaphor of culture as 'like a language' has a great deal to recommend it, it is not sound thinking to allow language to be separated off from practices since language is always embedded in practice. Further, all practices signify so that there is no special layer of signifying practices as such. Indeed, **Foucault**'s much-used concept of discourse refers to a unity of language and practice and not simply to rule-governed combinations of statements.

According to **Wittgenstein**, we learn language as an integral part of learning how to *do* things so that language is not necessarily best described as a coherent system or set of structural relations. Rather language is 'action' and meanings are temporarily stabilized by social convention for practical purposes in the context of their usage. Signification does not occur in a separate domain from other practices; all practices signify, and meaning is the product of the indistinguishability of signs and social practice. The 'propositions' or world-views that constitute culture and guide us are not made up simply of words, sentences and discourses but also of practices.

Much of our bedrock of convictions is a part of what **Giddens** calls our 'practical consciousness', that is, a condition of being that is rarely made discursively explicit but which is embedded in the practical conduct of social life. This involves the intertwining of language as a social institution and the taken-for-granted stocks of knowledge/practices of everyday life. Conversely, we also undertake a number of practices that are productive of ourselves, those which Foucault describes as 'techniques of the self', that is, the practices that generate the self.

Links **Discourse, language, language-game, meaning, semiotics**

Pragmatism A philosophical tradition of US origin that includes the work of William James, John Dewey and, more recently, Richard **Rorty**. Pragmatism has a radically contingent view of the world where truth ends with social practice and progress is a retrospective value judgement based on trial and error experimentalism. Here all problems are problems of conduct and all judgements are implicitly judgements of value.

Pragmatism is a form of anti-representationalism whereby language is not thought able to represent the world in ways that correspond to an independent object world. This is to argue that there are no pieces of language that line up with or correspond to chunks of reality. Above all, there is no Archimedean vantage point from which one could verify the universal 'truth' of any correspondence between the world and representation. The anti-foundationalism that follows from this argument suggests that we cannot ground or justify our actions and beliefs by means of universal truths. We can describe this or that discourse, chunk of language, as being more or less useful and as having more or less desirable consequences. However, we cannot claim it to be true in the sense of correspondence with an independent object world.

For Rorty, the contingency of language leads us into irony where this concept means holding to beliefs and attitudes which one knows are contingent and could be otherwise, that is, they have no universal foundations. This in turn leads us to ask about what kind of human being we want to be since no transcendental truth and no transcendental God can answer this question for us. This includes questions about us as individuals – who we want to be – and questions about our relations to fellow human beings – how shall we treat others? These are pragmatic questions requiring political-value responses and not metaphysical or epistemological issues.

These arguments turn our attention away from the search for universal truth and towards justification as the giving of reasons. This reason-giving is a social practice so that to justify a belief is to give reasons in the context of a tradition and a community. Here, reasons have an intersubjective base in the community norms for reason-giving and tend towards agreement on claims that have been merited by practice. Thus, justification is a part of an ongoing 'conversation' of humanity and however we characterize 'truth' we have no reliable source for it other than our ongoing conversation with each other.

Richard Rorty, the main contemporary exponent of pragmatism, has often been called a postmodern philosopher though he has on occasion tried to distance himself from this nomination. However, like postmodernism, pragmatism is against 'grand theory', being in sympathy with **Lyotard**'s 'incredulity towards metanarratives'. However, this does not mean that all theory is to be jettisoned, but rather that local theory becomes a way of re-describing the world in normative ways.

Since pragmatism understands the universe as always 'in the making', the future has ethical significance so that we can, it is argued, make a difference and create new 'better' futures. Here pragmatism embraces a form of 'ethical naturalism' by which ethics do not need metaphysical foundations to be justified, that is, ethics do not require to be grounded in anything outside or beyond our beliefs and desires. In this sense, pragmatism insists on the irreducibility of human agency even as it recognizes the causal stories of the past. Pragmatism shares with poststructuralism and post-Marxism the idea that social and cultural change is a matter of 'politics without guarantees'. That is, politics is centred on small-scale experimentalism, value-commitment and practical action and not on any claimed universal 'laws' of history or human conduct.

As a philosophy, pragmatism is not necessarily supportive of any particular political stance. However, Rorty's politics are those of 'Liberalism' in a broad sense while in its particulars he has repeatedly described himself as of 'the Left'. The hope of Liberalism for Rorty is to find ways for human beings to be freer, less cruel, more leisured and richer in goods and experiences while trying to maximize people's opportunities to live their lives as they see fit. That is, to pursue a private project founded on their own values and beliefs while not causing suffering to others. Since liberal democracy and cultural pluralism work imperfectly, it is entirely acceptable to Rortian Liberals to critique those aspects of our societies and cultures that restrict freedoms and cause suffering.

Links **Epistemology, foundationalism, irony, language-game, Liberalism, representation, truth**

Praxis We commonly think of a practice as a way of doing things, an action, application or performance that is contrasted to theory or abstract thinking. This counterpoising of theory to the practical is a legacy of Aristotle's classification of disciplines as theoretical, productive or practical. However, Aristotle also introduced the idea of 'praxis', which is not merely a mechanical making but a conceptually inspired 'creative doing'. Thus the concept of praxis, which derives from the Greek word for 'action that shapes the world', seeks to dissolve the distinction between theory and practice.

The concept of praxis involves a deconstruction of the binary pair of theory and practice involving recognition that each belongs to and in the other. For example, theory is not an unproblematic reflection or discovery of objective truth about an independent object world but a culturally situated practice. Equally, the meaning of a practice does not inhere within the action itself and no amount of stacking up of empirical data about practice can produce a meaningful story outside of the structures of language and theory. This overcoming of the divide between theory and practice is the meaning of praxis that has most concerned modern users of the concept.

The development of Marxism proved to be a significant moment in the modern extension of the use of the concept of praxis into the social and cultural domain. Thus Marx is critical of all previous forms of materialism for conceiving of 'reality' *only* as an object of contemplation rather than as a practice. However, as Marx argued, while humans are practical beings the ground on which they act has already be determined for them. Thus, on the one hand the consciousness of human beings is the product of particular historical material conditions, but on the other hand we are able to change those conditions, which by implication, leads to further alterations in human thinking. Thus the very knowledge produced by people under specific historical conditions enables them to bring about material change and as a consequence to change themselves. Thus does the circle of praxis keep turning.

As well as dissolving the distinction between 'theory' and 'practice', the notion of praxis can also be understood as overcoming the binary divide between 'thought' and 'action' as well as between 'agency' and 'determination'. The concept of praxis helps us to grasp the actor as simultaneously culturally situated, that is, determined, and as a choice-making actor. Theoretical knowledge and practice can never be separated so that culture can be understood as the embodied praxis of performances. For example, the creative, expressive and symbolic work of youth subcultures is constituted by a situated creative doing – the praxis of performativity. Thus, according to **Hebdige**, British Punk was a 'revolting style' that was not simply responding to the crisis of British decline manifested in joblessness, poverty and changing moral standards but performed and dramatized it in an angry, dislocated, but self-aware and ironic mode of signification.

Links **Agency, determinism, Marxism, practice, performativity, structuration, structure**

Psychoanalysis Psychoanalysis is a body of thought and therapeutic practice developed from the nineteenth-century writings of Sigmund **Freud** and which has been further refined and modified by subsequent thinkers. It has been the version of psychoanalysis developed by **Lacan** in the 1970s and interpreted by Judith **Butler** and Julia **Kristeva** amongst others that has been the most influential stream within cultural studies. For its supporters, the great strength of psychoanalysis lies in its rejection of the fixed nature of subjects and sexuality in favour of exploring the construction and formation of subjectivity.

Psychoanalysis points us to the psychic, non-linear, arational and emotional aspects of culture, subjectivity and identity. The main interest of cultural studies writers in psychoanalysis has centred on the formation of gendered subjectivity. For **Hall**, writing about identity in the 1990s, psychoanalysis has particular significance in shedding light on how discursively constructed subject positions are taken up (or otherwise) by concrete persons through their fantasy identifications and emotional 'investments'.

According to Freud, the self is constituted in terms of an ego, or conscious rational mind, a superego or social conscience, and the unconscious, the source and repository of the symbolic workings of the mind that functions with a different logic from reason. Here the self is by definition fractured so that the unified narrative of the self can be understood as something we attain over time through entry into the symbolic order of language and culture. Freud argued that the libido or sexual drive does not have any pre-given fixed aim or object, rather through fantasy, any object, which includes persons or parts of bodies, can be the target of desire. Thus, an almost infinite number of sexual objects and practices are within the domain of human sexuality. Subsequently, Freud's work is concerned to document and explain the regulation and repression of this 'polymorphous perversity' through the resolution (or not) of the Oedipus complex into the normative fate of heterosexual gendered relationships.

In Lacan's reading of Freud the resolution of the Oedipus complex marks the formation of the unconscious as the realm of the repressed and the moment of entry into the symbolic order that enables the very possibility of subjectivity. For Lacan, the symbolic order is the overarching structure of language and received social meanings that constitutes the domain of human law and culture. Crucially, subjectivity is gendered as the Phallus serves to break up the mother–child dyad and stands for entry into the symbolic order. Indeed, it is the Phallus as 'transcendental signifier' that enables entry into language (for both sexes) and, by standing in for the fragmented subject, allows the construction of a narrative of wholeness.

For Lacan the unconscious is the site for the generation of meaningful representations that are structured 'like a language'. Not only is language the route to the unconscious, but the unconscious is a site of signification, that is, of meaningful activity. In particular, the mechanisms of condensation and displacement, which Freud saw as the most important of the 'primary processes', are held by Lacan to be analogous to the linguistic functions of metaphor and metonymy.

Both Freud and Lacan have been criticized for being phallocentric. That is, their work is said to be a set of male-centred discourses in general and more specifically ones that are focused on the Phallus. Further, though psychoanalysis claims to be a scientific method it rarely produces empirical and testable experimental evidence in its support. Thus, psychoanalysis is a historically specific way of understanding persons even though it makes claims to universality. Indeed, in so far as psychoanalysis relies on linguistic and cultural processes that are deemed to be ahistorical and universal, since they mark the psychic processes of humankind across history, then at the very least it sits uncomfortably within a cultural studies that emphasizes the cultural construction of subjectivity. Whatever its strengths and weaknesses, psychoanalysis must be taken as a historically specific account of human sexuality and subjectivity.

Links **Identification, mirror phase, Oedipus complex, Other, phallocentric, subjectivity, symbolic order**

Public sphere A space for democratic public debate and argument that mediates between civil society and the state in which the public organizes itself and in which 'public opinion' is formed. Within this sphere individuals are able to develop themselves and engage in debate about the direction of society. The concept of the public sphere plays a particularly important role in the work of Jürgen **Habermas**, who traces its historical development from the rise of literary clubs, salons, newspapers, political journals and institutions of political debate and participation in eighteenth-century European 'bourgeois society'. In this context, argues Habermas, the public sphere was partially protected from both the church and the state by the resources of private individuals. Here the public sphere was in principle, though not in practice, open to all.

Habermas documents what he sees as the subsequent decline of the public sphere in the face of the development of capitalism towards monopoly and the strengthening of the state. The increased commodification of everyday life by giant corporations and the proliferation of the non-rational products of the advertising and public relations industries transform people from rational citizens into consumers. In a parallel erosion of the public sphere, the state has taken increased power over our lives through its economic role as a corporate manager and into the private realm of the family, where it acts as the superintendent of welfare provision and education. Nevertheless, Habermas attempts to ground the renewal of the public sphere in the notion of an 'ideal speech situation' where competing truth-claims are subject to rational debate and argument so that the public sphere is conceived as a space for debate based on conversational equality.

There has been considerable criticism of the historical accuracy of Habermas' account of the public sphere and of its male orientation. Further, some writers, such as **Giddens**, have suggested that the modern media have actually expanded the public sphere. More philosophically, some postmodern critics, particularly **Lyotard**, have argued that Habermas reproduces the totalizing discourse of 'Enlightenment reason' ignoring its repressive character. However, whatever the historical problems with Habermas' work, the idea of a public sphere retains a strong *normative* appeal. Postmodernists, poststructuralists and neo-pragmatists would all think Habermas mistaken in his attempt to construct a universal and transcendental rational justification for the public sphere. Nevertheless, it can be justified on the pragmatic grounds of cultural pluralism without the need for such a universalizing epistemological defence.

Links **Citizenship, Enlightenment, ideal speech situation, nation-state, politics, rationality**

Q

Queer theory Queer theory is a term that has been applied to a body of work that has explored gay, lesbian and bisexual life experience. Crucial to queer theory is the recovery of the concealed and repressed presence of gay and lesbian 'actors' and activities within social and cultural life. More broadly, queer theory has explored the processes through which sexual identities are constituted within contemporary culture. Here queer theory has advanced anti-essentialist claims regarding the cultural construction of sexual identities including their plurality and ambivalence.

The word 'queer' has been re-articulated and re-signified by ACT-UP, Queer Nation and other communities of queer politics to deflect its injurious effects and turn it into an expression of resistance. Thus the term 'queer' is a provocative re-nomination that appropriates earlier offensive descriptions of gay and lesbian life and turns them to its advantage. To 'be queer' is to adopt a non-straight lifestyle and 'to queer' is to estrange or de-familiarize identities, texts and attitudes that had otherwise been taken for granted. According to Judith **Butler**, who is one of the high-profile writers associated with queer theory, while the use of the term 'queer' as an affirmative has proved politically useful it continues to echo its past pejorative usage. This suggests that identity categories cannot necessarily be redefined in any way whatsoever.

Butler conceives of sex in terms of performativity produced as a reiteration of the regulatory apparatus of heterosexual hegemonic norms. The identification involved in the construction of sexual identity constitutes an exclusionary matrix by which the processes of subject formation simultaneously produce a constitutive outside. That is, identification with one set of norms, say heterosexuality, repudiates another, say homosexuality. Indeed, the abjection or 'throwing out' of gay and lesbian sexuality by the heterosexual 'imperative' is one of Butler's particular concerns. Nevertheless, she has suggested that through a miming of gender norms drag can recast and destabilize them through a re-signification of the ideals of gender. Drag suggests that all gender is performativity and as such destabilizes the claims of hegemonic heterosexual masculinity as the origin that is imitated. However, as she points out, drag is at best always ambivalent and can be itself a reiteration and affirmation of the Law of the Father and heterosexuality.

Links **Anti-essentialism, gender, identification, identity, performativity, sex**

R

Race For cultural studies, 'race' is a signifier indicating categories of people based on alleged biological characteristics, including skin pigmentation. Thus, the distinctiveness of the cultural studies approach to the topic lies in its treatment of race as a discursive-performative construction; that is, race is taken to be a form of identity. Race is understood not as a universal or absolute existent 'thing' but rather as a contingent and unstable cultural category with which people identify. However, racial categories are not entirely arbitrary either; rather, what they mean is temporarily stabilized by social practice. Indeed, race appears to be one of the more enduring 'nodal points' of identity in modern Western societies.

Understood as a form of identity, race does not exist outside of representation but is forged as a meaningful category in and by symbolization in the context of social and political power struggles. Thus, observable characteristics are transformed into signifiers of race, including the spurious appeal to essential biological difference. In this context, cultural studies has explored the shifting character of cultural understandings of race and ethnicity in terms of representation. That is, the cultural politics of race as a 'politics of representation'.

The representation of race continues to bear the traces of its origins in biological discourses that stress 'lines of descent' and 'types of people'. Here the concept of race refers to alleged biological and physical characteristics, the most obvious of which is skin pigmentation. These attributes are frequently linked to 'intelligence' and 'capabilities' and then used to rank groups in a hierarchy of social and material superiority and subordination. The process by which a group is 'turned into' a race through racial classifications constituted by power is known as 'racialization'. The concept of racialization refers to the way in which social relations between people have been structured by the signification of human biological characteristics. Thus, the idea of 'racialization' or 'race formation' is founded on the argument that race is a social construction and not a universal or essential category of biology.

The historical formation of 'races' has been a process dependent on power and subordination so that people of colour have generally occupied structurally subordinate positions in relation to every dimension of 'life-chances'. For example, British Afro-Caribbeans, African Americans and Australian Aboriginal peoples have been disadvantaged in the labour market, the housing market, the education system and within the media. In this context, race formation has been inherently racist, for it involves forms of social, economic and political subordination that are lived through the categories and discourses of race. Indeed, an anti-essentialist understanding of race entails recognition that race is always articulated with other categories and divisions such as class, gender and ethnicity.

The meanings of 'race' change and are struggled over so that different groups are differentially racialized and subject to different forms of racism. Thus there are racism*s* rather than a single racism. Further, the meanings of race differ between, say, the United States and Britain. In Britain, the arrival of migrants from the Caribbean and Indian sub-continent in the 1950s enabled racialization to occur in and through the category of national identity. However, the history of the modern United States began with the dispossession and genocide of native American peoples and continued through the long history of slavery. Thus, questions of race are posed at the very inception of the United States in ways that are more longstanding, but less concerned with nationality, than in Britain.

Links **Anti-essentialism, ethnicity, identity, national identity, performativity, representation**

Radway, Janice (1949–) Janice Radway is Frances Hill Fox Professor in Humanities at Duke University (USA). Radway has written extensively on issues of gender, popular culture, ethnography and the subjects of reading and literary consumption in the age of mass media. Her current research interests are in the history of literacy and reading in the United States, particularly as they bear on the lives of women. She is perhaps best known for her book *Reading the Romance*, an ethnographic study of the ways women read romantic fiction and the uses to which it is put. She has also explored the act of reading in relation to the Book-of-the-Month Club where she examines issues of class, gender and literary taste.

- **Associated concepts** Active audience, consumption, gender, reading, text, writing.
- **Tradition(s)** Cultural studies, ethnography, feminism, hermeneutics.
- **Reading** Radway, J. (1987) *Reading the Romance: Women, Patriarchy and Popular Literature*. London: Verso.

Rationality The concept of rationality refers to the grounds on which beliefs are held: namely, that they are coherent, logical and compatible with experience. That is, rational beliefs and actions are said to be the outcome of sound reasoning and valid inference. Since it is irrational to hold beliefs known to be false, then rationality implies that the grounds for holding beliefs are the foundations of truth.

The modern and/or Enlightenment conception of rationality has upheld the idea of a universal rationality that underpins science and other logical methods by which to pursue and discover immutable truths. Enlightenment philosophy of the seventeenth and eighteenth centuries, whose legacy still remains in contemporary realist epistemology, championed rationality as the source of progress in knowledge and society as it demystified religion, myth and superstition. By contrast, poststructuralism, postmodernism and pragmatism all argue that truth and knowledge are perspectival in character and do not possess metaphysical, transcendental or universal properties. In this view, since truth and knowledge are specific to particular times and spaces, there cannot be a single form of rationality that is able to grasp the 'objective' character of the world.

Most writers in cultural studies accept the idea that rationality is grounded in the rule-governed social and cultural conventions of local reason-giving rather than in a universal metaphysics. Here rationality is understood to be a form of social agreement and praise founded on cultural procedures rather than a universal given. That is, rational action is that which can be *justified* within a specific cultural context. This way of thinking understands the rationality of the physical sciences to be a set of specialized languages that form a cultural classification system. That is, the sciences consist of sets of conceptual tools that are the achievement of agreed procedures rather than the revelation of objective truth.

Links **Enlightenment, epistemology, modernism, postmodernism, poststructuralism, pragmatism, truth**

Reading The idea of 'the reader' and of 'reading' is a widely deployed metaphor in cultural studies that is frequently used as an expansive synonym for the practices associated with the interpretation of texts. Within cultural studies a text is taken to be any term of signification generated through the organization of signs into meaningful representations. Thus, just as a text is a literary metaphor for the products of signifying practices so a reader is a metaphor for the reception or decoding of texts.

There is something of a tension between 'democratic' and 'elite' meanings of the concept of reader when it is used within cultural studies. On the one hand reading is understood to be an activity undertaken by all competent actors, while on the other hand it is sometimes attributed to the critics' particularly insightful act of interpretation armed as they are with the tools of semiotics, discourse analysis or literary theory. Further, textual analysis will commonly ascribe a 'reading position' to a textual structure; that is, the text is said to position empirical readers into a particular way of understanding it. However, and by way of contrast, reception-oriented cultural studies have stressed the need to explore the actual grounded readings of culturally situated actors whose production of meanings may depart from those of the critic. In this view, the critic is just another kind of reader and not one with any particularly privileged access to its meanings.

A central issue for hermeneutics, a philosophical endeavour concerned with textual interpretation, has been the degree to which the generation of meaning resides in texts and/or is produced by readers. Likewise, the 'encoding–decoding model' of the text–audience relationship explores the congruence and/or divergence of 'readings' developed by the producers of texts and their readers/audiences. In general terms, whatever analysis of textual meanings a critic may undertake, it is far from certain which of the identified meanings, if any, will be activated by actual readers/audiences/consumers. Thus it is clear that audiences bring previously acquired cultural competencies to bear on texts in order to be active creators of meaning.

Links **Active audience, encoding–decoding, hermeneutics, subject position, text**

Realism (a) An epistemological claim that the truth is identifiable as that which corresponds to or pictures the real. As such, realism is another name for representationalism and readers interested in this understanding of the concept of realism should explore the links below.

173

Links **Discourse, Enlightenment, epistemology, language-game, representation, truth**

(b) Realism is a form of artistic representation commonly found in novels, films, plays, paintings and so forth that make claims to be picturing an independent object world as if looking through an unmediated 'window' onto it. Realism purports to show us 'things as they really are' and in doing so disguises its own status as an artifice. Realism also constructs narratives that have rationally ordered connections between events and characters. The narrative of realism sets its self up in a position of knowledge as an overarching 'metanarrative' of truth in the form of the narration of events. This metalanguage privileges and disguises the editorial position. Given that cultural studies deconstructs or takes apart texts in order to show how they are put together, then it is necessarily critical of the epistemological claims of realism. Thus cultural studies understands realism to be a set of *aesthetic conventions* by which texts create 'reality effects'.

For many writers from within cultural studies realism is a politically conservative and authoritarian mode of representation. Thus, anti-realists forge aesthetic practices that reveal their own techniques and allow for reflection upon the processes of signification. Historically, such work has been identified with the 'alienation effects' of Brechtian theatre, for example direct address to the audience or the disruption of the pretence of realism by the spectacle of singing. Later, similar effects are said to have been achieved through the modernist techniques of directors like Jean-Luc Godard which show the operation of cameras and refuse the smooth flow of realist narrative by jumping without 'motivation' from place to place or time to time. In this vein, stories do not follow the established convention of linear causality or the 'ordinary' flow of everyday time. More recently, it has been claimed that postmodernism challenges the domination of realism in television, but unlike modernism, does this through accessible popular culture.

However, the deconstructive work is itself a construction, a language of its own, which can be a problem where large numbers of people do not speak that language. Thus non-realist transgressive performances may not be read as such by audiences who do not already understand the 'rules' being violated and the purposes of the performance. Since the success of styles of cultural intervention is closely connected to the context of their occurrence, realist and naturalist modes of representation are not always politically mistaken because realism may be the only possible language of communication for a particular audience.

Links **Aesthetics, avant-garde, modernism, narrative, representation, soap opera**

Reductionism Reductionism is a form of explanation by which one category or phenomenon is likened to and explained solely in terms of another category or phenomenon. Here, to reduce means to lessen, contract and diminish since one component of human endeavour is deemed to have no specificity of its own but rather is the product of another form of activity. In particular, many cultural studies writers have argued against forms of economic reductionism by which the meanings of cultural texts are accounted for in terms of political economy. It is suggested that understanding culture cannot take the form of an economic explanation alone because culture has its own specific forms and it own particular mechanisms of operation. These specific features of culture cannot be reduced to (that is, explained in terms of) the activities of wealth production and distribution (though these are important facets of any culture).

Cultural studies has also been opposed to biological reductionism by which human behaviour is grasped in terms of invariant features of human genetic endowment that are resistant to change. A reductionist argument suggests that genetics alone can provide a sufficient explanation for features of human culture such as aggression no matter what other factors are present. Thus a biological reductionist claim might involve saying that all men are more aggressive by nature, whatever the environment, than are women. However, we need to 'deconstruct' the opposition of nature and culture that is inherent in such arguments. On the one hand culture is an outgrowth of human beings learning and adapting within their natural ancestral environment, but on the other hand nature is already a concept in language (and not a pure state of being beyond signs). Further, the natural world has come under the sway of human knowledge and institutions so that we speak of the 'socialization of nature' and through the investigations of genetic science we are learning to intrude even further into the 'natural' human body.

Since we are complex biological and cultural creatures, any plausible attempt to understand ourselves must embrace the idea of holism and complex system analysis where objects of analysis are considered not only in isolation but also within their systemic context. Indeed, the human and physical worlds are so interconnected both within themselves and between each other that everything can be said to affect everything else. As such reductionism is in general an unacceptable form of analysis and explanation of human behaviour. Nevertheless, it may be useful to adopt a distinction put forward by the philosopher Daniel Dennett between 'greedy reductionism' and 'good reductionism'.

Greedy reductionism seeks to reduce all human behaviour to one phenomenon without recourse to intermediate causal steps, while good reductionism attempts to explain phenomena through causal chains without resort to mysteries or miracles. While greedy reductionism is unacceptable the adoption of 'good reductionism' is merely to suggest that we can discover *causal chains* and explanations for human behaviour. Traditional science disciplines are reductionist in the sense that they break down objects of analysis into smaller and smaller parts that are subsequently related to each other in an explanatory causal chain. In terms of the relationship between culture and economy we can see something of this in the 'circuit of culture' approach that is focused on the articulation of production and text rather than on one-way determination.

Links **Circuit of culture, cultural materialism, deconstruction, determinism, evolutionary psychology.**

Reflexivity At one level reflexivity can be understood as a process of continuous self-monitoring including the use of knowledge about personal and social life as a constitutive element of it. In this way the modern person can be grasped as a 'reflexive project', that is, the ordering of self-narratives through self-reflection constitutes self-identity. Here identity is understood in terms of the self as reflexively understood by persons in terms of their biography. On a more institutional level, increased social and organizational reflexivity is manifested in the desire of institutions to know more about the population who are the object of their surveillance. This involves increased forms of observation and supervision from cameras in shopping centres and 'quality management' at work to the increased significance of marketing. Thus, institutional reflexivity involves the paradox that it appears to enhance individual creativity and control over the direction of lifestyles while at the same time serving forms of social control.

Reflexivity involves constructing discourses about personal and social experience so that to engage in reflexivity is to partake in a range of discourses and relationships while constructing further discourses about them. The cultural rise of reflexivity is connected to the emergence of modernity in that modern life involves the constant examination and alteration of social practices in the light of incoming information about those practices. Traditional cultures value stability and the place of persons in a normatively ordered and immutable cosmos so that the order of things in life is the way it is because that is how it should be. Here, identity is primarily a question of social position. By contrast, modernism values change, life planning and reflexivity so that for moderns identity is a reflexive project.

Without the certainties of traditional religious and cultural beliefs modern life may appear as a series of proliferating choices to be made without foundations. This encourages us to be more reflexive about ourselves since we have no certainties to fall back on. Here reflexivity has been associated with the 'late' modern or postmodern in that it enables increased possibilities for the playful self-construction of multiple identities. It also requires that we compare our traditions with those of others. Consequently, for some critics postmodern culture invites the 'other' of modernity, those voices that had been suppressed by the modern drive to extinguish difference, to find ways to speak.

Reflexivity appears to have particular resonance with the themes of postmodernism since it encourages an ironic sense of the 'said before', that is, the feeling that one cannot invent anything new but merely play with the already existent. Eco gives a good example of this with the person who cannot, without irony, say 'I love you' but prefaces it with the words 'As Barbara Cartland would say'. The thing is said, but the unoriginality of the words is acknowledged. Indeed, irony understood as a reflexive understanding of the contingency of one's own values and culture is the key sensibility of postmodernism. Further, a widespread reflexive awareness of the history of film, television, music and literature promotes a culture of ironic knowingness.

Links **Irony, modernism, postmodernism, self-identity, surveillance**

Relativism Epistemological relativism is the argument that one cannot judge between forms of knowledge that have radically different grounds of validity. That is, one cannot identify absolute and universal forms of truth, but rather knowledge is true only within the domain of its formation and operation. Thus relativism involves the rejection of overarching universal rules or procedures for deciding between truth-claims. Cultural relativism is the extension of that argument to different cultures leading to the suggestion that beliefs that appear to be invalid in the context of one culture are not so in another. Thus, the claim that 'X is an act of witchcraft' will not hold up within the confines of Western science but can be said to be valid within a culture for which witchcraft is a truthful practice.

It is common to suggest that relativism is a self-defeating argument since the very statement 'all truths are relative' must itself be held to be relative to the domain of its utterance. Equally, to say that the statement 'all truths are relative' is universally true is a contradiction in terms. Poststructuralism, postmodernism and pragmatism, streams of philosophical thought that are strong within cultural studies, have all been 'accused' of relativism. This is so because they all reject the validity of universal truth-claims. They argue that no universalizing epistemology is possible because all truth-claims are formed within discourse or language-games so that all truth is culture-bound.

The postmodern philosopher **Lyotard** does seem to embrace relativism when he argues that language is made up of islets each of which is governed by a system of rules that is untranslatable into those of others. Here truth and meaning are constituted by their place in specific local language-games and cannot be universal in character. Some other postmodern writers also embrace relativism arguing that truth is/should be an outcome of debates between competing claims. They suggest that the consequence of saying that truths are only truths within specific language-games is to accept the legitimacy of a range of truth-claims, discourses and representations of reality.

Richard **Rorty**, the leading contemporary exponent of pragmatism, also rejects the idea of universal truth since there can be no access to an independent object world from an Archimedean vantage point from which one could neutrally evaluate claims. For Rorty the notion of truth refers at best to a degree of social agreement within a particular tradition. However, he rejects the idea that such an argument is a form of relativism. This is because all knowledge is culture-bound and thus one cannot see across different forms of knowledge in order to regard them as of equal value. Rather, we are always positioned *within* acculturated knowledge so that the true and the good are what 'we' believe. Judgements can only be made by reference to 'our' values and not to a transcendental truth. Nevertheless, 'our' values can (and for Rorty they should) accept the moral right of others to hold different points of view. In other words, cultural pluralism is a value of 'our' tradition.

Critics of relativism argue that rejecting the possibility of a universal knowledge in favour of accepting its culture-bound character leads to the problem of incommensurability. That is, without a 'meta' or universal language one culture cannot talk to or understand another because their foundations of knowledge are radically divergent. However, Rorty argues that if we consider languages (and thus culture) as constituted not by untranslatable and incompatible rules but as learnable skills, then incommensurable languages could only be unlearnable languages, which, it is argued, is not possible. Though exact translation of languages or cultures is not feasible we can learn the skills of other languages and so enable dialogue and the attempt to reach pragmatic agreements.

Links **Constructionism, epistemology, language-game, postmodernism, poststructuralism, pragmatism, truth**

Representation The commonsense meaning of the concept of representation is that of a set of processes by which signifying practices appear to stand for or depict another object or practice in the 'real' world. Representation is thus an act of symbolism that mirrors an independent object world. However, for cultural studies representation does not simply reflect in symbolic form 'things' that exist in an independent object world, rather, representations are constitutive of the meaning of that which they purport to stand in for. That is, representation does not involve correspondence between signs and objects but creates the 'representational effect' of realism.

The philosophies of language (that form of representation par excellence) that have most informed cultural studies have suggested that representations are meaningful as a consequence of being a system of differential signs that generate significance through difference. That is, meaning is relational and unstable rather than referential and fixed. Representation endows material objects and social practices with meaning and intelligibility and in doing so constructs those maps of meaning that are constitutive of culture. Thus, the investigation of culture has often been regarded as virtually interchangeable with the exploration of the processes of representation. While culture is not just a matter of representations but also of practices and spatial arrangements, it can nevertheless be argued that it is the process of representation that makes practices meaningful and significant to us.

Since representations are not innocent reflections of the real but are cultural constructions, they could be otherwise than they appear to us. Here representation is intrinsically bound up with questions of power through the process of selection and organization that must inevitably be a part of the formation of representations. The power of representation lies in its enabling some kinds of knowledge to exist while excluding other ways of seeing. Consequently, cultural studies writers often talk about a 'politics of representation'. When we ask the question what does it mean to be a certain kind of person – male, female, young, old, black, white, gay, straight and so forth – we are engaged in a politics of representation. For example, the identity of being black does not reflect an essential state of being but rather is one that has to be represented and learned. **Hall** argues that a 'politics of representation' must register the arbitrariness of signification and generate a willingness to live with difference. That is, a politics of representation inquires into the power relations inherent in the representation of 'blackness' while simultaneously deconstructing the very terms of a black–white binary.

Links **Discourse, language, language-game, meaning, poststructuralism, pragmatism, semiotics, truth**

Resistance The common use of the term resistance refers to opposition or insubordination that issues from relationships of power and domination. That is, resistance takes the form of challenges to and negotiations of the ascendant order. However, resistance is not a singular and universal act that defines itself for all time, rather it is constituted by repertoires of activity whose meanings are specific to particular times, places and social relationships. That is, resistance needs to be thought of in relational and conjunctural terms. Further, resistance is not an intrinsic quality of an act but a category of judgement about acts and as such is a judgement that classifies the classifier.

It is common to understand resistance as an essentially defensive relationship to cultural power experienced as external and 'other' by subordinate social forces. Here, resistance arises where a dominating culture is seeking to impose itself on subordinate cultures from without. Consequently, resources of resistance are to be located in some measure outside of the dominating culture. This is the way that resistance has commonly been understood by cultural studies writers when they talk about class conflict, ideological struggle or counter-hegemonic blocs. This is to grasp resistance in terms of a zero-sum model of power that involves constraint. For example, subcultural style was understood as a dynamic and creative signifying practice of spectacular subcultures that was contrasted to passive consumption of cultural industry commodities and as such was a manifestation of symbolic resistance.

An alternative account of resistance (associated with **De Certeau** and **Foucault**) conceptualizes the resistive practices of everyday life as always already in the space of power. Consequently, there are no 'margins' outside of power from which to lay an assault on it or from within which to claim authenticity. Thus, where resistance is taking place in contemporary culture it is happening 'inside' consumer lifestyles, transforming commodities and using the mass media. For example, since there is no outside to commodified culture from which external resistance can be mounted, youth cultural styles are not formed outside and opposed to consumer culture and the media but within and through them. Here resistance is not to be thought of as a simple reversal of the order of high and low, of power and its absence, but rather of ambivalence and negotiation as exemplified by the transgressive character of the 'carnivalesque'.

Links **Carnivalesque, class, hegemony, ideology, power, style, youth culture**

Rhizome A rhizome is a form of botanical growth that, unlike a single root structure, produces different points of equal growth across a lateral path. In cultural studies the concept is deployed as a metaphor of logic or conjunction that stresses non-linear patterns of interconnection and feedback loops. This forms a contrast to the culturally predominant arboreal metaphors of 'root and branch' in which the image of the tree predominates, with causality running in straight lines. Burrows in their interconnected layout and multiple functions of shelter, supply, movement, evasion and breakout are rhizomorphic in character as are the bulbs and tumours of potatoes.

In the context of cultural studies the idea of the rhizome is particularly associated with the work of **Deleuze and Guattari**, whose 1988 book *A Thousand Plateaus* works across a range of perspectives or plateaus including psychoanalysis, subjectivity, the state, maps, language, forms of writing and so forth in a non-linear multi-perspectival way. However, the idea of the rhizome has wider application than the work of Deleuze and Guattari in so far as it stresses multiplicity, complexity, multi-dimensionality and chaos in contemporary cultural arrangements. The logic of the rhizome resists reductionism and embraces holism and as such shares something with the idea of différance in the work of **Derrida** and the capillary character of power as articulated by **Foucault**.

Links **Deconstruction, determinism, différance, power, reductionism**

Rorty, Richard (1931–) A Professor at Stanford University (USA), Rorty is the leading contemporary writer in the tradition of pragmatism. Rorty advocates anti-representationalism by which language is unable to represent the world in ways that more or less correspond to an independent object world. This leads him to adopt an anti-foundationalism that suggests that we are unable to ground our actions or beliefs in any form of universal truth. For Rorty, language is best understood through the metaphor of the tool rather than that of a mirror, and politics justified from within the values of specific traditions rather than seeking universal foundations. Knowledge is not a matter of getting a true or objective picture of reality but of learning how best to cope with the world. For Rorty the contingency of language underpins irony, that is, holding to beliefs and attitudes which one knows are contingent and could be otherwise. Rorty advocates both a politics of 'new languages' or 're-description' and a reforming Left Liberalism based on hope in the struggle for social justice.

- **Associated concepts** Epistemology, ethnocentrism, foundationalism (anti-), holism, irony, language-game, Liberalism, truth.
- **Tradition(s)** Postmodernism, pragmatism.
- **Reading** Rorty, R. (1989) *Contingency, Irony and Solidarity*. Cambridge: Cambridge University Press.

S

Said, Edward (1935–2003) Said was born in Palestine but emigrated to the United States where he was educated at Princeton and Yale before becoming a Professor at Columbia University (New York). The central themes of Said's work were those of culture and imperialism and he is regarded as one of the foremost writers in the domain of postcolonial literature and theory. In particular, his landmark work *Orientalism* is concerned with the application of **Foucault**'s theories of discourse and power to the political and cultural relationship of the West to the East. Thus, the Orient was understood by Said to be a historically specific discursive construction constituted by Western imagery and vocabulary which generated an Orient that reproduced the hegemony of the West. At the same time, he rejected the idea that the Orient remained passive during and after the process of Western imperialism.

Associated concept Cultural imperialism, discourse, Orientalism, Other, power.

Tradition(s) Marxism, postcolonial theory, poststructuralism.

Reading Said, E. (1978) *Orientalism*. London: Routledge.

Saussure, Ferdinand de (1857–1913) Saussure was a Swiss linguist whose posthumously published book *Course in General Linguistics* (reconstructed from his notes by students) laid the basis for what became structural linguistics or semiotics, the 'science' of signs. Saussure's influence on cultural studies comes indirectly through the work of other thinkers who were influenced by him. It was perhaps Roland **Barthes**' 1972 book *Mythologie*s that most clearly demonstrated the relevance of semiotics to cultural studies and heralded the field's interest in language, signs and culture mediated through Saussure's thinking. The central tenet of Saussure's argument is that language is to be understood as a sign system constituted by interrelated terms without positive values (that is, meaning is relational). *Langue*, or the formal structure of signs, is said to be the proper subject of linguistics.

- **Associated concepts** Language, meaning, signs, structure, text.
- **Tradition(s)** Semiotics, structuralism.
- **Reading** Saussure, F. de (1960) *Course in General Linguistics*. London: Peter Owen.

Self-identity The concept of self-identity refers to the way we think about ourselves and construct unifying narratives of the self with which we emotionally identify. That is, self-identity can be grasped as a reflexive and discursive construction of self, a story we tell ourselves about our self. Stuart **Hall**'s influential conceptualization of identity conceives of it as the suturing or stitching together of the discursive 'outside' with the 'internal' psychic processes of subjectivity. That is, one's identity refers to points of temporary emotional attachment to the subject positions which discursive practices construct for us.

The cultural repertoire of the self in the Western world assumes that we have a true self that can become known to us and that is expressed through forms of representation. Here identity exists as an essential, universal and timeless core of the self that we all possess. However, cultural studies has adopted an anti-essentialist stance by which self-identity is a culturally contingent production that is specific to particular times and places. That is, what it means to be a person is social and cultural 'all the way down'. While there is no known culture that does not use the pronoun 'I' and which does not therefore have a conception of self and personhood, the manner in which 'I' is used, what it means, does vary from culture to culture. Some writers argue that the very concept of 'I' as a self-aware object is a modern Western conception that emerged out of science and the 'Age of Reason'. Certainly people in other cultures do not always share the individualistic sense of uniqueness and self-consciousness that is widespread in Western societies. Rather, identity is inseparable from a network of kinship relations and social obligations.

For **Giddens**, self-identity is constituted by the ability to build up a consistent feeling of biographical continuity through identity stories that attempt to answer the critical questions: 'What to do? How to act? Who to be?' Thus individuals attempt to construct a coherent identity narrative by which the self forms a trajectory of development from the past to an anticipated future. Here self-identity is constituted not by the possession of traits but rather as a reflexively understood biographical project. An identity project builds on what we think we are now in the light of our past and present circumstances in conjunction with what we think we would like to be, that is, the trajectory of our hoped-for future.

Links **Identification, identity, identity project, narrative, reflexivity, subject position, subjectivity**

Semiotics Semiotics is the study (or 'science') of signs and signification that has developed from the pioneering work of **Saussure**. Semiotics is commonly understood to be a form of structuralism because it seeks to explain the generation of meaning by reference to a system of structured differences in language. That is, the rules and conventions that organize language (*langue*) are given priority over the study of the specific utterances that individuals deploy in everyday life (*parole*). Within semiotic theory a signifying system such as a language is understood as an ordering of signs that constructs meaning from within itself through a series of conceptual and phonic differences. In language, it is argued, there are only differences without positive terms. That is, meaning is not generated because an object or referent has an essential and intrinsic meaning but is produced because signs are different from one another. The sign 'good' signifies the quality good because it is not bad which is not evil and so forth.

According to Saussure, meaning is produced through the selection and combination of signs along the syntagmatic and paradigmatic axes. The syntagmatic axis is constituted by the linear combination of signs that, in verbal languages, form sentences. Paradigmatic refers to the field of signs (that is, synonyms) from which any given sign is selected. Meaning is accumulated along the syntagmatic axis, while selection from the paradigmatic field alters meaning at any given point in the sentence. Thus, to read the sequence 'the cat sat on the mat' from left to right is to follow the syntagmatic order. To replace the word cat with tiger or lion would be to make a paradigmatic alteration.

While Saussure's contribution was to the study of a narrowly defined field of linguistics he predicted the possibility of a wider 'science' that would study the life of signs within society. Thus **Barthes** and others from within the field of structuralism applied semiotic analysis to the practices of popular culture with an eye to showing how it generates meaning. Indeed, it was argued that because all cultural practices depend on meanings generated by signs all cultural practices are open to semiotic analysis. Hence both the importance of semiotics to cultural studies and the suggestion that culture works 'like a language'.

Links **Anti-essentialism, culture, language, meaning, signs, structuralism**

Sex The concept of sex is commonly taken to refer to natural or essential properties of an individual as male or female that derive from biological characteristics of the body such as hormones, genitals and the reproductive system. As such the concept of sex is often contrasted with the more culturally oriented idea of gender which alludes to the cultural assumptions that govern the practices of men and women. The so-called Nature *vs* Nurture debate frequently centres on the degree to which the behaviour of men and women can be attributed to the forces of biology and/or culture.

However, there is a strand of cultural theory identified with the work of Judith **Butler** and Donna **Haraway** amongst others that holds the distinction between biological sex and cultural gender to be untenable. Here the differentiation between sex as biology and gender as a cultural construction is broken down on the grounds that there is in principle no access to biological 'truths' that lie outside of cultural discourses and therefore no 'sex' which is not already cultural. Thus, sexed bodies are always already represented as the production of regulatory discourses so that the category of 'sex' is a normative one that functions as a 'regulatory ideal' and produces the bodies it governs. Discourses of sex are ones that, through repetition of the acts they guide, bring sex into view as a necessary norm. While sex is held to be a social construction, it is an indispensable one that forms subjects and governs the materialization of bodies. This does not mean that 'everything is discourse', but rather, as Butler argues, discourse and the materiality of bodies are indissoluble.

The majority of writers within cultural studies have adopted the view that biology has little of value to say on the subject of sex and gender. The reason why this view is so popular within cultural studies is not difficult to discern; it leaves the door open to unlimited changes in gender and the possibility of full equality (as sameness) of the sexes. However, there is now a good deal of accumulated evidence that points to the *predictability* of a range of male and female capabilities and behaviour that derive from genetics and biochemistry.

The idea that scientific discourses about sex are constitutive of the meaning of 'sex' does not invalidate claims for the usefulness of genetic science to understanding and predicting the actions and life choices of human bodies who have taken on the cultural identities of male and female. In any case, cultural diversity and the evidence for a genetic core to sexual difference are not contradictory stances. Biochemical similarity is able to co-exist with cultural divergence not least because similar genetic predispositions can have widely different outcomes within divergent contexts.

Links **Acculturation, constructionism, gender, identity, performativity, subjectivity**

Signs Signs stand in for or represent concepts and can be understood as marks and noises that generate or carry meaning through their relationship with other signs. The study of signs and the way they work is the domain of semiotics wherein the components of a sign are called the signifier and the signified. A signifier is taken to be the form or medium of signs, for example a sound, an image, the marks that form a word on the page, while the signified is to be understood in terms of concepts and meanings. The activities that generate meaning through the ordering of signs are signifying practices, for example writing or painting, while the totality of signs that one can draw from to write or paint is a signifying system. The process by which signs generate meaning is known as signification.

As understood by semiotics the relationship between the sounds and marks of language, the signifiers, and what they are taken to mean, the signified, is not held in any fixed eternal relationship. Rather, their arrangement is arbitrary in the sense that the animal we call a 'cat' as it sits on the 'mat' could equally be signified by 'tac' and 'tam' or by 'el gato' and 'la estera'. Because it is arbitrary, the combination of signifiers and signifieds at any particular moment of time is contingent upon cultural and historical processes. Indeed, signs are commonly organized into a sequence or code that generates meaning through the cultural conventions of their usage within a particular context.

The relationship between signifiers and signifieds may be arbitrary in the sense of 'could have been otherwise' that is, conventional rather than universal and essential. However, it is not arbitrary in the sense that, given the history of language and culture, words do have temporarily fixed meanings and uses in the world. This temporary 'fixing' is the consequence of the routine indissolubility of language, practice and power.

Links **Code, language, meaning, polysemy, representation, semiotics, structuralism**

Simulacrum A simulacrum is an imitation or copy without an original (or referent) in which the simulation becomes more real than the real, indeed, the apparent reality of the simulation is the measure of the real. The widespread appearance of the simulacrum as a central feature of contemporary culture is associated with the idea of postmodern culture in the work of **Baudrillard** and **Jameson** in particular.

For Baudrillard, we live in a world where a series of modern distinctions – the real and the unreal, the public and the private, art and reality – have broken down, or been sucked into a 'black hole'. In particular, for Baudrillard, television is the heart of a culture marked by an all-encompassing flow of fascinating simulations and facsimiles. That is, a hyperreality in which we are overloaded with images and information. The prefix 'hyper' signifies 'more real than real' – a real retouched in a 'hallucinatory resemblance' with itself. Baudrillard describes a process leading to the collapse of boundaries, which he calls 'implosion', between the media and the social. Here the news – 'reality' – and entertainment – 'fiction' – blur into each other so that 'TV is the world'. Thus, television simulates real-life situations not so much to represent the world as to execute its own as simulacrum.

The idea of a simulacrum has also been applied to Disneyland and Disney World, two of the most significant multimedia symbolic public spaces of the twenty-first century. Thus Disney presents a simulacrum of 'Main Street USA', where the American urban landscape takes on symbolic and imaginary form. In this copy of city life USA there are no guns, no homeless people, no drugs and no fear, which is thus a far cry from the streets of New York City. Disney World's stimulating/simulated visual culture is the new model for public space whose principles are echoed in numerous shopping malls.

Links **City, hyperreality, postmodernism, postmodernity, realism, signs, symbolic**

Soap opera A popular form of serial television that has received considerable attention from cultural studies writers, especially since the mid-1980s, both in terms of its textual construction and its audience responses. As a text, soap opera has been the butt of high cultural aesthetic disdain and a number of cultural writers have been concerned to demonstrate that this has been the outcome of distinctions of taste formed by cultural power rather than a matter of any lack of intrinsic worth or complexity as a text. Thus it has been argued that soap opera is a complex popular form marked by:

- Open-ended narratives without the sense of closure to be found in the feature film or the 13-episode series.
- Core locations that establish a sense of geographical space that the audience can identify with and to which the characters return again and again.
- The tension between the conventions of realism and melodrama so that soap operas can be differentiated from one another in terms of the balance struck between these conventions.
- The pivotal themes of inter-personal relationship wherein marriages, divorces, break-ups, new alliances, arguments, acts of revenge and acts of caring are at the core of the soap opera narrative and provide the dynamic and emotional interest.

The manner in which women have been addressed and represented in soap opera has been pursued by a number of feminist writers because it is frequently suggested that soap opera is a women's space in which women's motivations are validated and celebrated. Broadly speaking, writers have concluded that soap opera offers contradictory representations in which there is both protest and acceptance by women of their traditional cultural status.

A number of researchers, such as **Ang** and **Radway**, have sought to explore why it is that soap opera has been so popular amongst women. It has been argued that women are active creators of meaning in relation to soap opera and demonstrate a complex understanding of the genre. Women, it is said, gain pleasure from representations that chime with their concerns and use them as a part of a social glue, a topic of conversation within a network of female friends and relatives. The studies of the genre's audience played a significant part in the development of the 'active audience' paradigm.

Links **Active audience, aesthetics, feminism, narrative, realism, representation, text**

Social The idea of the social is commonly taken to mean 'of or in society', where society is understood to be an autonomous sphere of activity formed through the organization of rule-governed human relationships and interactions. However, many cultural studies theorists influenced by poststructuralism hold the 'social' to have no object of reference. For such writers, the social is not an object but a discursively constructed field of contestation in which multiple descriptions of self and others compete for ascendancy.

This argument springs from a critique of essentialism and foundationalism that rejects the idea of essential, universal concepts such as class, history or society that refer to unchanging entities in the world. Thus, the 'social' is not a proper object of analysis but a discursive construction of reality. Consequently, 'society' is understood to be an unstable system of discursive differences in which sociopolitical identities represent the open and contingent articulation of cultural and political categories.

Thus **Laclau** and Mouffe argue that the 'social' is to be thought of not as a totality but rather as a set of contingently related aggregates of difference articulated or 'sutured' together. Those aspects of social life (identities or nation or society) which we think of as a unity (and sometimes as universals) can be thought of as a temporary stabilization or arbitrary closure of meaning. Needless to say, a criticism of cultural studies voiced by sociologists in particular is that it has collapsed the idea of the social into the cultural and discursive.

Links **Articulation, discourse, foundationalism, poststructuralism, social formation**

Social formation The concept of a social formation is analogous to the idea of the social or society. However, rather than grasping the social as a 'whole' or totality it is conceived of as a concrete historically produced complex assemblage composed of different practices (ideological, political, economic). A social formation is said to consist of levels of practice, each of which has its own specificity, that are articulated together in particular conjunctures where there is no necessary or automatic correspondence or relationship to each other.

This understanding of a social formation has its origins for cultural studies in **Althusser**'s structuralist Marxism of the 1970s that describes the social as constituted by complex structures or regularities. Here a social formation is not grasped as a totality but rather as a complex structure of different instances, levels or practices that are articulated together to form a unity. This totality is not the result of a single one-way base–superstructure determination, as in orthodox Marxist theory, but rather is the product of determinations emanating from different levels. Thus a social formation is the outcome of 'over-determination' by which is meant that any given practice or instance is the outcome of many different determinations. These distinct determinations are levels or types of practice with their own logic and specificity that cannot be reduced to, or explained by, other levels or practices.

This conceptualization of a social formation was welcomed by key cultural studies writers because it allows theorists to examine cultural phenomena as a separate signifying system with its own effects and determinations. That is, structuralism does not dissolve culture back into the economic (as in the Marxist base–superstructure model) but instead emphasizes the irreducible character of the cultural as a set of distinct practices with its own internal organization or structuration. Thus, **Hall** argues that we must try to grasp a society or social formation as constituted by a set of complex practices each with its own specificity that is articulated unevenly to other related practices. Here, that unity thought of as 'society' is considered to be the unique historically specific temporary stabilization of the relations and meanings of different levels of a social formation.

Links **Base and superstructure, holism, Marxism, reductionism, social, structuralism**

Space Following Einstein's general theory of relativity, space and time are not to be thought of as separate entities but as inextricably interwoven together. That is, space is not an absolute entity but is relationally defined since at least two particles are required for space to occur. Further, time is constituted by the movement of these particles, which simultaneously establishes both time and space. It is not that time moves across a static space, but that space and time constitute each other enabling us to speak of time–space.

Traditionally, modern social theory has been more interested in time than space since time was understood to be the dynamic field of social change whereas space was regarded as dead, fixed and immobile, traversed by the movement of history. However, since the 1970s there has been a growing interest within cultural theory in questions of space inspired in particular by the work of **Foucault** and his focus on the construction of space by discourse, power and discipline. Here space can be understood as a social construct with the social itself being spatially organized. Thus space is constituted by a dynamic set of proccesses that are implicated in questions of power and symbolism.

It is necessary to grasp human activity as distributed in space since human interaction is situated in particular spaces that have a variety of social meanings. For example, a 'home' is divided into different living spaces – front rooms, kitchens, dining rooms, bedrooms etc. These spaces are used in diverse ways within which are carried out a range of activities with different cultural meanings that enable them to be constituted as emotionally charged places. Accordingly, bedrooms are private intimate spaces whereas a front room or parlour is available for more public encounters.

The symbolic and power-saturated character of space can be grasped in relation to the concept of gender since gender relations vary across space and spaces are symbolically gendered. The classical Western gendering of space is manifested in the division between 'home' and 'workplace' which is articulated with the 'private' and the 'public'. Thus, the home is regarded as the domain of the 'private' and the feminine whereas sites of paid work have been coded masculine within the public sphere. Homes have been cast as the unpaid domain of mothers and children, connoting the secondary values of caring, love, tenderness and domesticity. In contrast, places of paid work have been regarded as the domain of men, connoting the primary values of toughness (either physically or mentally), hardness, comradeship and reality.

Links **Code, gender, place, power, public sphere, symbolic**

Speech act The concept of a speech act is associated with the work of Austin who, after **Wittgenstein**, developed a philosophy of language that conceives of it in terms of actions. Hence the title of Austin's 1962 book, *How To Do Things With Words*. By saying 'I promise', we are not simply offering information to our audience about promising, rather, we are enacting or performing a promise. That is, we are engaged in a speech act. In the same way, saying 'I name this ship' or 'I take you as my wedded wife' is performing the action of naming the ship and getting married. In order to name a ship or get married people say words that constitute the acts they name. Thus, a 'performative' is a statement which puts into effect the relation that it names as in the marriage ceremony's 'I pronounce you . . .'. In addition, Austin introduced the notion of felicity conditions by which speech acts in order to be felicitous, that is, in order to work, must satisfy certain conditions. Consequently, for an order to be felicitous it must be issued by someone deemed to have the power to do so.

Speech act theory is pertinent to discourse analysis within cultural studies and also to the widespread use of the concept of performativity, that is, it is a discursive practice that enacts or produces that which it names through citation and reiteration. Though originated by Austin in the context of speech act theory, Judith **Butler** popularized the concept of performativity within cultural studies during the 1990s through her work on the construction of gendered identities. In particular, Butler conceives of sex and gender in terms of citational performativity and an iterable practice secured through repetition.

Links **Conversation, discourse analysis, language, language-game, performativity**

Spivak, Gayatri Chakravorty (1942–) Indian-born Spivak is currently a professor in the Humanities Department of Columbia University in New York. She frequently cites **Derrida** as a major influence on her work, a claim that is evidenced in her deconstructive style of intellectual exploration and writing. At the same time her work seeks to maintain a strong connection to the cultural politics of feminism and the marginalized subjects of the postcolonial world. Spivak is aware of the difficulty of being a privileged academic in the USA speaking for/about the silenced subjects of the world so that the reflexive examination of the conditions of her own voice is also a theme of her work.

188

- **Associated concepts** Cultural politics, deconstruction, subaltern, subjectivity, subject position.
- **Tradition(s)** Feminism, Marxism, postcolonial theory, poststructuralism.
- **Reading** Spivak, G. (1993) 'Can the Subulatern Speak?', in P. Williams and L. Chrisman (eds), *Colonial Discourse and Post-Colonial Theory.* London: Harvester Wheatsheaf.

Stereotype A stereotype is a vivid but simple representation that reduces persons to a set of exaggerated, usually negative, character traits and is thus a form of representation that essentializes others through the operation of power. That is, a stereotype suggests that a given category has inherent and universal characteristics and that furthermore these characteristics represent all that such a person is or can be. A stereotype commonly takes the form of a conventionalized idea constructed according to a rigid formula into a hackneyed image that typecasts people.

Stereotyping commonly involves the attribution of negative traits to people who are different from us, a process that points to the operation of power in stereotyping. In particular it highlights the role of stereotyping in the exclusion of 'difference' from the social, symbolic and moral order since stereotypes commonly relate to those who have been excluded from the 'normal' order of things. Stereotyping thus simultaneously establishes who is 'us' and who is 'them'.

In Britain and the United States the more obvious racial stereotypes echo colonial and slave history respectively. A central component of British imperial representations of black people was the theme of non-Christian savages who required civilizing by British missionaries and adventurers. In more recent times the imagery of black youth as dope-smoking muggers and/or urban rioters has come to the fore. As **Gilroy** has argued, hedonism, evasion of work and the criminality of black culture are becoming closely entwined motifs of British media stereotypes.

American plantation stereotypes also partake in the binary of white civilization and black 'naturalness' or 'primitivism' so that African Americans have often been represented as naturally incapable of the refinements of white civilization, being by nature lazy and best fitted for subordination to white people. Many contemporary representations of race on US television continue to stereotypically associate black people, specifically young men, with crime and social problems. Thus, a common portrayal of African Americans in newscasts is as criminals connected to guns and violence. In particular, poor black people are constructed as a 'menace to society' having moved beyond the limits of acceptable behaviour through their association with crime, violence, drugs, gangs and teenage pregnancy.

Links **Essentialism, gender, Orientalism, Other, postcolonial theory, race, representation**

Strategic essentialism The idea of strategic essentialism involves philosophical acceptance of the anti-essentialist argument that there are in principle no essential identities while nevertheless suggesting that in practice people act, and need to act, as if there were. Thus strategic essentialism means acting 'as if' identities were stable for specific political reasons. For example, one might temporarily accept the category of 'woman' as a stable unity for the purposes of mobilizing women in feminist political action. Here, it is argued, the practical character of social and political life can render the theoretical distinction between essentialism and anti-essentialism somewhat redundant.

The concept of strategic essentialism is deployed in order to modify anti-essentialist conceptions of identity, arguing that such discourse-based theories efface human agency. In particular, for their critics, anti-essentialist arguments about identity are said to be of no *practical* value. That an identity category can be 'deconstructed' does not mean that people do not and cannot mobilize around it as a device for the improvement of the human condition. This is an argument that has some merit for practical purposes and indeed 'strategic essentialism' may be the process that is enacted in practice in day-to-day life as well as in political action. That is to say, any sense of identity and community of identification (nations, ethnicities, sexualities, classes etc.) are necessary fictions that mark a temporary, partial and arbitrary closure of meaning. Some kind of strategic cut or temporary stabilization of meaning is necessary in order to say or do anything.

Nevertheless, as the basis for political strategy, the idea of strategic essentialism is open to the criticism that at some point certain voices have been excluded. Thus, the strategic essentialism of feminism in taking 'woman' to be an essential category for tactical reasons may lead to differences between women, for example between white, black or Hispanic women, being ignored. The idea of strategic essentialism always raises the question of where to draw the tactical line and can lend itself towards ethnic or gender 'absolutism'. The trick is to try to hold both the plasticity and the practical fixity of identity in mind at the same time thereby enabling one to oscillate between them for particular purposes.

Links **Anti-essentialism, cultural politics, essentialism, feminism, identification, identity, poststructuralism**

Structuralism Structuralism is best approached as a method of analysis concerned with social and cultural structures or predictable regularities that lie outside of any given person. As such, structuralism is anti-humanist in its de-centring of human agents from the heart of inquiry. Instead, structuralism favours a form of analysis in which phenomena have meaning only in relation to other phenomena within a systematic structure of which no particular person is the source. Thus, a structuralist understanding of culture is concerned with the 'systems of relations' of an underlying structure (usually language) and the grammar that makes meaning possible.

Structuralism can be traced back at least to the nineteenth-century sociologist Durkheim who searched for the constraining patterns of culture and social life that lie outside of any given individual. Durkheim rejected the empiricist view that knowledge is to be derived from direct experience seeking instead for what he called 'social facts' that are socially constructed, culturally variable and *sui generis* of particular consciousness. That is, they exist beyond individuals. For example, the beliefs, values and norms of religions, specifically the contrast between Catholicism and Protestantism, are said to account for variable patterns of suicide. In other words, the most individual act possible, suicide, is accounted for by normative social structures of belief.

However, it has been the work of **Saussure** rather than that of Durkheim which has been most influential within cultural studies. Structuralism in this sense takes signification or meaning production to be the effect of deep structures of language that are manifested in specific cultural phenomena or human speakers. Here meaning is not the outcome of the intentions of actors *per se* but of the language itself. Thus, structuralism is concerned with how cultural meaning is generated and understands culture to be analogous to (or structured like) a language. Saussure argued that meaning is generated through a system of structured differences in language so that significance is the outcome of the rules and conventions that organize language (*langue*) rather than the specific uses and utterances which individuals deploy in everyday life (*parole*). In short, Saussure, and structuralism in general, is concerned more with the structures of language that allow linguistic performance to be possible than with actual performance in its infinite variations.

Structuralism extends its reach from 'words' to the language of cultural signs in general so that human relations, material objects and images are all analysed through the structures of signs. In the work of Lévi-Strauss we find the manifestation of structuralist principles when he describes kinship systems as 'like a language' so that family relations are held to be structured by the internal organization of binaries. For example, kinship patterns are structured around the incest taboo that divides people into the marriageable and the prohibited. Also typical of Lévi-Strauss' structuralism is his approach to food that he declares to be not so much good to eat, as good to think with. That is, food is a signifier of symbolic meanings wherein cultural conventions tell us what constitutes food and what does not, the circumstances of its eating and the meanings attached to it.

Lévi-Strauss tends towards the structuralist trope of binaries: the raw and the cooked, the edible and the inedible, nature and culture, each of which has meaning only in relation to its opposite. Cooking transforms nature into culture and the raw into the cooked. Further, the edible and the inedible are marked not by questions of nutrition but by cultural meanings. An example of this would be the Jewish prohibition against pork and the necessity to prepare food in culturally specific ways (kosher food). Thus binary oppositions of the edible–inedible mark another binary, insiders and outsiders, and hence the boundaries of the culture or social order. During the late 1960s and 1970s **Barthes** was to extend the structuralist account of culture to the practices of popular culture and their naturalized meanings or myths. He argued that the meanings of texts are to be grasped not in terms of the intentions of specific human beings but as a set of signifying practices. In sum, structuralism:

- Understands culture to be an expression of the deep structures of language that lie outside of the intentions of actors and constrain them.
- Is synchronic in approach so that structuralist analysis focuses on the structures of relations in a snapshot of a particular moment.
- Asserts the specificity of culture and its irreducibility to any other phenomenon.

Links **Culture, language, myth, poststructuralism, semiotics, structuration, structure**

Structuration Structuration theory, which is associated with the work of Anthony **Giddens**, centres on the way agents produce and reproduce social structure through their own actions. Structuration offers a way to understand human social and cultural activity as involving both agency and structure. Here regularized human activity, or structure, is not brought into being by individual actors as such, but is continually re-created by them via the very means whereby they express themselves as actors. That is, in and through their activities agents reproduce the conditions that make those activities possible. For example, having been constituted as a man or a woman by the structures of gendered expectations and practices, and having learned to be a father or mother, we then act in accordance with those rules reproducing them once again.

Giddens argues that social order is constructed in and through the everyday activities and accounts (in language) of skilful and knowledgeable actors (or members). The resources that actors draw on, and are constituted by, are social in character. Indeed, social structure (or regular patterns of activity) distributes resources and competencies unevenly between actors. That is, regularities or structural properties of social systems, which are distinct from any given individual, operate to structure what an actor is.

Central to the theory of structuration as developed by Giddens is the concept of the 'duality of structure' by which structures are not only constraining but also enabling. That is, while individual actors are constrained and determined by social forces that lie beyond them as individual subjects, it is those very same social structures that enable subjects to act. For example, what it means to be a mother in a given society may mean that we cannot undertake paid employment and in that sense we are constrained. However, the structures of motherhood also allow us to act as a 'mother', to be close to our children, to form networks with other mothers, and so forth. Likewise with language: we are all constructed and constrained by a language that pre-exists us, yet language is also the means and medium of self-awareness and creativity. That is, we can only say what is sayable in language, yet language is also the medium by which we can say anything at all.

Links **Agency, determinism, holism, praxis, reductionism, structuralism, structure**

Structure A structure can be understood in terms of regularity or stable patterns. Thus the structures of language are said to be the secure and predictable rules and conventions that organize language (*langue*). A social structure is constituted by the recurrent organization and patterned arrangement of human relationships. Social and cultural structures are often said to be constraining and determining of actors and action and as such are often contrasted to the notion of agency.

For example, class structure can be understood as a classification of persons into groups based on shared socio-economic conditions who are a part of a system of relations involving other classes in the context of an overall stratification system. As such, a class structure is a relational set of patterned inequalities with economic, social, political and ideological dimensions. However, in both the linguistic and social sense structures are 'virtual' in that they do not exist as things or entities that one can find. Rather, a structure exists in the mind of the beholder and is deployed as an analytic tool for specific purposes.

Links **Agency, determinism, poststructuralism, semiotics, structuralism, structuration**

Style The idea of style played an important part in the early youth subculture theory developed within cultural studies and in the work of Dick **Hebdige** in particular. In this context, style was constituted by the signifying practices of youth subcultures, including the display of codes of meaning achieved via the transformation of commodities as cultural signs. Here style involves the organization of objects in conjunction with activities and attitudes through active bricolage to signify difference and identity.

Thus, according to Hebdige, British Punk style of the late 1970s was both ordered and meaningful even as it signified noise and chaos. Punk was a 'revolting style' that created an ensemble of the perverse and abnormal: safety pins, bin liners, dyed hair, painted faces, graffitied shirts and the iconography of sexual fetishism (leather bondage gear, fishnet stockings, etc.). In Hebdige's account, Punk was not simply responding to the crisis of British decline manifested in joblessness, poverty and changing moral standards but *dramatized* it in an expression of anger and frustration. At the same time, Punk was an especially dislocated, self-aware and ironic mode of signification.

Other members of the **Centre for Contemporary Cultural Studies** had also argued that youth subcultural style can be understood as a form of symbolic resistance. For example, it had been suggested that youth subcultures sought to reinvent the lost community and values of the working class through stylization. Thus, Skinheads were held to be enacting an imaginary recapturing of working class male 'hardness' through their cropped hair, boots, jeans and braces. Their style stressed the resources of working class collectivism and territoriality through the coherence and loyalty of 'the gang' of mates.

It should be noted that cultural studies writers have tended to explore the more spectacular youth cultures. That is, the visible, loud, different, avant-garde youth styles that have stood out and demanded attention. Further, critics of Hebdige argued that the concept of style in his hands had become over-inflated as resistance while resistance was reduced to questions of style. Thus it was said that style had been robbed of its elements of fun and flattened down to become only a political question.

Links **Bricolage, code, homology, identity, resistance, semiotics, subculture, youth culture**

Subaltern The idea of the 'subaltern' came into cultural studies through the influence of **Gramsci**, who spoke about the 'subaltern classes' as the politically unorganized popular masses. However, the word now has a greater association with postcolonial theory through a collective of Indian writers headed by Ranajit Guha called 'subaltern studies'; and even more so through the writings of Gayatri **Spivak**.

Spivak, who draws on deconstructionism, Marxism and feminism, asks the question in a famous essay of the same name: 'Can the Subaltern Speak?'. Her answer is in the negative since the subaltern subject is irretrievably heterogeneous and cannot invoke a unified voice. Further, there are no subject positions in English or Indian discourse that would allow the subaltern to know or speak itself. This is doubly so for subaltern women in colonial contexts who have neither the conceptual language to speak nor the ear of colonial and indigenous men to listen. It is not that subaltern women cannot literally communicate but that there are no subject positions within the discourse of colonialism that would allow them to articulate themselves as persons and they are thus condemned to silence.

Links **Cultural imperialism, deconstruction, postcolonial theory, subject position**

Subculture The signifier 'culture' in subculture has traditionally referred to a 'whole way of life' or 'maps of meaning' that make the world intelligible to its members. The prefix 'sub' has connoted notions of distinctiveness and difference from the dominant or mainstream society. Hence a subculture is constituted by groups of persons who share distinct values and norms which are held to be at variance with dominant or mainstream society and offers maps of meaning that make the world intelligible to its members.

A significant resonance of the prefix 'sub' is that of subaltern or subterranean. Thus, subcultures have been seen as spaces for deviant cultures to renegotiate their position or to 'win space' for themselves. Hence, in much subculture theory the question of 'resistance' to the dominant culture comes to the fore. In particular, for cultural studies writers of the 1970s, subcultures were seen as magical or symbolic solutions to the structural problems of class. Subcultures attempt to resolve collectively experienced problems and generate collective and individual identities. Thus subcultures legitimize alternative experiences and scripts of social reality and supply sets of meaningful activities for their 'members'.

For many cultural studies writers (for example, **Willis**), the cultural symbols and styles by which subcultures express themselves represent a 'fit' (or homology) between the group's structural position in the social order and the social values of the subculture's participants. Thus particular subcultural items parallel and reflect the structure, style, typical concerns, attitudes and feelings of the group. Consequently, the creativity and cultural responses of subcultures are not random but expressive of social contradictions. Indeed, the creative, expressive and symbolic works of subcultures are read as forms of symbolic resistance expressed as style.

Contemporary critics of subculture theory have suggested that it relies on unsustainable binaries; namely, mainstream–subculture, resistance–submission, dominant–subordinate. In particular, it is argued that subcultures are not formed outside and opposed to the mainstream culture, as represented by the mass media, but are instead formed within and through the media. Further, subcultures are not unified but marked by internal differences so that youth cultural difference is not necessarily a form of resistance but is better grasped as cultural capital or distinctions of taste. Indeed, such is the fragmentation of youth culture and the loss of 'authenticity' and 'style' that we are said to be in a post-subculture period where style marks not the politicization of youth but the aestheticization of politics.

The deconstruction of authenticity at the level of theory does not prevent participants in youth subcultures from laying claim to it. Indeed, authenticity claims remain at the heart of contemporary youth subcultures. Further, subcultures can be understood as domains of creative consumption by which members act as bricoleurs selecting and arranging elements of material commodities and meaningful signs as the basis of multiple identity construction. This is now the topsy-turvy postmodern world in which style is on the surface, subcultures are mainstream, high culture is a subculture and fashion is retro.

Links **Authenticity, bricolage, cultural capital, homology, popular culture, style**

Subject position A subject position can be understood in terms of the empty spaces or functions in discourse from which the world makes sense. Here, discourse constitutes the 'I' through the processes of signification and the speaking subject is dependent on the prior existence of discursive positions. Thus, for **Foucault**, bodies are 'subject to' the regulatory power of discourse by which they become 'subjects for' themselves and others. In this conception, the speaking subject is not the author or originator of a statement but depends on the prior existence of discursive positions. Virtually any individual can fill a particular subject-position when he or she formulates a statement and the same individual may occupy a series of different positions and thus assume different forms of subjectivity. Through identification or 'emotional investment' with the subject positions of discourses we create an identity that embodies an illusion of wholeness.

Links **Agency, discourse, identification, identity, poststructuralism, subjectivity**

Subjectivity Subjectivity can be described as the condition of being a person and/or the processes by which we become persons, that is, how we are constituted as subjects and come to experience ourselves. Thus, to ask about subjectivity is to pose the question 'what is a person?' and to answer the question is to construct a narrative or story about the self. For cultural studies, subjectivity is often regarded, after **Foucault**, as an 'effect' of discourse because subjectivity is constituted by the subject positions that discourse obliges us to take up.

According to Foucault, the discourses of disciplinary power that constitute subjectivity can be traced historically so that we can locate particular kinds of 'regimes of the self' in specific historical and cultural conjunctures. That is, the subject is held to be wholly and only the product of history generated by discourses that enable speaking persons to come into existence. Foucault describes a subject that is the product of power that individualizes those subject to it. Here power is not simply a negative mechanism of control but is *productive* of the self. The disciplinary power of schools, work organizations, prisons, hospitals, asylums and the proliferating discourses of sexuality produce subjectivity by bringing individuals into view. They achieve this by categorizing, naming and fixing subjects in writing via the discourses of, for example, medicine.

Foucault's account of subjectivity has been of concern to a number of cultural writers because it appears to rob subjects of agency. Thus, if subjects are docile bodies generated by discursive practices then how can we conceive of persons as able to act since subjects appear to be 'products' rather than 'producers'. However, agency can be said to be a subject position within discourse, that is, the capacity for agency is discursively determined and as such is best understood as the socially constructed capacity to act.

Foucault attacks what he calls the 'great myth of the interior' and adopts an anti-essentialist position in which the subject is not unified but fractured. The Enlightenment or Cartesian subject as understood through the work of Descartes has grasped persons as unique unified agents endowed with the capacities of reason, consciousness and action. Thus Descartes' formulation 'I think, therefore I am' places the rational, conscious *individual* subject at the heart of Western philosophy. By contrast the so-called fractured or postmodern subject conceives of the subject in terms of discursively constructed shifting, fragmented and multiple identities. Persons are composed not of one but of several, sometimes contradictory, identities because they have been subjected to and formed as subjects by a variety of discourses located in a range of social spaces. If we feel that we have a single identity it is because we have constructed a unifying narrative of the self.

Links **Agency, discourse, identity, self-identity, structuration, subject position**

Surveillance The process of surveillance involves the monitoring and collection of information about subject populations with an eye to the supervision and regulation of activities. Thus the idea of surveillance refers to the collection, storage and retrieval of information as well as to the direct supervision of activities and the use of information to monitor subject populations. It is widely argued that while modernity did not invent surveillance *per se* it did introduce new, more complex and extensive forms of surveillance. These included shifts from personal to impersonal control as marked by the bureaucratization, rationalization and professionalization that form the core institutional configurations of modernity.

In particular, the rise of modernity is associated with organizations intrinsic to which are attempts to regularize control of social relations across time and space. For example, the emergence of the industrial labour process included an increase in the size and division of labour in tandem with the mechanization and intensification of work. The workshop and factory were then utilized as a means of exerting discipline and the creation of new work habits. That is, they marked new forms of surveillance.

In the current period increased social and institutional reflexivity is manifested in the desire of institutions to know more about their workforce, customers and clients. Thus contemporary life has increasingly been put under surveillance through the use of electronic technologies such as CCTV cameras in urban centres, security systems surrounding houses, police helicopters using infra-red cameras and the use of electronic shopping cards that record information for store management regarding consumer spending patterns. Indeed, this is not simply the province of capitalism but is also a marked activity of the state which has taken increased authoritarian powers over questions of 'law and order', morality and internal surveillance.

Links **Capitalism, city, modernity, reflexivity, urbanization**

Symbolic A symbol is a mark that appears to stand in for another object or meaning. Thus, symbolism is a form of representation founded on signs. As with all sign systems, meaning is not generated because the object of symbolic reference has an essential and intrinsic meaning but rather is produced because signs/symbols are different from one another. The use of metaphor, which involves the replacement of one signifier by another, is a symbolic act. Indeed language is clearly a symbolic system that relies on metaphor to the point that all language use is metaphorical. The relationship between the sounds and marks of a symbolic system and its meanings is not fixed or eternal but rather is governed by the cultural conventions of usage within particular contexts.

Links **Language, metaphor, representation, semiotics, signs, symbolic economy, symbolic order**

Symbolic economy (a) One meaning of the term symbolic economy refers to the organization of symbols into meaningful representations That is, the grammar of language and other forms of signifying system. To explore this sense of the concept see the following links.

Links **Language, meaning, representation, semiotics, signs**

(b) Another use of the term symbolic economy refers us to the way in which the symbolic practices of culture are also productive activities of a monetary economy. This has been particularly marked in urban redevelopment practices such as the transformation of old wharfs and canals into shopping centres or areas of leisure activity during and since the 1980s. Here the symbolic economy is manifested as material economic power. Indeed, the redevelopment of urban spaces and places is commonly forged through the synergy of capital investment and cultural meanings.

Symbolic culture plays an economic role in branding a city by associating it with desirable 'goods'; for example, movie representations of the New York skyline and the Sydney Opera House. Further, culture industries such as film, television and advertising lend glamour to cities, bringing direct employment and other economic benefits. Finally, symbolic houses of culture such as museums and theatres provide convivial spaces of consumption for business meetings and tourism. Thus, Paris is famous for its architectural history and gastronomic reputation rather more than its manufacturing base.

Links **City, postmodernism, symbolic, urbanization**

Symbolic order: The symbolic order is constituted by the grammar of signs and symbols as organized into the meaningful representations that constitute culture; that is, the patterned forms of significance or meaning constituted by the relations of difference between signs. The idea of the symbolic order plays a special part in the psychoanalytic theory of **Lacan** that has acquired considerable currency with some cultural studies writers. Here the symbolic order is the overarching structure of language and received social meaning, entry into which is the condition for the very possibility of subjects. According to Lacan, the symbolic order is the domain of human law and culture whose composition is materialized in the very structure of language. In particular, language enables subjectivity by virtue of the subject positions it provides from which one may speak, so that outside of the symbolic order lies only psychosis.

Links **Language, meaning, psychoanalysis, representation, symbolic, semiotics, subject position**

Synergy The idea of synergy is a concept drawn from political economy that refers to the bringing together of previously separate activities or moments in the processes of production and exchange to produce higher profits. Synergy, in the context of the communications industries, involves the assembling of various elements of production and distribution so that they complement each other to produce lower costs and greater profitability. In particular, the preoccupation with combining software and hardware can be seen when films are marketed simultaneously with pop music soundtracks and virtual reality video games all owned by the same company. This is now not so much the exception as the rule.

The search for synergy has fuelled the growth of multimedia giants who dominate key sectors of the market. Thus the world's largest multimedia corporation, AOL-Time Warner, is the product of a series of mergers and take-overs that united first Time and Warner in 1989, followed by the 1995 acquisition of Turner Broadcasting (CNN) and finally the buy-out by AOL in 2000. Likewise, the acquisition by News Corporation of the Hong Kong-based Star TV for $525 million gave them a massive satellite television footprint over Asia and the Middle East. Allied to other television holdings, notably BskyB (UK) and Fox TV (USA and Australia), and the acquisition in 2003 of Direct TV (USA), News Corp's television interests have a global reach of some two-thirds of the planet.

However, it is not just the spatial breadth of the corporation's ownership that is significant but also the potential link-ups between its various elements. In Twentieth-Century Fox and Star TV, News Corp acquired a huge library of film and television product that can be channelled through their network of distribution outlets to create the possibility of a lucrative global advertising market as well as the advantages of cross-promotion. This is synergy at work.

Links **Convergence, globalization, multimedia corporation, political economy, television**

T

Television No other medium can match television for the volume of popular cultural texts it produces and the sheer size of its audiences. As such, television is one of cultural studies' longstanding interests. Television is a resource open to virtually everybody in modern industrialized societies and can be grasped as a significant resource in the construction of identity projects. It is a source of popular knowledge about the world and brings us into mediated contact with ways of life other than our own.

While television can be valuably understood in terms of its political economy, cultural studies' main contribution has been through textual analysis and audience research. Cultural studies writers have sought to study television as a socially and culturally informed activity that is centrally concerned with meaning so that the main focus of interest has been on the interplay between texts and audiences. Here texts are understood to be polysemic, that is, they are carriers of multiple meanings only some of which are taken up by audiences. Consequently, differently constituted audiences will work with different textual meanings. Audiences are understood to be active creators of meaning in relation to texts and do so on the basis of previously acquired cultural competencies forged in the context of language and social relationships.

The founding work on television within cultural studies during the late 1970s and early 1980s was concerned with the production and reproduction of ideology in the context of a hegemonic model of cultural power. Here ideology is bound up with the broader role of television in cultural reproduction. However, the generation of ideology was not seen as an outcome of proprietorial manipulation and conspiracy but of the routine attitudes and working practices of television staff. There had been a tendency to understand the reproduction of ideology in audiences as a passive process of 'hailing' or injection in the manner of a hypodermic needle. However, the development of the 'active audience' paradigm during the 1980s demonstrated that audiences were creators of meaning not simply passive dopes. The notion of the active audience was then linked to the idea of ideological resistance. However, the fact that audiences/consumers are *always* active does not guarantee a challenge to the contemporary social order since activity is required to take up world-views or 'ideology' as well as to resist it.

Today cultural studies has a concern with the globalization of television and its role in the creation of a global electronic culture whereby cultural artefacts and meanings from different historical periods and geographical places can mix together and be juxtaposed to constitute a jumbled-up flow of images and ideas. Here television contributes to the networks of meaning in which people are involved that extend far beyond their physical locations. The globalization of television and other communications technologies has created an increasingly complex semiotic environment of competing signs and meanings that has been understood by certain writers to be postmodern. For some critics the globalization of an electronic TV culture is understood as a process of cultural mixing, matching and exchange in the production of hybridity though for others it represents a form of cultural domination or imperialism.

Links **Active audience, globalization, hegemony, identity, ideology, postmodernism, soap opera, text**

Text The everyday use of the concept of a text refers to writing in its various forms so that books and magazines are understood to be texts. However, it is an axiom of cultural studies that a text is anything that generates meaning through signifying practices. That is, a text is a metaphor that invokes the constitution of meaning through the organization of signs into representations. This includes the generation of meaning through images, sounds, objects (such as clothes) and activities (like dance and sport). Since images, sounds, objects and practices are sign systems which signify with the same fundamental mechanism as a language we may refer to them as cultural texts. Hence, dress, television programmes, images, sporting events, pop stars etc. can all be read as texts.

Texts can be analysed in terms of the arrangement of signs into sequences or codes that generate meaning through the cultural conventions of their use within a particular context. Textual analysis usually involves deconstructing the practices of cultural coding to show us how the apparent transparency of meaning is an outcome of cultural habituation. Any kind of textual analysis involves a somewhat arbitrary drawing of boundaries for particular purposes since meaning is unstable and cannot be confined to single words, sentences or particular texts. This is so because meaning has no single originatory source; rather it is the outcome of intertextuality, that is, the relationships between various sites of meaning. Here there is no 'outside' of a text since other texts form the exterior of any given text. Since texts are constitutive of their outsides so we may say with **Derrida** that there is nothing outside of texts or nothing but texts. However, this does not mean that there is no non-textual material world, rather it suggests that meaning is a product of textual arrangements.

Texts, as forms of representation, are polysemic; that is, they contain the possibility of a number of different meanings that have to be realized by actual readers who give life to words and images. While we can examine the ways in which texts work, we cannot simply 'read-off' audiences' meaning production from textual analysis. At the very least, meaning is produced in the interplay between text and reader, that is, the hermeneutic circle.

Links **Code, hermeneutics, intertextuality, polysemy, representation, semiotics, signs**

Theory Theory can be understood as a form of narrative that seeks to distinguish and account for the general features that describe, define and explain persistently perceived occurrences. It can also be grasped as a tool, instrument or logic for intervening in the world through the mechanisms of description, definition, prediction and control. Theory is not an unproblematic reflection or discovery of objective truth about an independent object world. Rather, theory construction is a self-reflexive discursive endeavour that seeks to interpret and intervene in the world. It involves the thinking through of concepts and arguments, often re-defining and critiquing prior work, with the objective of offering new tools by which to think about our world.

Theoretical work has maintained a high profile position within cultural studies and can be thought of as a crafting of the cultural signposts and maps of meaning by which we are guided or, as argued in the introduction to this dictionary, as a toolbox of concepts. Cultural studies has rejected the empiricist claim that knowledge is simply a matter of collecting facts from which theory can be deduced or against which it can be tested. That is, 'facts' are not neutral and no amount of stacking up of 'facts' produces a story about our lives without theory.

Theory permeates all levels of cultural studies, which can itself be understood as a body of theory generated by thinkers who regard the production of theoretical knowledge as a political practice. Here, theory is not held to be a neutral or objective phenomenon but a matter of positionality, that is, of the place from which one speaks, to whom, and for what purposes. Within the domain of cultural studies there are a variety of theoretical perspectives that compete for ascendancy, the most prominent of which are Marxism, structuralism and poststructuralism.

Links **Epistemology, Marxism, narrative, poststructuralism, structuralism, truth**

Time–space geography Given the complexity of contemporary life it is a requirement on us all to move across and through a variety of spaces and places, including places of work, leisure, sleep, eating, shopping and so forth. Time–space geography is a domain of study that has been concerned to map the movements and pathways of persons through these physical environments and is especially interested in the physical, technological, economic and social constraints on such movement. Time–space geographers trace the variety of social activities that occur and the constraints which material and social factors place on the patterns of our movement. Time–space geographers claim to demonstrate how society and culture are constituted by the unintended consequences of the repetitive acts of individuals.

On a larger scale, time–space geography has been concerned with explanations for globalization expressed in terms of concepts like 'time–space compression' and 'time–space distanciation'. Thus globalization can be understood in terms of an intensified compression of the world, that is, globalization is constituted by the ever-increasing abundance of global connections. According to **Harvey**, since the early 1970s we have witnessed a phase of accelerated globalization marked by a new dimension of time–space compression propelled by transnational companies' search for new sources of profit.

As understood by **Giddens**, time–space distanciation refers to the processes by which societies are 'stretched' over shorter or longer spans of time and space. Of particular significance is the development of abstract clock time, which allows time, space and place (locales) to be separated from each other and then enables social relations to develop between people who are not co-present. The development of new forms of communication and information control also allows transactions to be conducted across time and space so that any given place is penetrated and shaped by social influences quite distant from it. For example, the development of money and electronic communications allows social relations to be stretched across time and space in the form of financial transactions conducted 24 hours a day throughout the globe.

Links **City, globalization, glocalization, modernity, place, space**

Truth Contemporary common sense and Enlightenment philosophy both understand truth to be constituted by a description that corresponds to or pictures an independent object world in a neutral language of observation. The adoption of this form of epistemology, known as representationalism, leads thinkers to seek out universal propositions that apply across time, space and cultural difference. All the modern social sciences from sociology to economics and psychology were founded on the premise that conceptual and empirical truth can be discovered. This includes cultural studies in so far as one of its early theoretical pillars was Marxism.

However, representationalism has now largely been displaced within cultural studies by the influence of poststructuralism (for example, **Foucault**), postmodernism (for example, **Lyotard**), neo-pragmatism (for example, **Rorty**) and other anti-representationalist paradigms. Here truth is a matter of expression in language where sentences are the only things that can be true or false with acculturated authority arbitrating between sentences. That is, truth is a matter of interpretation of the world and of whose interpretations count as truth, that is, it is an issue of power. Thus instead of truth, Foucault speaks about particular 'regimes of truth' whereby statements are combined and regulated to form and define a distinct field of knowledge/objects that is taken to be true. That is, truth and knowledge do not possess metaphysical, transcendental or universal properties but are specific to particular times and spaces.

Richard Rorty, from within the parameters of neo-pragmatism, shares the view that knowledge cannot mirror an independent object world but is inherently culture-bound in character. In particular, Rorty argues that there is no Archimedean vantage point from which one could verify any claimed correspondence between the world and language. From this it follows that we cannot hold our descriptions of the world to be true in the sense of correspondence with an independent object world. Instead, the word truth is best understood as indicating a social commendation rather than an accurate picture of an independent object world. That is, we give reasons that seek to justify our statements and actions in the context of intersubjectively formed constitutive rules regarding what establishes legitimate forms of reasoning. There is no final vocabulary of language that is true in the sense of accurately picturing an independent object world called reality. Our vocabularies are only final in the sense of currently without tenable challenge.

Having said that, some descriptions of the world are undoubtedly more useful than others in relation to particular purposes. Thus while the physical sciences do not have privileged access to a deeper truth, their empirical methods have yielded useful and workable knowledge of the material world. Science has produced levels of predictability that have underpinned a degree of consensus or solidarity amongst the scientific community, leading them to call particular statements true. The arguments of these sciences should be understood not as the revelation of objective truth or the correspondence of language with an independent object world but as the achievements of agreed procedures.

These arguments do not mean that material reality does not exist or that we are 'out of sync' with that reality. Rather, language, by which we seek to represent truth, is an evolutionary tool developed through practice by human beings in order to achieve various purposes. When language is conceived as a tool for action rather than a mirror for representing the world, then it cannot be at odds with reality. Language can only misrepresent the world if it is also able to accurately represent it. Since the former is not possible, then the latter is an irrelevancy and to ask about it is to pose a poor, because literally sense-less, question.

Links **Enlightenment, epistemology, language, language-game, meaning, poststructuralism, pragmatism, representation**

U

Unconscious On a mundane level the idea of the unconscious simply suggests that there are aspects of our minds and bodies of which we are not self-conscious and that can be described as causes of our actions. However, the notion of the unconscious is more commonly attributed to the domain of psychoanalysis, where it has specific and technical meanings. For cultural studies, the unconscious is pertinent to theories of subjectivity, identity and representation in particular.

In classic psychoanalysis the unconscious is the realm of the repressed that is generated initially by the resolution of the Oedipus complex. This repressed or unconscious domain is comprised of symbolic memories originating in primal fantasies or scenes involving forbidden sexual knowledge, fears, desires and so forth. Subsequently, the primary processes of drives and wishes are censored and regulated by secondary processes of internalized social control. **Freud** found his evidence for the unconscious in people's obsessions, slips of the tongue, neurotic symptoms and dreams. In his later work Freud tended to speak of the id, ego and superego rather than primary and secondary processes, though the notion of the unconscious remained intact.

In **Lacan**'s influential reading of Freud the resolution of the Oedipus complex and the formation of the unconscious mark the very possibility of gendered subjects as established through entry into the symbolic order. In Lacanian terms, the unconscious is not just the site of the repressed but also a location for the generation of meaningful representations. Here the unconscious is said to be structured 'like a language', that is, not only is language the route to the unconscious but also the unconscious is a site of signification. In particular, the mechanisms of condensation and displacement, which Freud saw as the most important of the 'primary processes', are held by Lacan to be analogous to the linguistic functions of metaphor and metonymy. Condensation is the mechanism by which one idea comes to stand-in for a series of associated meanings along a chain of signifiers (as with a metaphor) while displacement involves the redirection of energy due to one object or idea onto another (not unlike a metonym).

Links **Identity, mirror phase, Oedipus complex, psychoanalysis, subjectivity, symbolic order**

Under erasure Under erasure is a concept that is derived from the work of **Derrida** and forms part of the vocabulary of deconstructionism. To deconstruct is to take apart, to undo, in order to seek out and display the assumptions of a text. In particular, deconstruction involves the dismantling of hierarchical binary oppositions that serve to 'guarantee' truth through excluding and devaluing the 'inferior' part of the binary. However, when Derrida deconstructs the binaries of Western philosophy and attacks the 'metaphysic of presence' (that is, the idea of a fixed self-present meaning) he must use the conceptual language of the very Western philosophy he seeks to undo. In Derrida's view there is no escape from reason, that is, from the very concepts of philosophy, and to mark this tension he places his concepts 'under erasure'.

To place a word under erasure is to first write the word and then cross it out, leaving both the word and its crossed-out version, for example, Reason ~~Reason~~. This procedure indicates that the word is inaccurate or unstable but is nevertheless necessary. The use of accustomed and known concepts 'under erasure' is intended to destabilize the familiar as at one and the same time useful, necessary, inaccurate and mistaken. Thus does Derrida seek to expose the *undecidability* of metaphysical oppositions, and indeed of meaning as such. He does this by arguing within and against philosophy and its attempts to maintain its authority in matters of truth.

Links **Deconstruction, logocentricism, meaning, poststructuralism, representation, text, truth**

Urbanization The idea of urbanization refers to the social, economic and cultural practices that generate metropolitan zones and involves turning parts of the countryside into a cityscape as one of the features of capitalist industrialization. Urban life is both the outcome and symbol of modernity and is indicative of the ambiguity of modernity itself. Thus, Durkheim, **Marx** and Weber, the so-called 'founders' of sociology and students of the nineteenth-century urban developments of modern capitalism, all regarded urbanization with ambivalence. Durkheim hoped that urban life would be a space for creativity, progress and a new moral order while fearing it would be the site of moral decay and anomie. For Weber, urban life was the cradle of modern industrial democracy whilst also engendering instrumental reason and the 'iron cage' of bureaucratic organization. Marx viewed the city as a sign of progress and the great leap of productivity which capitalism brought about while also observing that urban life was a site of poverty, indifference and squalor.

The development of urban studies owes much to the Chicago School of the 1960s, who advanced a functionalist urban ecology approach to the study of city life. The typical processes of expansion of the city can best be illustrated according to the Chicago School by a series of concentric circles that radiate outwards from the Central Business District (CBD), with each zone said to be inhabited by a particular type or class of people and activities. A more contemporary emphasis in the study of urbanization is on the political economy of cities, especially as it operates as an aspect of globalization. Here the stress is on the structuring of space as a created environment through the spread of industrial capitalism. The geography of cities is held to be the result of the power of capitalism in creating markets and controlling the workforce. In particular, capitalism is sensitive to the relative advantages of urban locations, including factors such as labour costs, degrees of unionization and tax concessions.

Other approaches to the study of urban life put more stress on the cultural aspects of the city, including questions of class, family life, lifestyle and ethnicity. For those in a position to enjoy them cities offer unrivalled opportunities for work and leisure, the context for mixing and meeting with a range of different kinds of people and high degrees of cultural activity and excitement. In big cities as nowhere else one can eat, listen to music, go to the movies, dress up, set off on travels and play with identities.

The city can also be understood in terms of representation, that is, it can be grasped as a text. Representing urban life involves the techniques of writing – metaphor, metonymy and other rhetorical devices – rather than a simple transparency from the 'real' city to the 'represented' city. Representations of cities – maps, statistics, photographs, films, documents etc. – summarize the complexity of the city and displace the physical level of the city onto signs that give meaning to places. Representations of the spatial divisions of cities are symbolic fault lines of social relations and a politics of representation needs to ask about the operations of power that are brought to bear to classify environments. By revealing only some aspects of the city, representations have the power to limit courses of action or frame 'problems' in certain ways.

Links **Capitalism, city, modernity, political economy, power, representation**

V

Values An item of value is something to which we ascribe worth and significance relative to other phenomena. Cultural studies has been concerned with questions of value in relation to (a) aesthetics, (b) political and cultural objectives and (c) the justification of action.

The philosophical domain of aesthetics is concerned with the definition of Art and also with the means by which to distinguish so-called good Art from bad Art. As such it is centred on the making of artistic and cultural value judgements. Cultural studies has been critical of the attempt to construct universal aesthetic criteria, seeing them as class-based and elitist, and has shifted the axis of value judgement from the aesthetic to the political. Having said that, there is a paradox in the fact that cultural studies writers do value popular culture often over and above high culture.

Cultural studies has not produced a political manifesto or clear-cut statement of its values and no doubt various writers in the field would disagree about what values should be adopted were it ever to do so. However, cultural studies does seem to be marked by a mix of values that centre on a democratic tradition that holds *equality, liberty, solidarity, tolerance, difference, diversity* and *justice* to be contemporary 'goods'. These values suggest support for cultural pluralism and the representation of the full range of public opinions, cultural practices and social-geographical conditions. They suggest a respect for individual difference along with forms of sharing and co-operation that are genuine and not enforced. Indeed, our best chance of maintaining difference and pursuing a private identity project is to live in a culture that values heterogeneity.

Cultural studies is for the most part anti-foundationalist in its stance, which means that the adoption of particular values cannot be justified by recourse to universal truth. Critics of this view have feared that the abandonment of foundationalism leads to irrationalism and the inability to ground any radical politics. However, we do not need universal foundations to pursue a pragmatic improvement of the human condition on the basis of the values of our own tradition. It is not possible to escape values any more than we can ground them in metaphysics, so that historically and culturally specific value-based knowledge is inevitable and inescapable. Nevertheless, values do require justification. Such reason-giving is a social practice, so that to justify a value is to give reasons in the context of a tradition and a community. Here, the acceptability of reasons has an intersubjective base in the community norms for reason-giving.

Links **Aesthetics, cultural politics, difference, epistemology, ethnocentrism, foundationalism, pragmatism, truth**

W

West, Cornel (1953–) West is one of the most prominent public intellectuals in the United States, mixing traditional academic scholarship with more populist writings, particularly in relation to issues of democracy, spirituality and race. West was educated at Princeton and Harvard, where he is currently a professor. An African American, West's work involves an unusual mixture of Christianity, Marxism (notably **Gramsci**) and pragmatism. While his work ranges over a wide domain, his public face is as a champion for racial justice. For West, 'prophetic criticism' requires social analysis that is explicit and partisan in its moral and political aims. Further, the development of critical positions and new theory must be linked with communities, groups, organizations and networks of people who are actively involved in social and cultural change.

- **Associated concepts** Capitalism, citizenship, cultural politics, hegemony, ideology, race, resistance.
- **Tradition(s)** Cultural studies, Marxism, pragmatism.
- **Reading** West, C. (1993) *Keeping Faith*. London and New York: Routledge.

Williams, Raymond (1921–1988) Raymond Williams' background in working class rural Wales before attending Cambridge University (UK) as both student and professor is significant, in that the lived experience of working class culture and a commitment to democracy and socialism are themes of his writing. Williams' work was extremely influential in the development of cultural studies through his understanding of culture as constituted by 'a whole way of life'. His anthropologically inspired grasp of culture as ordinary and lived, sometimes dubbed 'culturalism', helped to legitimize the study of popular culture. Williams' work engages with Marxism, most notably through the notions of ideology and hegemony, but he critiques a reductionist notion of base and superstructure. Williams argues for a form of cultural materialism that explores culture in terms of the relationships between the elements in an expressive totality.

- **Associated concepts** Base and superstructure, capitalism, class, common culture, cultural materialism, culture, experience, hegemony, ideology.
- **Tradition(s)** Culturalism, humanism, Marxism.
- **Reading** Williams, R. (1981) *Culture*. London: Fontana.

Willis, Paul (1945–) Paul Willis was one of the first postgraduate students at the Birmingham **Centre for Contemporary Cultural Studies** during the 1970s and has been associated with the emergence of cultural studies as a discipline. In particular, he has been one of cultural studies' foremost proponents of ethnographic research into culture as sensual lived experience. On a theoretical level, Willis has been influenced by both Marxism and the work of Raymond **Williams** and as such has been connected to the ideas of 'culturalism'. In his most famous work, *Learning to Labour*, Willis explored, via an ethnographic study of 'The Lads', the way that a group of working class boys reproduce their subordinate class position. Some of his later writing examines the creative symbolic practices of young people at the moment of consumption in the context of the creation of a common culture.

- **Associated concepts** Common culture, consumption, experience, homology, popular culture, subculture, youth culture.
- **Tradition(s)** Culturalism, cultural studies, ethnography, Marxism.
- **Reading** Willis, P. (1977) *Learning to Labour*. Farnborough: Saxon House.

Wittgenstein, Ludwig (1889–1951) The Austrian-born philosopher Ludwig Wittgenstein did much of his work at Cambridge University (UK). He is one of the pillars of post-Enlightenment philosophy whose linguistic anti-essentialism and holism have been a significant 'behind-the-scenes' influence on constructionism in general and postmodernism, poststructuralism and pragmatism in particular. For Wittgenstein, 'language' is a context-specific tool used by human beings where the meaning of the word is forged in use. Wittgenstein argued that words do not derive meaning from the essential characteristics of an independent referent but rather meaning arises in the context of a language-game. While language-games are rule-bound activities, those rules are not abstract components of language (as in structuralism) but rather they are constitutive rules. That is, rules which are such by dint of their enactment in social practice.

- **Associated concepts** Anti-essentialism, holism, language, language-game, meaning, truth.
- **Tradition(s)** Ordinary language philosopher who has been influential on constructionism, postmodernism, poststructuralism and pragmatism.
- **Reading** Wittgenstein, L. (1953) *Philosophical Investigations*. Oxford: Basil Blackwell.

Women's movement The idea of the women's movement and the concept of feminism are virtually interchangeable. However, we may make the gentle distinction that while feminism is marked by strong theoretical inclinations, the idea of the women's movement designates a concern with political strategies by which to intervene in social life in pursuit of the interests of women. It also registers the material gains and losses of the movement for women's emancipation.

It is commonplace if somewhat crudely schematic to discuss the women's movement in terms of three waves. The first wave of feminism is constituted by the nineteenth-century suffragette movement that sought after political and property rights for women, including the right to participate within the democratic process. The second wave of the women's movement began in the 1960s and engaged with a wider set of social and cultural issues, including male violence, the representation of women, the exclusion of women from positions of economic and political power, equality of pay, abortion rights and so forth. A good deal of emphasis was put upon achieving both cultural and legislative change and it was during this period that the description 'feminism' was given greater prominence. Finally, the third wave of the women's movement refers to contemporary feminism during a period in which a number of women's rights have been enshrined in the legislation of leading Western societies. Here there has been a greater theoretical concern with what is meant by the very concept of a woman and the place of women within culture, as well as with the possibilities for a global women's movement. For some commentators this represents not so much a third wave of feminism as the condition of post-feminism.

Links **Cultural politics, feminism, men's movement, New Social Movements, patriarchy, post-feminism**

Writing A commitment to writing is important to cultural studies because this is the prime activity of most of its practitioners and also the form in which most of what we call cultural studies actually appears. As such, there is something of a tension within cultural studies between its populist rhetoric of cultural politics and the fact that in practice most of the published work in the field reaches a very limited readership.

Cultural studies writers have commonly justified themselves with the argument that cultural criticism is a demystifying aspect of cultural politics and yet for the vast majority of people cultural studies writing appears to be obscure. This is not to say that the most 'obscure' and convoluted piece of writing possible is not valid in its own terms, for writing is obscure to the degree that it enacts a language used by a limited number of people. However, this does raise the question of the purposes of intellectual activity and of cultural studies in particular.

The work of **Derrida** has had a significant influence within cultural studies and he uses the idea of writing in a rather more technical way to raise philosophical questions about the nature of meaning. The idea of writing plays an important part in Derrida's work, by which he means not simply text on a page but what he calls *arche-writing*, a concept intended to remind us that there is no 'outside' of the text. Writing is always already part of the outside of texts so that texts form the outside of other texts in a process of intertextuality. It is this sense that Derrida has in mind when he argues that there is nothing but texts.

For Derrida, writing is not held to be secondary to speech (as self-present meaning) but rather is a necessary part of speech and meaning. That is, there is no meaning that is outside of or free from writing or that writing gives expression to. Rather, meaning and truth-claims are always already dependent on writing and are subject to its rhetorical claims and metaphors. Thus the strategies of writing are constitutive of any truth-claims and can be deconstructed in terms of those strategies. Further, since writing is 'a sign of a sign', then the meaning of words cannot be stable and identical with a fixed concept. Rather, as Derrida indicates with his concept of différance, meaning is deferred by dint of supplement of meaning by the traces of other words.

Links **Deconstruction, différance, intellectuals, intertextuality, poststructuralism, text**

Y

Youth culture The post-Second World War Western world has been marked by the emergence and proliferation of distinct musical forms, fashion styles, leisure activities, dances and languages associated with young people. These assemblages of meanings and practices have become known as youth cultures. The question of youth cultures has had a significant place in cultural studies and raises a number of important concerns and themes that echo down and across the pathways of its development. These include the cultural classification of persons into social categories (youth), the demarcations of class, race and gender, the questions of space, style, taste, media and meaning (that is, issues of culture), the place of consumption within capitalist consumer societies and the vexed question of resistance.

The category of youth is not a universal of biology but a changing social and cultural construct that appeared at a particular moment of time under definitive conditions. As a discursive construct, the meaning of youth alters across time and space according to who is being addressed by whom. **Hebdige** has remarked that youth has been constructed within and across the discourses of 'trouble' (youth-as-trouble: youth-in-trouble) and/or 'fun'. For example, through the figures of football hooligans, motorbike boys and street corner gangs youth has been associated with crime, violence and delinquency. Alternatively, youths have been represented as playful consumers of fashion, style and a range of leisure activities. This is figured by the partygoer, the fashion stylist and, above all, by the consuming post-1950s 'teenager'.

While the concept of the 'teenager' has framed much popular discourse on young people, cultural studies was drawn instead to the analytic concept of subculture wherein youth subcultures were explored as stylized forms of resistance to power. Youth subcultures are marked, it was argued, by the development of particular styles that are said to 'win space' for themselves from both the parent culture and the hegemonic class culture through symbolic resolutions of the class contradictions they faced.

Today the lines of style that separated one youth subculture from another seem to have collapsed. Consequently, it can be argued that we live in a post-subculture phase in which young people are the creative bricoleurs of a postmodern consumer culture. This involves picking and choosing aspects of a variety of styles and putting them together in a process of mix and match. Further, contemporary communications technologies have constructed commodities, meanings and identifications of youth culture that cut across the boundaries of races or nation-states, leading to global rap, global rave and global salsa. We might then ask about whether or not there is now a global youth culture. If so, we must speak of youth cultures that have 'family resemblances' not a homogenized culture. This is so because youth cultures are not pure, authentic and locally bounded. Rather, they are syncretic and hybridized products of interactions across space.

Links **Bricolage, common culture, consumption, cultural capital, homology, resistance, style, subculture**